-Warren,

you there.

# I'll Take You There

# I'll Take You There

## Pop Music and the Urge for Transcendence

### BILL FRISKICS-WARREN

**continuum**

NEW YORK • LONDON

2005

The Continuum International Publishing Group Inc
15 East 26 Street, New York, NY 10010

The Continuum International Publishing Group Ltd
The Tower Building, 11 York Road, London SE1 7NX

www.continuumbooks.com

Printed in the United States of America

Library of Congress Cataloging-in-Publication Data

Friskics-Warren, Bill.
    I'll take you there : pop music and the urge for transcendence / Bill
Friskics-Warren.
        p. cm.
    Includes bibliographical references, discography, and index.
    ISBN-13: 978-0-8264-1700-8 (hardcover : alk. paper)
    ISBN-10: 0-8264-1700-0 (hardcover : alk. paper)
    1. Popular music—History and criticism   2. Music—Philosophy and
aesthetics.   3. Transcendence (Philosophy)   I. Title.
ML3470.F746   2005
782.42164'11—dc22                                              2005020280

ISBN 0-8264-1700-0

# CONTENTS

# AUTHOR'S NOTE AND ACKNOWLEDGMENTS

I SPENT THE BETTER PART OF A YEAR WRITING THIS BOOK, BUT in some respects I have been working on it most of my life. I started gearing up for it in earnest during the 1980s, when, at the age of twenty-one, I moved to Nashville from Chicago and increasingly began to hear pop music as an expression of the urge for some sort of transcendence. This preoccupation doubtless was inevitable given my vocational and avocational pursuits at the time. As a graduate student in theology at Vanderbilt I spent countless hours pouring over the writings of philosophers like Husserl and Merleau-Ponty and those of theologians ranging from Gutièrrez to Cone, Tillich to Teilhard de Chardin. When I wasn't studying I usually was combing the bins of record stores and flea markets for old LPs or camped out in the clubs.

That said, the groundwork for this book was already being laid while I was growing up in suburban Chicago. This certainly was the case by the time I was in high school, when I spent ridiculous amounts of time trying to unlock the transcendental mysteries of albums like *Astral Weeks* and *Music from Big Pink*. Yet even before that I couldn't get enough of the punchy, evocative dispatches from the AM band that I heard by groups like Creedence Clearwater Revival and Sly & the Family Stone. In some underlying existential sense I suppose I was at work on a version of this project as far back as kindergarten, when I used to stand in the shadows of my cousin Frankie's basement when he and his high school buddies would bring home the latest 45s. I still have vivid memories of hearing some of those singles for the first time, everything from the Standell's "Dirty Water" to Sam & Dave's "Hold On! I'm Comin'." I'll never forget my first encounter with "Paint It, Black," a record that scared the hell out of me even as I hoped my cousin would play it again, and even as

I proceeded to buy safer 45s by the Monkees and the Young Rascals to play at home.

My foremost musical epiphany, though, came late one Sunday afternoon in 1964 when Frankie and my cousins sent me running home to lobby my parents to let me watch the Beatles on *The Ed Sullivan Show* that night. I had just turned four. Dashing through the crisp February twilight with my unbuttoned red cardigan flapping like a cape in my wake, I felt the sense of wonder and anticipation that comes when something extraordinary is about to break into the everyday. I had tasted transcendence on a par with this at church the previous Easter when the pealing trumpets, the heady musk of the lilies, and the oceanlike roar of the choir transported me to similar heights. I couldn't say, at this remove, which revelation was more formative, my experience that Easter or seeing the Beatles on *Ed Sullivan*. However, I can say that I've long been uncomfortable with hard-and-fast distinctions between the sacred and the secular and that, whether consciously or otherwise, I've been trying to sort out what that means ever since.

Not that such deliberations made me want to write about music, not even after I became acquainted with *Rolling Stone*, *Creem*, and *Crawdaddy*, none of which I read with any regularity. More than anything else, my immersion, while in college and graduate school, in the work of writers like James Agee, Zora Neal Hurston, Wendell Berry, Langston Hughes, Will Campbell, and Virginia Woolf is what prompted me to explore the yearning for transcendence that suffuses so much popular music. I didn't know the difference, for example, between Robert Palmer and Greil Marcus until a friend recommended their books *Deep Blues* and *Mystery Train* to me while I was at Vanderbilt. Both volumes got their hooks in me soon enough, though, distracting me to such a degree that I was forced to invent pretexts for taking incompletes in my seminars on Nietzsche and Whitehead.

Thus began my dissociation from academic pursuits, a process that was accelerated by my subsequent involvement and employment with the Nashville Coalition for the Homeless. That, however, is another story. For the purposes of this discussion, suffice it to say that I got religion, so to speak, after my exposure to *Deep Blues* and *Mystery Train*. I soon discovered Robert Christgau's pithy, occasionally abstruse consumer guides in the *Village Voice*, and then Ellen Willis's

bracing columns from old issues of the *New Yorker* and Peter Gural-
nick's empathetic profiles in *Lost Highway* and *Feel Like Going
Home*. Dave Marsh's book *The Heart of Rock & Soul*, an uncom-
monly smart, passionate argument for a way of listening to music
(and of being in the world), also was crucial. As were two volumes
edited by Greil Marcus: *Stranded*, a 1979 collection of essays on "de-
sert-island discs" by leading rock critics (not to be missed are Lang-
don Winner's meditation on *Trout Mask Replica* and M. Mark's
luminous treatment of Van Morrison), and *Psychotic Reactions &
Carburetor Dung*, a compilation of writings by the late Lester Bangs.
The works of other socially-conscious critics, especially Mikal Gilmore, Ann Powers, Michael Eric Dyson, and Jon Pareles, but also
Howard Hampton, R. J. Smith, Evelyn McDonnell, Sarah Vowell,
Colson Whitehead, Emily White, Danyel Smith, Leslie Berman, and
Terri Sutton likewise made their mark on me before I gave any real
thought to writing about music. Directly or indirectly, I owe all of
them, and others whom I have failed to mention, a word of thanks.

A more express word of appreciation goes to everyone who contributed directly to this project. This includes people who burned or
loaned me records, made bibliographical and other suggestions,
forced me to reexamine my thinking at points, read or offered to read
portions of my manuscript, gave me space in print to work out some
of my ideas, or shared their weekend hideaways with me so that I
could work without distraction. For one or more of these things I
thank Malcolm Alcala, Grant Alden, Emily Askew, Eric and Paige
LaGrone Babcock, Peter Blackstock, Diane and Buddy Benedict,
David Cantwell, Holly George-Warren, Richard Harrington, Will
Hermes, Peter Kaufman, Wendy Kurland, Dave Maddox, Scott Manzler,
Jonathan Marx, Barry Mazor, Michael McCall, John Pancake, Leo
Rauh, Jim Ridley, Fletcher Roberts, Alexander Philip Shashko, Craig
Werner, Ron Wynn, and Mark Zimbicki.

Special thanks to my agent Sarah Lazin, who immediately "got"
what this book was about and without whom I likely still would be
trying to find a publisher; to David Barker, who believed in the book
enough to publish it; to my brother Bill Harkins, who ferrets out the
transcendent at nearly every turn; to my brother Paul Shupe, an ardent theologian and listener of music who read every page of this
manuscript and improved it immeasurably; and to my mentor Ed Far-

ley, whose lectures and writings inspired this project and whose non-directive guidance helped plug a gaping lacuna in it by posing a timely question and by creating the space for me to answer it. I dedicate this book, with the utmost gratitude, to Paul and Ed.

I am deeply grateful to my family as well. To my wife Kate, who with grace and steadfastness supports what I do even as she works wonders in the real world. To our son Marshall, whose irrepressible spirit compels him to overhear the likes of Public Enemy's "Bring the Noise" and Randy Newman's "Political Science" and beg to hear more. To my gifted, generous brother Scott, who read much of this manuscript and greatly enriched it. To my Aunt Karen and Uncle Bob, who persistently expand my world. To my parents Bill and Ann, who continue to trust that I'm doing what I'm supposed to be doing, or at least traveling on a worthy path.

All of which brings me to the use of the first-person in the book's title. I would of course like to think that everyone who reads this book will find aspects of it transporting. The presence of the first person in its title nevertheless does not stake a claim for my ruminations so much as allude to the music of the artists whose work I explore. The "I" in "I'll Take You There" refers to musicians like Marvin Gaye, Polly Harvey, and Bruce Springsteen who, by giving voice to their hunger for transcendence, create a window to something transformative for the rest of us. In many ways, the "I" in "I'll Take You There" refers to all of those cited in these acknowledgments whose insights and observations have taken me "there" as well. Indeed, the "I" in question ultimately describes a collective sense of the first person reminiscent of the wonderful Rastafarian adaptation of the Hebrew expression "I and I." Born of a distaste for divisive personal pronouns like "you" and "me," the phrase "I and I" reinforces the interconnectedness of all people. It testifies to the existence of an intersubjective "I," a transcendental "we" that embodies and participates in something that is greater than the sum of its parts.

This is to say nothing of the enthralling monument to transcendence that supplies this book with its title. A No. 1 pop hit for the Staple Singers in 1972, "I'll Take You There" is very much of a piece with the Rastafarian notion of "I and I." When, impelled by one of the leanest, funkiest vamps ever, Mavis Staples vows to take listeners to a wondrous place where nobody is crying, worried, lying or being lied to, she isn't just promising to lead *them* there. Moaning in that gruff, voluptuous alto of hers, Staples also is imploring them to help *her* get to that place, which is just what her sisters Yvonne and Cleo pledge to do when they shout "I'll take you there" by way of response. Though more glorious and with much greater urgency, the Staples' recording of "I'll Take You There" is a lot like the processes of call-and-response that resulted in the creation of this book. It witnesses to how reaching a transcendental plane often involves people taking *each other* there, to how transcendence often is more a matter of "I and I" than anything else.

# PROLOGUE

## I Want to Take You Higher

About the time that I began writing this book, the local department of public works started putting in a dog park behind the community center near our house in east Nashville. Piled upon the basketball court behind the field house were several mounds of dirt, each maybe five or six feet high, that the workers had dug up to pour the forms for the sidewalk. One of the mounds sat directly in front of the backboard and rim at the south end of the court. Each afternoon when I cut behind the community center on my run I could count on seeing a few kids around the age of nine or ten dunking basketballs from that elevated station. It was a natural enough thing for them to be doing, an impulse, born of their impatience with the limitations of their age and stature (and, no doubt, of visions of NBA glory), to reach higher than they otherwise could have. Seeing that mix of kids striving, day after day, to grasp what was beyond their normal reach stuck with me. It struck me as an apt metaphor, however prosaic, for our innate hunger for transcendence, and for how that hunger is expressed by the musicians discussed in this book.

Talking about pop music in the same breath as transcendence might strike some people as high-minded or over-earnest, if not as altogether quixotic. Such a reception almost certainly would have greeted this book during the irony-clad decade that preceded this one, and this despite the unabashed striving for transcendence evident in the music of tragic pop icons like Kurt Cobain and Tupac Shakur. Or, for that matter, in that of Jimi Hendrix and Janis Joplin a generation before them. Yet spirituality—and that is precisely what the language of transcendence refers to—has lately made a comeback. After the attacks of September 11, 2001, the U.S. invasion of Iraq, and the heightened sense of global insecurity with which we now live, people seem increasingly conscious, certainly in the persistently narcissistic United States, of the brokenness that pervades our world. Perhaps due to this keener awareness of our vulnerability and finitude, more people are reflecting on things that point beyond the quotidian or the everyday; more are preoccupied, as the theologian Paul Tillich put it, with things of ultimate, as opposed to penultimate, concern. This even is true of pop music, where recent recordings as disparate as rapper Kanye West's "Jesus Walks" and Hoobastank's modern-rock hit "The Reason" not only resonated spiritually with listeners; they topped the charts, sold millions of copies, and won Grammy Awards.

Pop music perennially has been viewed as disposable—or worse, as spiritually bankrupt. Yet from "A Change Is Gonna Come" to "Smells Like Teen Spirit," pop records long have given voice to an urge to "move on up" or "get higher." This talk of elevation or "higher ground" notwithstanding, this book is not a work of philosophy or theology, at least not in any strict academic sense. Entire portions of it do not even, for example, refer to God, and many make more of the absence or inscrutability of the divine than anything else. Nor is this book an apologetic for the convictions of any of the musicians under consideration. More than anything it is a volume of criticism that looks at the different ways that people seek, express, and experience transcendence, a definition of which I unpack in the introduction that follows. Drawing on various philosophical and theological frameworks, as well as on different types of social analysis and arts criticism, this book attempts to expand the ways in which we understand not just the spiritual impulses of the musicians in question, but our own as well.

This is a book, in other words, about spirituality with what might be termed a small "s" instead of spirituality as it tends to be promulgated by organized religion, which, being a human construct, often codifies spiritual impulses and suppresses them. My aim, in contrast to this religious inclination, is to broaden or push back the horizon of what people commonly view as spirituality. Part of this simply involves making room for manifestations of spirituality that typically are not understood as such by recognizing the spiritual impetus at work in, say, eroticism, negation, or resistance. Part of it also has to do with seeing the continuity between these commonly unacknowledged expressions of spirituality and more overt embodiments of it like prophecy, contemplation, and empathy. Ultimately this means engaging the music discussed in these pages—a great deal of music, in fact—as inherently spiritual rather than as incidentally or accidentally so. In this way, and in what I hope proves a transcendental move of its own, I hope that the eight chapters that follow do for you something akin to what the music of the artists under consideration does for me: take you higher.

What follows, though, is not an attempt to lay out a systematic understanding of what is, perhaps uniquely, a human urge for transcendence, or even to chart the contours of human spirituality in general. Despite its overarching conceptual schematic, and despite the fact that it seeks to elucidate an encompassing array of ways that popular musicians express a striving for something deeper and more abiding than the everyday, this book is not a systematic undertaking at all. Nor is it an attempt to ascertain, in any definitive way, what the artists in question intend or might be trying to "say." Or, for that matter, to unearth religious nuggets from their work or to serve as an argument for the "hidden" Christianity, Buddhism, or whatever else might be mined from their recordings. More than anything this book is an attempt to engage in dialogue with these artists and the bodies of work that they have created in order to illuminate and understand the hunger for transcendence at the heart of human experience.

My interest lies in *popular* music, rather than in gospel, "contemporary Christian," or other types of religious music. This is not to disparage the latter, the examination of which I happily leave to others. My concern is with those epiphanies, if only for their power to unite people across faiths and cultures, that have in some way broken into or out of the cultural mainstream. My interest lies with those articulations of the urge for transcendence that have found their way into the popular zeitgeist without recourse to dogmatic or sectarian agendas. It is not only for this reason, though, that pop recordings form the backbone of the discussions that take place in this book. As far as Western popular music goes, the so-called secular expressions of spirituality with which I take up here have, with the exception of the black and Southern gospel genres, accounted for vastly superior music than those that have come from, say, contemporary Christian circles.

I also have chosen to explore the work of some thirty individual artists, as opposed to clusters of recordings made by a much broader array of musicians grouped together under certain rubrics. As listeners we relate to and identify with individual musicians and bands and follow their careers in the press. Looking in depth at the larger bodies of work of particular artists lends the book's discussions a familiar, or at least discernible, trajectory. Examining entire careers also affords a better glimpse of the way that the artists' expressions of the urge for transcendence change over time, which many invariably do. Moreover, pursuing this tack helps uncover how the broader social, historical, and cultural contexts from which the artists emerged gave rise to both their music and their striving.

The discussions that follow are not, in any case, artist profiles or reportage. Compared with most contemporary writing about pop, rock, and hip-hop, they might seem a little light on biographical material, relying more on the analysis of artists' recordings and on the examination of the larger contexts from which their music arose. And by recordings, I mean just that—words *and* music. This book seeks to gainsay the logocentric tendency, which is all too prevalent in writing about pop music, of privileging a record's lyrics over everything else. The unfortunate effect of that practice is to reduce recordings to works of "poetry" backed by beats, guitars, or what have you instead of treating them as potentially rich arrangements of notes, rhythms, silences, and effects that "say" more than the words that come from the singer's or the MC's mouth. I have sought, with considerable diligence, to avoid falling into this trap.

In much the same spirit of inclusion, the exegeses that follow constitute what I hope is an encompassing constellation of expressions—from rock and rap and industrial music to country and electronica and soul—of the urge for transcendence in contemporary pop music. I have focused almost exclusively on musicians who emerged or made their mark in the past three or so decades, the era, loosely speaking, of rock, soul, and rap (as opposed to rock 'n' roll[1]). Part of this has to do with the fact that these artists share many social and cultural reference points with the vast majority of people who might read this book. Just as crucial is the fact that whether we are talking about Bing Crosby, Billie Holiday, or Robert Johnson, or about Hank Williams, James Brown, or the Beatles, the artistic and spiritual outpourings of many early or transitional figures in the pop, jazz, blues, "hillbilly," and rock 'n' roll genres have been scrutinized exhaustively elsewhere. The work of some of the artists discussed in these pages has been considered at length as well. None of it, however, has been looked at primarily in terms of how it gives voice to a hunger for transcendence. Certainly none of it has been examined as part of a larger undertaking like the one that this book represents.

I chose to include some of the artists, in what is perhaps quintessential postmodern fashion, because they best helped expound the categories that I use to examine the urge for transcendence in popular music. In most cases I could have selected other artists, and they might have served the book's purposes just as well—the Clash, for example, instead of the Mekons, Ani DiFranco instead of Sleater-Kinney, the Coup or Rage Against the Machine instead of Spearhead, Prince instead of Marvin Gaye or Madonna. This, however, is not a book solely about first-generation punk bands, post-feminist rockers, leftist agit-rappers, or pop artists of a sensualist bent. I had to make choices, not only to keep from repeating myself, but also to account for a sufficiently broad range of articulations of spirituality in popular music. Such is the heretical imperative, or burden of choice, inherent in any project of this scope. Less crucial, in the end, is exactly which artists I included—someone else could have written a comparable book using other exemplars—but whether my engagement with the work of the musicians that I *have* selected adequately illuminates my subject. And again, my concern is with *popular* music, which explains why, with maybe a handful of exceptions, the artists discussed here will be familiar to most readers who follow pop music, rather than just to cultists or critics.

Some of the musicians discussed here might not be able to articulate exactly what it is that, driven by their spiritual restlessness, they are searching for. Some of them might not even be able to see beyond the antipathy that colors their lives and music to envision what might satisfy that striving. Ultimately this does not matter. The fact that these artists are reaching at all, and that they have the presence of heart and mind to express their restlessness through music, is evidence of their desire to participate in something greater than what they know and thus is transcendental. This is not to say that these artists do not know what they are talking about or feeling, or in any way to patronize them or their work. Nor is it, once again, to ascribe philosophical or dogmatic aims to what they are trying to say. It is merely to acknowledge the transcendental impulse that the striving of these artists, as conveyed by their music, betrays.

Some musicians might be conspicuous in their absence from these pages. For example, the Velvet Underground, who, while in some ways perfect exemplars of the negation that I explore in Chapter 4, were just too hedonistic and thus uttered too loud a "Yes" to life to fit there. Pere Ubu, Captain Beefheart, and Parliament-Funkadelic are other cases in point, all of them far too mercurial, and inscrutably so, to lend themselves to the fairly circumscribed discussion at hand. All of which is to say nothing of Bob Dylan, who simply towers over the field. Dylan was the wedge who cleaved the hitherto hermetic universe of pop music, a world that still clung to ill-fitting distinctions between the sacred and the profane, the eternal and the mundane. Even if such claims for Dylan's legacy might overreach somewhat—Ray Charles and Sam Cooke, after all, shattered their share of assumptions during the 50s and early 60s—Dylan blew open the aperture, forever altering the pop landscape and how we survey it. Even devoting a chapter to his music and the tectonic shift that it set it motion would seem trifling in this context, especially with so many attempts to do some version of this already in print; plus, you can't do it all.

My decision to focus on some musicians and not others nevertheless is not, in the end, a subjective one, as if there were such a thing in a world that is as interconnected as ours is. If nothing else, the shared nature of how we engage popular music makes my choices profoundly intersubjective. My decisions are informed not only by the myriad conversations in which I have taken part, either with other writers or fans, but also by my immersion in the cultural currents from which the music and the conversations that surround it have sprung. None of which is to deny that personal taste is reflected in my choices, but there is no disgrace in that. "To patronize the faculty of taste is to patronize oneself," wrote Susan Sontag in *Notes on*

"*Camp.*" "Taste governs every free—as opposed to rote—human response."[2]

Finally, I have chosen to look at articulations of the urge for transcendence in the work of musicians, instead of, say, film directors or playwrights (although I'd warrant that similar treatments of movies and theater still might go begging). I have concentrated on pop music in part because, as a critic, it is what I follow most closely, but also because it has served, along with fiction, as the most profound point of convergence between art and spirituality in my life. Pop music functions this way in the lives of a great many people, and it played this totemic role long before the advent of modern recording technology. Everything from the Anglo-Celtic ballad tradition to the centuries-old art of West African drumming and storytelling has shown us that. All of which is not to privilege the likes of PJ Harvey, Curtis Mayfield, or Public Enemy over, say, Robert Altman, August Wilson, or Jean-Luc Godard. It merely is to acknowledge that of the various founts of pop culture from which I have imbibed, I have drunk at the well of popular music more deeply and have gotten higher there more often than anywhere else. This book examines the work of some of the artists whose music has taken me to that place, much as those mounds of unearthed dirt did for the kids on the basketball court behind the community center in my neighborhood. My hope is that some of what follows will take you a little higher as well.

# INTRODUCTION

## Cleaning Windows:
## Of Restlessness, Records,
## and Transcendence

I nterest Surges in Voodoo, and Its Queen" trumpeted a headline in the November 30, 2003 edition of the *New York Times*.[1] The story that ran beneath it bore a New Orleans dateline and was accompanied by a pair of photos. The first was of pilgrims visiting the tomb of Marie Laveau, the woman renowned as the "queen of voodoo." The second was a picture of a contemporary voodoo priestess. Her name was Miriam Chamani and she was leaning over an altar, lighting a candle in the icon-crowded backroom where she performs rites for people experiencing physical, financial, and other hardships. Her clients, the story reported, were among a growing number of people in the United States who are turning to voodoo to deal with life's mysteries and challenges. Not just people of a superstitious or esoteric bent either, but those of various races, classes, and nationalities, many of whom otherwise seek refuge in conventional religion. Voodoo's resurgence, the story concluded, is symptomatic of "an increasing desperation in our culture for spiritual meaning and direction."

Much the same spiritual urgency is evident in today's popular entertainment. *The Matrix* and its sequels have become Rorschach blots in this regard, inspiring not just vigorous popular discussion about the movies' transcendental themes, but considerable academic discourse as well. Some interpret the trilogy as a story of resurrection, others as one of reawakening, others as an allegory about the tyranny of institutional religion. *Buffy the Vampire Slayer*, the TV series about a young woman who defends her town against forces of evil, has also prompted a flurry of analysis plumbing the show's deeper meaning. One scholarly essay casts the protagonist Buffy Summers as a Kierkegaardian Knight of Faith.[2] Another is subtitled "A Comparative Study of Buffy and the Hindu Saint Antal on Identity and Self-Realization." This paper, which was written by a doctoral candidate at Boston College named Tracy Tiemeier, was presented at the Slayage Conference on *Buffy the Vampire Slayer* held in Nashville in 2004.[3]

*Buffy* and *The Matrix* are not anomalies; nor are they without precedent. English literature alone offers myriad cases of writers using their work to comment on society, to envision alternatives to it, and to spark debate—everyone from satirists like Jonathan Swift to social critics like James Baldwin to writers of utopian/dystopian fiction like Ursula K. LeGuin. Contemporary popular culture, it seems, is more rife than ever with expressions that do so with a strong spiritual bent. The *Lord of the Rings* movies reanimate J. R. R. Tolkien's meditations on good and evil for the age of globalization. *His Dark Materials*, a trilogy of novels by the British author Phillip Pullman, serves as a parable about the hegemony of Christendom. The writers of *Joan of Arcadia*, one of numerous TV series on the air right now that have religious overtones, have God appearing in assorted human guises to a reluctant high school student, drawing her out of herself and into the worlds of others. The show's theme song is a remake of the Joan Osborne hit that asks, "What if God was one of us?"

All of these things point to a pervasive restlessness in our culture, to a desire for more than just diversion, for something deeper and more enduring than the everyday. "There's this hunger, there's this quest—not for organized religion, but for spirituality," observed Alex Gee, the co-author of *Jesus and the Hip-Hop Prophets: Spiritual Insights from Lauryn Hill and Tupac Shakur*.[4] The yearning that Gee describes has been articulated in a variety of ways, but St. Augustine, the fourth century theologian, might have said it best in *The Confessions* when he asserted, "Our heart is restless until it rests in you."[5]

The restlessness to which Augustine refers is not an ordinary longing that comes and goes with our moods, such as lust, ennui, or some vague psychological discontent. Augustine is invoking the Platonic notion of eros, not eros understood as a mere sexual pull (i.e., Homer's "pulsing rush of Longing"), but eros as an unquenchable fire that fuels all of our urges, libidinous or otherwise. Augustine is talking about an ontological gnawing, a condition stitched into the fabric of our beings: the desire for something more than what we, in and of ourselves, can achieve or become. He is saying that people are restless and incomplete. That we cannot find peace without a connection to something that transcends our experience and can ground it.

For Augustine the object of this longing was God, and the experience of the divine, however it might be understood, is what many people associate with the language of transcendence. Yet transcendence can take place in other ways as well—indeed, wherever there is a portal to some higher realm. Transcendence can occur through mystical insight, through sexual intimacy, or through expressions of empathy. It can be occasioned by the likes of wonder, reverence, or reciprocity. It can be achieved by standing in solidarity with others, by resisting unjust powers and conditions, or by means of historical liberation. Transcendence takes place whenever there is a convergence or interpenetration of the temporal and the eternal, whenever something deeper and more abiding than the everyday breaks into and, if only fleetingly, transforms the present.

People understand the urge for transcendence in a variety of ways, much as they variously interpret how we might satisfy it. Yet regardless of how it is viewed, this hunger to participate in something greater and more lasting than what we have or know—a hunger born of our awareness of our mortality—is what defines us as spiritual beings. Spirituality thus is not something strange or otherworldly, much less a lifestyle choice like that associated with, say, adopting some strain of New Age philosophy. It is not something that we can choose to participate in or not, as we do with religion. Spirituality is the stuff of who we are. It is the overriding restlessness at the core of our beings and how we respond to it.

The urge for transcendence is especially pronounced in artistic pursuits, regardless of whether the artists involved are conscious of this impetus or not. An urge for some sort of transcendence is what makes most people want to write, paint, sculpt, or dance in the first place. Even narcissistic artists are responding to a calling or pull that draws them out of themselves and instills in them a desire to connect with others through the works that they create. This impulse can be misdirected or impeded and thereby thwart the pursuit of transcendence, such as when its expression serves banal, venal, or oppressive ends. A core restlessness nevertheless remains, no matter how compromised that striving might be. Some artists seek transcendence more transparently than others, using their work to express, embody, or comment on their search for it, even if that commentary only points to how transitory or elusive transcendence can be. If only by virtue of its existence, most every creative endeavor points beyond the artist in question to something more and, in that way, betrays a thirst for transcendence.

Pop music, despite being written off at times as ephemeral—or, more grievously, as demonic—is no exception. Popular recordings have long given voice to this urge for transcendence, even if the musicians who make them tend not to be as outwardly spiritual as, say, their gospel or sectarian counterparts. Pop acts are constantly pointing beyond themselves, whether it is to a better future, to some higher ideal, or to some vision of deliverance. The Beatles "Help!," the Rolling Stones' "(I Can't Get No) Satisfaction," Bob Dylan's "Like a Rolling Stone," Al Green's "Take Me to the River," Afrika Bambaataa's "Looking for the Perfect Beat," and U2's "I Still Haven't Found What I'm Looking For" are but a half-dozen of the hundreds of pop recordings that convey a longing for something beyond the everyday. And not just through their lyrics, but in how those words are sung or rapped, and in how the beats, melodies, and arrangements that accompany them amplify, deepen, or comment on the meanings that they transmit. What, other than transcendence, is Jimi Hendrix getting at in "Purple Haze" when he shouts, "'Scuse me, while I kiss the sky," before discharging an untrammeled blast of noise from his Stratocaster? Or Van Morrison, in "Caravan," when he implores us to crank up our radios and sail away with him into the mystic? Or Bruce Springsteen, in "Thunder Road," when the sound of that slamming screen door sends him—and the rest of us, if just vicariously—hurtling headlong toward freedom?

Heard in the right way, almost any pop record can speak to transcendental concerns, some to the point of galvanizing their historical or cultural moments. Chuck Berry's "Brown-Eyed Handsome Man," a song about a gifted baseball player, served as a veiled statement of black pride amid the last gasps of Jim Crow. Aretha Franklin's "Think," a lover's ultimatum issued at the height of the women's and the civil rights movements, doubled as a call for solidarity, and likely served as a masked word of caution about the war in Vietnam as well. Nirvana's "Smells Like Teen Spirit" captured the abandonment and rage felt by a generation come of age to the death rattle of AIDS on the one hand and to a future mortgaged by Reaganomics on the other. Even records that seem nonsensical, or those that express negation, can convey an urge for transcendence and become emblems of their eras. The anarchic, ID-driven "a-wop-bop-a-lu-bop" of Little Richard's "Tutti Frutti" is the very sound of rock 'n' roll's big bang. The relentless thudding of the Stooges' "I Wanna Be Your Dog," by contrast, channels the angst felt by legions of misfit teenagers who could not relate, among so many other things, to the increasingly hollow idealism of the 60s counterculture. Love songs, too, can reach vast heights and depths, whether explicitly, such as when Marvin Gaye weds sex and sanctification in "Let's Get It On," or implicitly, when Ray Charles, his soul in tatters, begs his lover, "Unchain My Heart."

Records that articulate an urge for transcendence, and a great number of them do, are not pegged as easily as the bins of retailers might suggest. Less the domain of genres like rock, soul, and rap, they might more appropriately be termed "transcendental music"—music that, regardless of stylistic signature or marketing niche, points beyond itself, urging listeners to look past the mundane and to see themselves and their striving in a new light. Those who make transcendental music understand how this works only too well. They typically have had their worlds opened up in much the same way. Johnny Cash, who struggled, as he sang, to "subdue the beast within," was drawn to the existential conflict expressed in the songs of Bob Dylan and Kris Kristofferson, just as Dylan and Kristofferson were enthralled by the work of the Beat Poets and the French symbolists before them. Al Green, a soul singer who eventually became a preacher, identified with the spiritual desolation of Hank Williams's "I'm So Lonesome I Could Cry." Polly Harvey, a post-punk, art-school dropout from rural England, sought cathartic renewal in the blues, much as her Irish counterpart Van Morrison first did some thirty years before her.

Records of a transcendental bent, those made by people trying to get higher—and often, to take us there as well—are not peripheral to the history of popular music; they lie at the heart of it. The restlessness that they express often speaks to people as profoundly as what they hear in church or at their mosque or synagogue—more profoundly at times, especially lately, as many wrestle with questions of providence in our seemingly more volatile world. Countless people in the United States, for example, looked to Bruce Springsteen and his album *The Rising* for comfort and insight after the attacks on the World Trade Center and the Pentagon in 2001. In today's post-Christian milieu—a world defined increasingly by multiculturalism and globalization—pop music frequently serves as a substitute for conventional religious observance, or at least provides spiritual clarity and guidance where it might be lacking. Pop music has for decades possessed the power, much as liturgies and sacred music have for centuries, to transport the human spirit and to serve as a vehicle for the transcendence that we seek.

Pop music that expresses the urge for transcendence is the focus of the explorations in the eight chapters that follow. Some of the musicians under consideration, such as the Reverend Al Green, singer-songwriter Jimmie Dale Gilmore, and the rapper Chuck D, operate from particular religious traditions, from Christianity to Buddhism to Islam. Others exercise their spirituality in more humanistic terms. Their particular spiritual leanings notwithstanding, all of the artists examined here manifest the urge for transcendence through what can be described as mystical, negative, or prophetic impulses. These postures invariably overlap and inform each other, yet one of the three tends, in each case, to predominate.

Musicians who express the urge for transcendence mystically strive for some deeper spiritual union, be it with God (however the divine is understood) or with some other person or elevated state of consciousness. Assertions of this mystical urge often result in music that is ecstatic, sublime, or singularly intense, as well as in music that explicitly engages transcendental or even religious themes. Perhaps the most recognizable manifestation of this impulse is the contemplative path or journey inward. Van Morrison's "Listen to the Lion," Jimmie Dale Gilmore singing, "You're just a wave, you're not the water," and Prince Be of the hip-hop duo P.M. Dawn ruing, "Reality used to be a friend of mine," all belong here. Each of these recordings is unique in sound and sensibility, yet all point beyond themselves and embody some greater spiritual ideal, even P.M. Dawn's, which exhibits considerable bewilderment over the ineffabilities of life.

Sensuality is another assertion of the mystical urge for transcendence. Sex does not spring to mind when people think of mystics; if anything, asceticism does, the denial of the flesh. The tension between the body and the soul, between sex and salvation, however, has long been at the heart of blues, jazz, country, gospel, soul, and rock 'n' roll music. Sensual expressions of the urge for transcendence can be witnessed in the way that people in church rock back and forth, as if releasing sexual energy, or in the way that soul singers seize on the transcendental properties of gospel lyrics, modifying them to convey erotic desire. Many records in this category, such as Al Green's "Belle" and Madonna's often maligned "Like a Virgin," articulate a hunger for sexual and spiritual renewal that points to their common wellspring.

A third mystical display of the urge for transcendence is empathy, the gift that some people have to enter into the suffering of others. Music that expresses this impulse can be interpersonal, such as the Pretenders' "I'll Stand by You" or 2pac's "Keep Ya Head Up." It also can be more broadly social in scope, such as Sinéad O'Connor's "Black Boys on Mopeds," an enormous outpouring of compassion—and exquisitely controlled rage—occasioned by the murderous racial profiling of the London police. Moby's "God Moving Over the Face of the Waters" likewise creates wider ripples, its brooding, earth-bound notes evoking a well of empathy that seems as divine as its title suggests.

Unlike mystics who seek some higher spiritual union (whether through contemplation, sensuality, or empathy), musicians who convey the urge for transcendence through negation are responding to a world that makes no sense to them and that holds out little hope of deliverance. Their restlessness is not evident in a pull toward anything, at least not outwardly, but in an aversion to their surroundings, and specifically, to the distortion or absence of any window to something more or better than they know. These musicians might not be able to see, or even to envision, what could bring transcendence about, but their striving typically is as intense as those who articulate their spiritual hunger mystically or prophetically. Though arrested or impeded, the yearning of these naysayers points beyond the mundane or the everyday and thus betrays spiritual leanings, no matter how profane some observers might find their expressions of frustration, brokenness, or despair.

Many artists who give voice to antipathy do so through music that reflects chaos and discord, such as Tricky, the British DJ and MC, and Trent Reznor, the auteur behind the industrial-rock band Nine Inch Nails. Tricky's music is claustrophobic and paranoid, depicting a world bereft of intimacy and trust in which the best that people can hope for is not to hurt each other too badly. Reznor's records are more implacable and abrasive, their cacophony born of feelings of despondency and self-loathing. Despite this overriding negativity, each manages in his way to move beyond dissolution, if only by virtue of his persistent expression of it. Each seems to need to scatter the gloom that engulfs him in order to have any hope of getting beyond it.

Others express their antipathy more radically, not just by echoing the desolation that they experience, but by going beyond evocation to embody or serve as a repository of it. Iggy Pop, for example, acts the idiot and debases himself as a way of confronting the "non-sense" that he experiences and divesting it of its power. Johnny Rotten of the Sex Pistols proclaimed himself an antichrist and threw himself into the role, assailing the social and economic stagnation of postindustrial England in order to clear the way for a future of his own making. The rapper Eminem embodied the hatred and degradation that he has known by becoming it in the person of his pernicious alter ego Slim Shady. Like that of many negationists, the music that Eminem makes is disruptive and can be off-putting, but it conveys an overriding urge for transcendence nonetheless.

This identification with or assumption of negation can be dangerous if taken too far, even to the point of extinguishing the urge for transcendence altogether. The Geto Boys' "Mind's Playin' Tricks on Me," a nightmarish, vérité-style dispatch from Houston's Fifth Ward, comes close to doing so as the gangsta rap duo brilliantly and all too convincingly convey how poverty, drugs, and violence loosen a person's grip on reality and erode their humanity. Transgressive rocker G. G. Allin, whose self-abasing shows saw him beating himself bloody as well as defecating and eating his feces onstage, presents a singularly disintegrating extreme. Allin vowed to commit suicide during a performance scheduled for Halloween 1993, but he died of an overdose of heroin before he could deliver on his threat. In cases like his, any hope of transcendence apparently has given way to nihilism or madness and been eclipsed by negation itself.

Why bother with expressions of negation in a book about transcendence? Why even listen to them, especially when the music and the messages that they convey can be unsettling and repugnant? Negation gives voice to the desolation that many people experience, an absence of hope and humanity akin to what the medieval mystic John of the Cross referred to as the "dark night of the soul."[6] As articulations of an urge for transcendence, these dispatches from the abyss might be profoundly impeded, but they betray a deep-seated striving just the same. Most point beyond despair if just by the force of their expression of it.

There is another reason to listen to and talk about shocking, even transgressive records like Eminem's "Criminal" or the Sex Pistols' "Holidays in the Sun." The revulsion and rage that these outpourings of negation contain often are fitting responses to violence, intolerance, and other forms of oppression. Such expressions, again, can be offensive, and some are not worth hearing, being neither redemptive nor good art. G. G. Allin, sadly, is ultimately a case of the former, the shock-rocker Marilyn Manson perhaps a case of the latter. The best naysayers, though, force us to confront things that we otherwise might not face, thereby opening the door to feelings like anger, understanding, and empathy—and, through them, to action that prevents inhumanity and keeps portals to transcendence open. Naysayers also remind us of our inability, in and of ourselves, to achieve the release that we seek; the clamor that they make serves as a corrective to cheap or false claims to transcendence. All of which is to say nothing of the cathartic thrill that comes from destroying idols and tearing down walls.

Prophetic articulations of the urge for transcendence point to what satisfying our underlying restlessness might mean on a larger social scale. These expressions often stem from impulses that are evident in their negative and mystical counterparts, such as outrage and empathy, yet they ultimately are more social and political in scope. Prophetic voices tend to be less transparently spiritual, more "worldly" or outward-directed, than their mystical counterparts. Prophetic

voices also are more visionary and constructive than those of negationists. When prophets resist unjust structures and conditions, they
do not merely decry or seek to dismantle them; they envision and, in
some cases, establish something better in their place.

Maybe the most prevalent expression of the prophetic impulse in
pop music involves lifting up and demonstrating solidarity with those
who suffer or are oppressed. The point, in this case, "is not to fight
the bad guys," as the singer Ani DiFranco put it; "it's to help the
good guys. The point is to make [the good guys] stronger."[7] Johnny
Cash did this with people living on society's margins when he
adopted the persona of the Man in Black. Vowing to wear mourner's
black in public "till things are brighter"—that is, until more was done
to lessen human misery—Cash became a voice for people who were
homeless or in prison, for those who languished on Indian reservations or lived with AIDS. A similar impulse is at work in Curtis Mayfield's message of equality and uplift in veiled civil rights anthems like
"Keep on Pushing," "People Get Ready," and "We're a Winner."
More than just calling attention to the struggles of the people that
they sing about, or even just encouraging them not to give up, prophets of uplift move beyond empathy to spur others to action.

Other artists articulate the urge for transcendence prophetically by
calling oppressive institutions into account. These musicians concen-
trate less on giving voice to the predicaments of individuals or whole
classes of people than they do on resisting the values and institutions
that keep people down. They "fight the bad guys," as DiFranco's col-
loquialism would have it. Thus we hear Michael Franti of the agit-rap
collective Spearhead confronting racially motivated police brutality at
home in the US and calling for an end to the bullying tactics of the
nation's military forces abroad. Or we have the Mekons, the aggro-
punk collective from the UK, assailing First World greed and aggression with music so indomitable that it sounds like it might be able to
obliterate those things all by itself. Or we have Public Enemy venting
their anger, by way of Chuck D's thundering raps and the group's
polyrhythmic maelstroms, not just at racism and Reagan/Bush-era
bad faith, but at apathy within middle-class black communities and
at gangsta rap's glorification of drugs, violence, and materialism. The
prevailing impulse of these prophets is resistance. Their expressions
are different from those of negationists insofar as they do not merely

lash out at the forces that thwart transcendence. They have a vision, whether of peace, justice, or equality, of what transcendence might hold.

Some prophets move beyond solidarity and resistance to personify the liberating alternatives that they envision, the way, for example, that Sly & the Family Stone did for a while during the late 1960s. The Family Stone not only embodied an alternative to segregation by making room in the band for members of various races and ethnicities, they made records that integrated styles of music that had increasingly become segmented along lines of class and race. Not only that, in contrast to the patriarchal norms that governed even the putatively liberated Woodstock generation of which they were a part, the group featured female members in lead as opposed to merely supportive roles. "Riot grrrl" offered a similarly liberating model a quarter-century later. A post-punk movement led by visionary feminist bands like Bikini Kill and Sleater-Kinney, riot grrrl called for "Revolution Girl Style" by promoting cooperative artistic and entrepreneurial ventures that went beyond identity politics to include men and to encompass global concerns.

Whether they do so mystically, negatively, or prophetically, musicians who express the urge for transcendence invariably point beyond themselves to something deeper and more abiding than the everyday. These artists do not necessarily have to be pointing to the divine, much less to visions of glory of the sort that have dominated Christian thinking for centuries (many of which run counter to the more earthbound model of the Jesus of the gospels). Transcendence occurs anytime that the eternal impinges on and, however briefly, transforms the present. Transcendence can be manifest in the empathy or sexual intimacy that takes place between two people. It can be present in the sense of wonder occasioned by an encounter with art or nature, or in the emergence of a liberating moment within history, such as the end of Apartheid in South Africa. Even feelings of antipathy that stem from alienation or despair can become portals to transcendence. Artists who express negation might not be able to articulate a vision of what transcending those conditions might entail, but by bearing witness to whatever impedes transcendence, they attest, if only indirectly, to the possibility of experiencing it.

Which is not to say that some artists do not obscure or corrupt the urge for transcendence. Those, for example, who make music born of banal, venal, or narcissistic impulses that lacks redeeming qualities, such as the "vapid spirituality" that the singer Morrissey has said that he hears in the music of Britney Spears.[8] I would not want to suggest that records that merely entertain us, as Spears's music can, do not have merit. Still, if only implicitly, Morrissey has a point. Records that give voice to an urge for transcendence not only have the capacity to speak to human restlessness and desire in ways that music that represses or masks that striving cannot. They also are vastly better equipped to serve as portals to the transcendence that we seek.

One such portal, and one that speaks explicitly to how pop music can function in this way, is Van Morrison's 1982 single "Cleaning Windows," an impressionistic, autobiographical wonder in which he revisits his childhood in East Belfast. Over the better part of five minutes of juking R&B that is in itself transcendent, Morrison looks back fondly on the odd jobs that he had as a boy, as well as on a variety of other quotidian comings and goings. He exults at some length in the transformative power of the music that he heard and the books that he read, mentioning everything from the records of Lead Belly and Muddy Waters to Jack Kerouac's *On the Road* and Buddhist scholar Christmas Humphrey's primer on Zen. The fact that Morrison mixes music, books, and spirituality is crucial here, particularly as it relates to washing windows, the song's central conceit. This image doubles as a metaphor for vocation, an undertaking understood not merely as labor or work, but as a basic calling. "What's my line?" Morrison asks as he heads into the chorus. "I'm happy cleaning windows," he answers, suggesting that for him, meaning, if not transcendence itself, is found in the everyday, or at least in that which breaks into the mundane and illuminates it. As he so often has, Morrison is talking about a way of orienting oneself to the world, about cultivating a posture of openness—in this case, a way of listening *and* seeing—that persistently seeks windows to something more. Just as important, he is reminding us of the value of keeping those panes clean.

# SECTION I

# MYSTICS

Contemplatives, Sensualists,
and Empaths

# chapter 1

## DWELLERS ON
## THE THRESHOLD

### Van Morrison, Jimmie Dale Gilmore,
### and P.M. Dawn

<small>INTO THE MYSTIC: LOOKING FOR THE VEEDON FLEECE</small>

"Man can embody truth but he cannot know it."

—William Butler Yeats[1]

"It's the great search, fueled by the belief that through these musical and mental processes illumination is attainable. Or may at least be glimpsed."

—Lester Bangs[2]

"I'm a dweller on the threshold and I'm waiting at the door. I'm standing in the darkness, I don't want to wait no more."

—Van Morrison, "Dweller on the Threshold"

Each of these passages speaks to the perennial quest for transcendence at the heart of Van Morrison's life and music. The first is from his fellow Irishman, a poet whose mystical streak, incantatory rhythms, passion for his homeland, and prodigious power over words prefigured Morrison's own. The second comes from a fevered essay by the late Lester Bangs, the insatiable rock critic who was drawn, among other things, to how through the repetition of a single word or syllable, Morrison coaxes the eternal from the now, or at least seems ever on the verge of doing so. The third quote, from the song "Dweller on the Threshold," is Morrison giving voice to his overwhelming desire for transcendence, a thirst that, while never quenched, and perhaps because of that, infuses all of his music and makes so much of it sublime.

Morrison's urge to connect with some abiding presence or force pervades his music's roiling grooves, its transporting hooks and horn choruses, its pregnant silences, and above all, his gruff, honking vocals. His evocative lyrics, too. "If I ventured in the slipstream / Between the viaducts of your dreams / Where the mobile steel rims crack / And the ditch and the back roads stop" begins the first stanza of "Astral Weeks." "Could you find me / Would you kiss, uh, my eyes / And lay me down / In silence easy / To be born again?" Morrison goes on to ask. He could be talking to a friend or to a lover here, or even to God, but it hardly matters; impelled by tensive strains of upright bass, drums, and guitar, his agitated delivery testifies to an urgency that goes well beyond the everyday.

Words, however, take Morrison only so far in his pursuit of transcendence. "My t-tongue gets ti-ed / Ee-ee-every-every-every time I try to speak," he stutters on "Cypress Avenue." He repeats these lines, which are sprung by a flurry of notes traded by flute and violin, before adding, "And my insides shake just like a leaf on a tree." On those occasions when Morrison exhausts a lyric, he avails himself of a more elemental brogue, a glossolalia through which he moans, stammers, and wrestles wordlessly, locked in a groove until he finds and awakens what in one staggering track he refers to as the lion inside him. Sometimes, resorting to concrete imagery, he sings of this mystical destination or state of consciousness as if it were a place outside himself, such as heaven or Caledonia, his mythical ancestral homeland. Other times he depicts it as a vehicle that can carry him there or otherwise enrapture him, as in "Celtic Ray," the title of which invokes not only Morrison's Irish heritage, but also both his late hero Ray Charles and outer space. In "Vanlose Stairway" Morrison beseeches us to send him our Bibles and our Bhagavad-Gitas via a celestial passageway that "reaches up to the moon" and doubtless beyond. The term "Vanlose" is Morrison's coinage, the loss to which it alludes seemingly a reference to his need to lose or die to himself in order, paradoxically, to find himself or to get home. Or, as he puts it in "Astral Weeks," to be born again, although not in the sense of embracing some orthodoxy or belief system, but of being transformed or, as he sings elsewhere, of being made whole.

As is often the case with spiritual omnivores like Morrison, the object of this striving does not always come into clear view, not for him or for the listener. Then again, used in this connection, the subject-object dichotomy that dominates Western thought ultimately might not prove helpful when plumbing the interpenetration of the temporal and eternal that distinguishes the experience of transcendence.[3] There are times when the goal of Morrison's quest seems to be communion with the traditional personal God of Judaism and Christianity. At others it could be communion with a transpersonal deity or some state of enlightenment. Whatever the case, the intensity with which Morrison engages in his pursuit of what he at one point deems "the mystic" seldom has been witnessed among rock 'n' rollers.

Dave Marsh, writing some twenty years ago about Bruce Springsteen, Bob Seger, Gram Parker, and others who might be considered Morrison's acolytes, argued that "none of these [other singers] has yet taken the spiritual basis of rock and R&B and the blues so far into an almost religious concept."[4] Springsteen has sought increasingly to do so with his arena shows, which adapt the liturgical trappings of Pentecostal worship to a secular setting. Yet Morrison, with his obsessive quest to reach a higher spiritual plain—indeed, to lose himself there (wherever "there" is or whatever it means)—remains rock 'n' roll's most ardent contemplative. Dozens of his recordings teem with this fervor, with "Into the Mystic" being the most emblematic and his albums *Astral Weeks* and *Veedon Fleece* being the most ineffable and sustained. Though rarely as intense, Morrison's later work often is luminous, large portions of it finding him more or less at home within the bosom of Christianity.

No single recording embodies Morrison's outsized thirst for transcendence more than "Listen to the Lion," the eleven-minute reverie that closes the first side of his 1972 LP, *St. Dominic's Preview*. The track begins as a ruminative variation of Wilson Pickett's "In the Midnight Hour" (itself an adaptation of an old gospel number), with Morrison singing about his love tumbling down as bass, snare drum, and acoustic guitar furnish him with a gently undulating bed of rhythms to land on. Morrison has extolled the mystical properties of sex before, and often, but that is not what is happening here. As he

heads into the second stanza he wearily starts searching his soul for
the lion within. His tears, not his sex, are flowing like water now.
Jazz-tinged figures played on a piano and a second acoustic guitar
punctuate the proceedings, which mount steadily, like the tide, until
five or six minutes into the piece, Morrison begins to scat. Even these
impromptu ramblings, though, are too confining for him—too medi-
ated or coherent or something. He finally abandons words altogether
and, with a chorus of singers chanting, "Listen to the lion," starts to
grunt and growl, and then to roar, tapping his leonine persona before
returning at last to concrete speech. Morrison's ship has set sail, he
tells us, abruptly switching metaphors. His vessel makes its way
around the world and, as the tempest dies down, "way up to Caledonia" and into the mystic, where he vows to make "a brand new start."

You can hear this overriding urge for transcendence, albeit expressed more menacingly than it later would be, in the records that
Morrison made during the mid-60s with the Belfast garage band
Them. One of those singles was called "Mystic Eyes," a relentless
vamp powered by Morrison's squalling harmonica, a thunderous
forcebeat, and some hard-charging organ and electric guitar. As Van
shouts the record's inchoate lyrics, the band sounds less like it is sum-
moning the lion within him than beating it out of him. Doubtless
some of this fury was born of the combo's teenage years playing in
R&B cover bands in cramped, noisy clubs in the red-light districts of
Hamburg and Scotland—and later, with a prototype of Them called
the Gamblers at Belfast's Maritime Hotel (with Morrison on sax,
harp, and vocals). Yet there also is an underlying desperation in the
group's records that betrays a fiercer need to be heard. Greil Marcus,
writing in *Rolling Stone*, called it an "angry need for freedom,"[5] and
Morrison would later bear this comment out when, on the otherwise
sublime "Tupelo Honey," he proclaims: "You can't stop us, on the
road to freedom / You can't stop us, 'cause our eyes can see."

Sibilant and on the brink of distorting, many of the records that
Morrison made with Them rage with pent-up desire. In "Could You,
Would You," one of his many early attempts to channel the ch'i of
James Brown, Morrison pours his fireplug self into each word as if he
is about to burst, perhaps believing that the effort alone could set him
free, or at least vent his urge for release. "Van Morrison is *obsessed*
with how much musical or verbal information he can compress into a

small space," Lester Bangs wrote in 1979, and Bangs's observation goes well beyond formal musical considerations.[6] "Gloria" ("G-L-O-R-I-A") is obsession writ large, at once sexy and scary, and in both cases even more so than Patti Smith's shamanic renewal of the song a decade later. Here as elsewhere, Morrison seems to be squeezing out every spark of emotion that he has ever felt, if only, at this early stage when he just let things blurt, to keep from overloading.

Such transmissions were befitting of the twilight years of AM radio's golden age, when records beamed from dashboard and transistor radios, broadcasting elemental outpourings like "Be My Baby," "I Want to Hold Your Hand," and "Papa's Got a Brand New Bag." Such eruptions seemed natural enough, too, coming from Morrison, a blue-collar tough who grew up in East Belfast under cover of the cranes of the Harland & Wolff shipyard, where his father, who played in skiffle bands, worked as an electrician. To a kid of six or seven those silhouetted hoists must have resembled radio towers, perhaps like that of Radio Luxembourg, which Morrison, enthralled by his father's jazz and blues records, tuned in to hear the latest pop and R&B hits. In 1991, looking back on those days and reflecting on their spiritual significance in his life, he sang:

> Take me back, take me way, way, way back
> On Hyndford Street
> Where you could feel the silence at half past eleven
> On long summer nights
> As the wireless played Radio Luxembourg
> And the voices whispered across Beechie River
> In the quietness as we sank into restful slumber in the silence
> And carried on dreaming, in God.

Music has long been a subtext of Morrison's records, and many of his references to it have had spiritual and religious overtones. But radio always has been something else altogether for him, an almost cabalistic totem of transformative power that connects people beyond the mundane precincts of space and time. "Hey, Mr. Deejay / I just wanna hear some rhythm and blues music on the radio / Uh huh, all right," he shouts in "Domino." Morrison sounds as if he is about to start speaking in tongues here. In "Caravan," maybe the greatest of his "radio" songs, he entreats us to crank up our receivers and, as he puts it in the track into which "Caravan" flows, let our souls and spirits fly "into the mystic." "Wavelength," a single from 1978, sets forth the redemptive properties that radio holds for Morrison. "When I'm down, you always comfort me / When I'm lonely, you see about me / You are everywhere you're supposed to be / And I can get your station when I need rejuvenation," he exults as surges of guitars and synthesizers and the "doo-doo's" of the backup singers carry him away.

Ironically given his faith in the medium—indeed, his obsession with it—Morrison's records rarely have fared well on commercial radio. He charted a few singles in the UK and the US with Them in the mid-60s, but only "Mystic Eyes" and "Here Comes the Night" reached the *Billboard* Top 40.[7] A handful of his solo records later reached the American Top 40, with "Domino" climbing the highest, topping out at No. 9 in 1970. The closest he came to radio perfection, though, was 1967's ebullient "Brown-Eyed Girl," its rumbling bass line making straight for the pelvic cavity and its indelible tagline, "Making love in the green grass, behind the stadium with you," ripe for the Summer of Love. "Brown-Eyed Girl" reached No. 10 during that conflicted season, just after Morrison left both Them and Ireland and moved to the United States. The record's effervescence could not have been more at odds with where he was emotionally. He was living in Boston at the time, renting a squalid flat with his first wife and her young son. He did not have a band and he was fighting with his record label and drinking heavily. More in keeping with his mood was "T. B. Sheets," a threnody depicting the ravages of tuberculosis that appeared with "Brown-Eyed Girl" on his first solo album, *Blowin' Your Mind*. Only radio provided any succor, with Morrison phoning in sodden requests to hear the likes of Muddy Waters and John Lee Hooker to an all-night deejay named Peter Wolf, who later befriended him and became the lead singer of the J. Geils Band.

Out of Morrison's dark night of the soul, though, came *Astral Weeks*, the first sustained upwelling of spiritual restlessness of his career. He made the album in a fever—a mere 48 hours. Impressionistic, introspective, and singularly intense, it was Morrison, then just twenty-three, leaving rock 'n' roll and R&B behind, or at least sublimating them, in the pursuit of what Dave Marsh called a "personal emotional equivalent of the blues."[8] Not that the music on the album, despite its nods to Lead Belly, Ray Charles, and others, reveals any outward debt to the twelve-bar, AAB strictures of the idiom. Played by the heady likes of Richard Davis (on upright bass) and the Modern Jazz Quartet's Connie Kay (on drums)—and filigreed with flute, soprano sax, and vibraphone—*Astral Weeks* is more akin formally to chamber jazz than anything else, although it is hardly as polite as that label suggests. Though often hushed, the album's impromptu arrangements are unfettered, as free of the beat as the outward bound "new thing" of Ornette Coleman and Eric Dolphy (with whom bassist Davis recorded). "I'm pushing at the door," Morrison announces in the title track, and it certainly sounds like it; buttressed by his collaborators, he bleats and moans like one consumed with the desire to break through.

The lyrics on *Astral Weeks* tend to be gospel-inspired, such as when, on the title track, Morrison sings, "I'm nothin' but a stranger in this world / I got a home on high / . . . Way up in, uh, heaven." The overriding impulse here, though, is that of the blues, particularly as Ralph Ellison—and later, Albert Murray—described it in terms of someone who fingers the jagged grain of a painful experience in order to transcend it.[9] This impression is most intense when Morrison gets stuck on a word or a phrase, as in when, in a hypnotic, sax-like burr, he moans, "You breathe in, you breathe out / You breathe in, you breathe out / You breathe in, you breathe out / You breathe in, you breathe out / And you're high," in what feels like stop-time rhythm. And if not in stop time, then definitely in time *out* of time. "Wrapped up in your magic shroud as ecstasy surrounds you / This time it's found you," Morrison goes on, as fluttering bass and swirls of flute render the gathering rapture palpable.

*Astral Weeks* is not a Christian record per se (heard one way, it could be about reawakening, about dying to oneself in order to be free), but most of its imagery and musical dynamics suggest death and resurrection. Still, as evidenced by the line, "This time it's found you," with its suggestion that previous connections had failed, transcendence is not a given; there is no hint of what theologians call "cheap grace" here. "Grab it, catch it / Fly it, sigh it / C'mon, *die* it," Morrison urges his partner over the fitful strings and cadences of "Ballerina." They reach any number of ecstatic heights on the album, yet, as black preachers often say, they have "come a mighty long way" to do so. Indeed, on the mournful "Slim Slow Slider" Morrison's partner rides a pale horse. She is dying and he cannot do a thing to save her.

*Moondance*, the album that followed *Astral Weeks*, is the sound of someone who has come through the storm. "When all the dark clouds roll away / And the sun begins to shine / I see my freedom from across the bay / And it comes right in on time," Morrison begins to the hymnlike piano and guitar of "Brand New Day." In this enchanted state he also flirts with gypsies who blast transcendental radios, he makes crazy love that leaves him feeling "righteous" and "whole," and he embarks on a foghorn-guided trip into the mystic. At one point he even gets stoned, not on smoke or drink, but on the rainwater that soaks him, "down to [his] soul," when he and a fishing buddy get caught in a summer cloudburst.

The albums that issued from this rebirth constitute the first flowering of what Morrison called his "Caledonia soul music," a transporting amalgam of country, jazz, rock, and R&B marked by sweeping melodies, swelling horn choirs, lilting guitar lines, and singalong choruses that, as he raves at one point, "head straight to your heart like a cannonball." Dense, punchy, and swinging, singles like "Domino," "Wild Night," and the juking "Blue Money," with its drunk-on-words shout-out, "Take five, honey," are typical of this phase, which is rooted more in traditional songform—and more groove-obsessed—than the untrammeled flights of *Astral Weeks*. The result, to borrow a phrase from Morrison's "Warm Love," is a sort of "jellyroll soul," a sweet signature sound owing to Motown, Curtis Mayfield, and the Hank Williams of "Hey Good Lookin'" that is every bit as sexy as the double entendre of that "jellyroll" tag suggests. *It's Too Late to Stop Now*, the blues-steeped concert document that Morrison made with the eleven-piece "Caledonia Soul Orchestra" that he had assembled at the time, remains one of the great live albums of the era.

*Van the Man*, a bootleg of live and studio tracks from 1971, might be even better. Among its greatest pleasures is Morrison's declamatory remake of Bob Dylan's "Just Like a Woman" (although his riotous segue from the opening lines of "Que Sera Sera" to his band's delirious take of "Hound Dog" is transcendent in its own way). Nothing on the album, however, approaches the glossolalia-suffused

"Caledonia Soul Music," a mostly wordless anthem in which Morrison and the guitar, piano, horn, and mandolin players ride a variation of the undulating groove from "Into the Mystic" for more than sixteen ecstatic minutes. The musical equivalent of a cross between Solomon's sexually charged "Song of Songs" and the Biblical balm in Gilead, this putative jam session rocks the body as steadfastly as it does the soul; if anything, it does not go on long enough. On the hymnal "Friday's Child," Morrison and his "Street Choir" second this emotion: Over and over they shout, "You can't stop now," as the track builds to a pumping climax.

Morrison's "Caledonia soul music" was in many respects the product of his courtship and marriage to his second wife, Janet Planet, a relationship that ushered in a period of domestic and pastoral tranquility reminiscent of the time that Dylan spent in Woodstock, New York while recovering from his fabled motorcycle accident in 1966. Biographer Robert Shelton called that time in Dylan's life a "retreat from significance," but Shelton was only half right.[10] Dylan indeed was moving away from the vitriol, irony, and abstruse statements of his volcanic outpourings of the previous year. His embrace of hearth and home, though, was not so much a retreat as a shift from one type of significance to another, and something similar was happening with Morrison as the 70s began. He was releasing glorious records, and the stoned, earthbound soul of *Moondance* was unquestionably as transcendent as the fantastic voyage of *Astral Weeks* (love's mysteries are no less ineffable than heaven's, after all). Yet apart from the exquisite "Tupelo Honey" and the exhilarating "Jackie Wilson Said (I'm in Heaven When You Smile)"—the latter an unremitting single from 1972 that obliterated distinctions between the body and the spirit— little of it evinced the restlessness that drove Morrison to his previous heights or depths.

Hints of unrest nevertheless remained, even amid the reveries of *Moondance*. Despite the assurances of the gospel-infused singers who back him on "Brand New Day," Morrison sings that it only "feels" and "seems" like a new day. He never comes out and says that it actually *is* one. Similarly, in "Into the Mystic," slipped in among his repeated declarations that he will be coming home—that is, that he will reach the incandescent state referenced in the song's title—he sings, "You know I *won't* be coming home," his qualification perhaps an acknowledgment that transcendence is fleeting, if finally unattainable. Not that Morrison won't die trying. He makes that plain enough when he sings the record's signature line, "It's too late to stop now," as the music draws to a close.

Tensive moments like this might not be necessary for making great art, but they certainly have driven Morrison's best, much as they did that of his Irish predecessor Yeats, whose outsized contradictions or "antinomies" were among the hallmarks of his early poems. "His lion thrives on ambiguity," M. Mark wrote in her inspired 1979 essay on Morrison, alluding to that conflicted line about him not coming home in "Into the Mystic."[11] Less a question of either/or, of getting home or not, Morrison's quest is more about living with the tension born simultaneously of being home and not being there, of undergoing mystical transformation yet never experiencing it fully, of being what he at one point calls a "dweller on the threshold."

This tension between what some theologians describe as the "already" and the "not yet," the tension between what is and what yet could be, lies at the heart of "Almost Independence Day," the roiling, ten-minute counterpart to "Listen to the Lion" that closes *St. Dominic's Preview*. "It's *almost* Independence Day," Morrison repeats over the track's heaving rhythms as if intoning that litany might hasten the event's arrival. He can sense that his day of liberation is coming, just as he could "see" his freedom from across the bay in "Brand New Day." He *knows* it is there. He even hears voices calling up and down the San Francisco coastline and, as the track fades, a foghorn hailing its coming, but his moment of release never quite arrives. "Almost Independence Day" expresses an eschatological tension, not one construed narrowly as having to do with some historical end of the world, but one that, in a broader existential sense, relates to the unquenchable thirst for transcendence that makes us human.

The restlessness that receded with the blissful likes of *Moondance* and *Tupelo Honey* was stirred up again by the time that Morrison made *St. Dominic's Preview* in 1972. It would not be long before he would divorce his wife, but perhaps more significantly, he had not been home to Ireland since leaving Them in 1966. He was longing for and felt somehow exiled from the land of his birth. The album's sweeping title track, inspired by a mass held at St. Dominic's Cathedral in San Francisco to promote peace in Northern Ireland, captured the dis-ease that Morrison was feeling at the time, even as it afforded him a measure of transcendence over it. At once an anthem of protest ("Everybody feels so determined not to be in anyone else's pain") and a glimpse or "preview" of release (Morrison is gazing upon "freedom marchers, out in the street"), this keening wonder was as majestic and lyrical a burst of Caledonia soul as any that he had made up to that point.

As a Celt, Morrison is, as Greil Marcus has pointed out, a spiritual descendant of St. Brendan, the Irish prelate who traveled in search of America fifteen centuries ago and, according to legend, reached his destination and established a community there.[12] Morrison's quest brought him to America as well, but unlike Brendan, he kept searching. He gravitated toward spiritual havens like Woodstock and the Bay Area, but he never really settled down, or stopped missing Ireland. He finally got back to Belfast in 1973, after his marriage to Janet Planet had ended, and it was there that he wrote the material that would appear on the luminous *Veedon Fleece*.

M. Mark called the record "a magnificently gentle album of Gaelic mysticism, lit from within—recorder, flute, and guitar music that sounds centuries old and utterly reborn."[13] The music *did* sound ancient and new—timeless, to invoke the reviewer's readymade. *Veedon Fleece* also was Morrison's most "Irish" album to date, one in which the pull of his homeland, not so much the war-torn nation that he knew as the mythical idyll of his ancestors, is strong, even if explicit references to it on the record are few. The songs are knotty and inscrutable, and most are arranged for strings and wind instruments. Several are sung in a gauzy falsetto and large portions of the album are bereft of the hooks and grooves that galvanize Morrison's sashaying Caledonia soul. *Veedon Fleece* contains everything from sprung country rhythms and relentless stuttering to an impressionistic apology for a tortured outlaw hero named Linden Arden and boundless outpourings of compassion and disdain. Included as well are an abundance of oblique, gorgeously sung couplets like, "You can hang suspended from the sky, wish on a toilet roll / You can just soak up the atmosphere, like a fish inside a bowl."

All of it converges on "You Don't Pull No Punches But You Don't Push the River," the numinous, nine-minute voyage that Morrison embarks on midway through the album. "Go and merge with the

river," he urges amid whirling flourishes of piano, flute, and guitar as
he steers his way through a Scylla and Charybdis of rocks and fog,
homing in on the lion within. This time, though, he is not alone.
"William Blake and the Eternals" and the "Sisters of Mercy" are there
with him, searching for the Grail-like fleece. "We're going out to the
country / [To] get down to the real soul / I mean the real soul / Talking about the real soul, people," Morrison growls, as if he is leading a
neo-Gothic tent revival. The entire company ultimately pushes west,
"to the cathedrals," then "down to the beaches" (to be baptized?)
and, finally, like the children of Icarus taking wing, "behind the
sun."[14]

*Veedon Fleece* proved to be a mystical apotheosis for Morrison, at
least for the 1970s, much as *Astral Weeks* had been during the previous decade. Yet it also sold poorly, causing him to withdraw further
and, it seemed, to lose his spiritual and emotional compass. Some of
the lyrics that he wrote after emerging from the self-imposed exile
that followed the album's release suggest that he might have become a
born-again Christian, while some people heard the joyous "Kingdom
Hall" as a nod to the Jehovah's Witnesses. (The reference likely was
inspired by Morrison's memories of his mother's passing ties to the
group.)

There nevertheless were flashes of transcendence during this phase,
especially as the 70s wore on. Most notable by far was the ecstatic
second half of 1979's *Into the Music*, in which Morrison gloriously
weds his sensual and mystical streaks, testifying profusely to his faith
in the healing power of music—and, to only a slightly lesser degree,
of sex. Three years earlier, riding the slow-drag, horn- and harmon-
ica-driven groove of "It Fills You Up," he declaims, "There's something going on / It fill you up, it fill you up, it fill up now." Morrison
repeats these lines, his guttural brogue gaining force, before delivering
the sphinx-like payoff, "But you don't know what it is / But you
don't have to know / You just dig it for what it is." Here again, Morrison does not so much sidestep the question of what he is searching
for as much as trust that whatever it is, he will find it.

*Beautiful Vision*, the album that contains "Cleaning Windows,"
"Vanlose Stairway," and "Dweller on the Threshold," got the 80s off
to an auspicious start (that is, if you overlook *Common One*, its som-
nolent, though admittedly mystical predecessor from the turn of the

decade). The inspiration evident on *Beautiful Vision*, though, vanished with Morrison's flirtations with the dodgy Church of Scientology, including his dedication of 1982's *Inarticulate Speech of the Heart* to the sect's founder, L. Ron Hubbard. That album's title might have served as an apt description of Morrison's leonine glossolalia; instead it proved a cautionary word about its noodling, New Age-derived contents. *No Guru No Method No Teacher* (1986) was not much better, its title a defensive jab at the critics who had tried to pin Morrison down spiritually during this mercurial phase of his career. The 80s, however, ended with a pair of relative high points, 1987's *Poetic Champions Compose*, which poses the mystical-existential question, "Did Ye Get Healed?" and *Avalon Sunset*, an uplifting, Christocentric record from 1989. *Avalon* also included the closest thing that Morrison had to a hit single in nearly a decade—a jaunty, Afro-pop-tinged duet called "Whenever God Shines His Light" that he recorded with one of his heroes, erstwhile teen idol Cliff Richard.

"He just wants to roll on, undulating from rhythmic hill to melodic dale," wrote Robert Christgau at the time, summing up Morrison's mostly blissed-out late 80s catalog.[15] Christgau's assessment is hardly as derogatory as it might have sounded, and it certainly proved prescient. Since then Morrison has been in something of a groove, gliding along the Celtic Ray, or, if you prefer, riding up and down the Vanlose escalator, exuding an aura of grace and a sense of vocation that has seen him offering *Hymns to the Silence* and wandering off in search of *Enlightenment*. He also has waxed nostalgic about his childhood and his musical touchstones, including variously inspired genre exercises in jazz (*What's Wrong with This Picture*), blues (*Too Long in Exile* and *Down the Road*), honky-tonk (*You Win Again*, with Linda Gail Lewis), Celtic ballads (*Irish Heartbeat*, with the Chieftains) and skiffle (*The Skiffle Sessions*, with Lonnie Donegan).

Some of Morrison's material, such as that on *Hymns*, is more explicitly spiritual—and frequently Christian or gospel in emphasis (i.e., "When Will I Learn to Live in God")—than his earlier, more mystically open-ended work. Many of these later recordings are quite good, even if they are not as transcendent as the self-surpassing likes of *Astral Weeks*, *Moondance*, and *Veedon Fleece*. All nevertheless are of a piece, issuing from Morrison's perennial pursuit of the lion within. "Down the highways and the byways / Still searching for my home," he confesses in 1998's "The Philosopher's Stone." Three years later, singing what amounts to the same song, he submits, "Trying to find my way back home / Further on down the road / Down the road of peace," to a restless shuffle-beat. "Too late to stop now" is how he put it some three decades earlier in "Into the Mystic." Even then it sounded like he never would.

## Just a Wave, Not the Water: The Search for Another Colorado

> "There's still time for heaven, though we're already there."
>
> —Jimmie Dale Gilmore, "Braver Newer World"

> "She would never see that this world's just not real to me."
>
> —Jimmie Dale Gilmore, "Tonight I Think
> I'm Gonna Go Downtown"

A steadfastness of purpose akin to Morrison's is evident in the spiritual quest of Jimmie Dale Gilmore, a singer-songwriter who, with Terry Allen, Jo Carol Pierce, Joe Ely, and Butch Hancock, has long been a mainstay of the so-called Lubbock Mafia, perhaps the most gifted and outré aggregation of musicians ever to come from Texas. Each member of this loose-knit collective has distinguished himself or herself not just in music, but in artistic pursuits that range from sculpting and painting to acting and photography. Each also has strong spiritual leanings, but Gilmore, who with Ely and Hancock is one of the cofounders of the evanescent country ensemble the Flatlanders, doubtless is the most contemplative of the lot.

Born, like Morrison, in 1945, Gilmore is one of the "War Children" who came of age with the Beat and rock 'n' roll generations that Morrison sang about. Yet whereas the Irishman's search for rebirth typically has been visceral or Dionysian, as much a matter of wresting transcendence from life as anything else, Gilmore's tends to be more heady or Apollonian. While Morrison roars about the lion within or pushes the river despite telling us that it cannot be done, Gilmore pursues a more serene journey inward, even during those times when he suffers heartbreak or is otherwise discomfited. "She would never see / That this world's just not real to me," he pines in a numinous quaver to the gauzy strains of "Tonight I Think I'm Gonna Go Downtown," one of his many metaphysical love songs. To the mariachi cadences of "Go to Sleep Alone" he tosses off cosmic-comic refrains about "referee[ing] the fight between the being and the seeming." Amid the shimmering cymbal washes and guitars of the Zen-like "Braver Newer World" he observes, "There's still time for heaven / Though we're already there / The daily bread will leaven / All hope, all pain, all care."

Like Morrison, Gilmore sometimes depicts this spiritual destination or transcendental realm as a place, a tendency that was underscored dramatically during an interview that I did with him at his home in the hill country outside Austin, Texas, in 2001. Gilmore's mind flitted over a dazzling array of subjects that bracing January afternoon. He touched on everything from Hinduism, Buddhism, macrobiotics, and Buckminster Fuller to cybernetics, psychology, the *Whole Earth Catalog*, and the philosophies of Bertrand Russell and Alfred North Whitehead. This is to say nothing of his freewheeling commentary on music and musicians. At one point, though, sensing that daylight was fading, he shoved his lanky frame back from the kitchen table and, dispensing with conversation, said, "I've got to show you something."[16]

Soon we were out the door with his dogs Lyra, Vega, Indra, and Maia, winding our way through cedars, boulders, live oaks, and prickly pear before coming to a steep ravine. We tromped another hundred yards or so along the rim of the gorge until Gilmore pointed to where it meets Lick Creek, which empties into the Pedernales River and, eventually, into the mighty Colorado. Just up the creek bed, he announced, was the "oldest known inhabited spot in North America," or at least the site that seems to have held that distinction for a time after archeologists at the University of Texas happened on it during the 1970s. "It's incredible, isn't it?" Gilmore asked, his graying mane and placid smile exuding the aura of a brujo. "I really wasn't interested in this house until our real estate agent brought me back here." He might as well have been talking about the mythical El Dorado that he sings about in "Another Colorado."

Gilmore lives for such epiphanies, the more ineffable and paradoxical the better. His sense of wonder, his hunger to come to terms with his place in the larger world, is evident in his study of metaphysics, in the meditation that he practices, and in the spiritual concerns that suffuse his lyrics. His records, which typically defy definition, likewise betray this omnivorous bent, embracing folk, blues, honky-tonk, rock 'n' roll, Cajun, and Tex-Mex Border music. "There is an encompassing spirituality here," Terri Sutton wrote of his 1993 album, *Spinning Around the Sun*, "a reconfiguration of rural music's tug between sin and salvation that speaks not of a judging God but of connections between people, the flexibility of time and space, the relative triteness of the ego."[17]

In Gilmore's case that ego is linked inextricably to being a "flatlander"—as a native of the Texas panhandle, of course, but also as a member of the mirage-like, yet widely influential band of that name. The original incarnation of the Flatlanders recorded just one album, after which, due to contractual obligations that prevented them from recording together, Gilmore and the group's two other singer-songwriters, Ely and Hancock, pursued solo careers. Ely went on, among other things, to open the shows that the Clash played in Texas during their 1980 tour of the United States, and the Flatlanders became, as the title of the 1991 reissue of their debut—and, at the time, only—album put it, "More a legend than a band." Gilmore, Ely, and Hancock nevertheless remained friends and continued to perform and write together, amassing what is today a voluminous body of work that in interviews they refer to self-effacingly as "communal property." This is not just talk. Often a song that one of the three has written becomes identified with another, such as Gilmore's 1993 version of Hancock's "Just a Wave." Gilmore had recorded the song before. He had been singing it at shows for years in fact, but this sublime take, from *Spinning Around the Sun*, has the ring of the truth as lived. It serves as the de facto credo by which Gilmore has sought to live for the better part of four decades now.

"Just a Wave" is a love song, but one with a twist. It doubles as a meditation on how, as Buddhists believe, selfish desire, the yoking of personal destiny to earthly fulfillment, causes suffering—in this case, Gilmore being cast aside by his lover. "I said, 'I've been your raging river, precious African queen / I've shown you everything that I've ever seen,'" he sings in disbelief, his fiddle-leavened tenor recounting the couple's parting conversation. "But she knew more than I taught her," Gilmore goes on, his narcissism beginning to fade, "When she said, 'Babe, you're just a wave, you're not the water.'" From here Gilmore pursues his love "with all of [his] will" until, finally seeing things for what they are, he draws near her, only to discover, his sighs echoed by heaving guitars, that his place in her heart, and in the larger cosmic scheme, has not changed. "Then up some old sad river, where snow white lilies float / I came to her for mercy, but I hardly rocked the boat / She seemed surprised that I had caught her / But she said, 'Babe, you're just a wave, you're not the water.'"

The opening lines of "Just a Wave"—"Thirst is not the answer / Oceans come and go"—all but give away the song's ending, distilling its message with aphoristic concision. They also can be heard as a poetic take on Buddhism's Second Noble Truth, in which the source of all suffering is identified (in Pali) as "thirst," as an urge that connotes craving and attachment.[18] Thirst then not only is not the answer, as Gilmore sings; thirst is the *cause* of suffering, if only because everything that people desire, whether lofty or base, is impermanent and inevitably fades away, thus leading to dissatisfaction.

Arriving at such a perspective on human striving, and on humanity's place within the universe, came naturally enough to Gilmore, growing up as he did on the wind-scoured plains of Tulia and Lubbock, where the expansive horizon dwarfs even the monumental, sand-sculpted landscape. Out on the Texas panhandle the firmament routinely becomes a theater for breathtaking funnel clouds and lightning shows. At night it is often a vault for stars so numerous and intense that a body feels lost in space. It can be humbling, and more than a little disorienting, stranded out there among all that earth and sky. The sense of isolation that it breeds, particularly given Lubbock's relative cultural barrenness, can be so alienating that Joe Ely likened living there to "being in a concentration camp on the moon."[19]

Yet Lubbock's environs also can be inspiring. Some believe that they account for the profusion of musicians who have come from the area, from Buddy Holly to Waylon Jennings (who got his start as a deejay at KLLL there) to Gilmore, Ely, and the rest of the Lubbock Mafia. The sense of possibility that the vastness of West Texas begets, one of connecting with things beyond the everyday like the famous UFOs, or "Lubbock Lights," that were sighted there in the 1950s, cries out for a response. From Gilmore it called forth music of singu-

lar beauty steeped in a mysticism that is both earthy and otherworldly, and that seems to thrive on the potential or liminal space
between the two. "So good to be home in the Borderland / Where
things are not what they seem / So good to be home in the
Borderland / Between the dawn and the dream," he drawls on the
chorus of one beatific track.

This dialectical sensibility, this at times paradoxical sense of geo-
graphical and spiritual ambiguity, or "between-ness," was heightened
by the fact that Gilmore's generation, the last off the farm and the
first to go to college and grow up with rock 'n' roll, was in transition
itself. Radio, however, was a constant—a beacon, much as it was for
Van Morrison when he was coming of age across the Atlantic. "Radio
was my matrix," Gilmore told one interviewer, and when he was
growing up in Lubbock in the early 50s, radio meant little more than
country music and the livestock report.[20] By mid-decade, though,
country music was undergoing a transformation of its own: the likes
of Elvis Presley and Carl Perkins were fusing "hillbilly" music with
the hopped-up rhythms of gospel and R&B and supplanting the stars
of the Grand Ole Opry on the country charts. Rockabilly acts routinely played Lubbock, which is where, in 1956 or so, Gilmore saw a
touring revue starring Elvis and Johnny Cash that inspired him to put
away his fiddle and trombone and pick up the guitar.

Epiphanies like this, coupled in the ensuing years with the advent
of Bob Dylan and the counterculture, paved the way for the Flatlanders, who in their initial incarnation were something of a Sons of the
Pioneers for the Aquarian Age. The first installment of the band was
together only briefly in 1971 and 1972, but the album that they left
behind, a bohemian-cum-hippie take on the "High Lonesome Sound"
called *Jimmie Dale & the Flatlanders*, was unlike any that came before
or after it. The record's sonic signature was the eerie whine of Steve
Wesson's musical saw, a high-pitched whir that sounded more like it
was produced by an oscillating Theremin than by the steel guitar that
it sought to imitate. Just as uncanny was Gilmore's tremulous tenor
(suggestive of a cross between Gene Autry and the Dalai Lama), and
the group's sweeping originals and musical ecumenism, which encompassed Western swing, Cajun music, and covers of antediluvian favor-
ites by the likes of Gilmore's namesake Jimmie Rodgers. Virtually
everything about the group's music was mind-expanding, but nothing

compared with the Day-Glo mystagogy of "Bhagavan Decreed" and its admonition, "You can burn your brain cells out just trying to get higher / But you'll find the highest place is underground." The recording is high plains existentialism in excelsis, a lysergic update of the cowboy classic "Tumbling Tumbleweeds."

"Dallas," Gilmore's impressionistic sketch of the central Texas city from the vantage point of a DC-9 at night, was the first and only single from the Flatlanders' ill-fated 1972 LP. The song's verses are plain-spoken yet poetic, personifying the town by turns as a fickle mistress, "a rich man who tends to believe his own lies," and as "a steel-and-concrete soul in a warm-hearted love disguise." Accented by the keening sighs of Wesson's saw and Ely's harmonica, Gilmore's evocative string of images constitutes a surreal update of country music's perennial cautionary tale about the risks of losing one's spiritual and emotional compass amid the glitter and snares of the city. Released as a promotional single to country radio, "Dallas" went nowhere, prompting Plantation Records, the Flatlanders' Nashville-based label, not to promote the album or to keep it in print. The record was available briefly, and only on 8-track tape, but it since has appeared in various guises, along with a couple of live CDs of similar vintage and a pair of recent studio albums.

Stuck with a record deal that they could not get out of—and, ironically, caught in the sort of big city trap that "Dallas" warns against— the Flatlanders retreated to Texas and were not heard from again until Ely began releasing solo albums toward the end of the decade. Gilmore was hit the hardest. The Flatlanders' contract was in his name and kept him from recording under another until Plantation released him from their agreement, a setback that only reinforced his appreciation for the relative insignificance of the human ego. Gilmore soon withdrew from the music business altogether, moving to Denver in 1975 to study metaphysics with a teenage guru from the Himalayas. He stayed there until 1980, when he returned to Austin, where he had led bands prior to forming the Flatlanders. He gradually began playing in clubs again and became a mainstay of the city's progressive country scene, but he didn't make another record until the late 80s, when, by then in his mid-forties, he released a pair of neo-honky-tonk albums on the independent HighTone label.

Both of those records include updates of vintage country hits by the likes of Webb Pierce and Marty Robbins, as well as interpretations of material written by Ely, Hancock, and other kindred spirits. Despite their considerable virtues, though, both albums found Gilmore operating within a limited, if contemporary, hard-country compass. Neither record was "out there" enough for his voice or spirit to take wing, something that is not the case with the three albums that he made in their wake. Their titles alone betoken larger themes, whether that means the earth's place within the solar system (*Spinning Around the Sun*), the bounds of human understanding (*"After Awhile"*), or possibilities for human communion scarcely imagined (*Braver Newer World*). The lyrics and arrangements on each of these albums evince a similar reach. The former speak persistently to transcendental concerns, from mindfulness to the impermanence of the self, while the latter open onto ambient, at times experimental musical settings that afforded Gilmore's music an expansive, new purchase.

The first disc in this triptych, 1991's *"After Awhile,"* is not a significant sonic departure from his late 80s albums. Apart from a version of Hancock's apropos "My Mind's Got a Mind of Its Own," though, Gilmore wrote all of its songs, and most betray a strong contemplative bent. Flecked with strains of gypsy fiddle and Flamenco guitar, "Chase the Wind" is a mystical love story with a hint of magical realism that turns on axioms like "The journey is worth the price of gold." "Midnight Train," by contrast, is a howling blues that taps America's vast repository of railroad songs, from the Woody Guthrie-associated "Little Black Train" to Sister Rosetta Tharpe's exhortatory "This Train" and Curtis Mayfield's eschatological "People Get Ready." "You might as well choose right now / It's love or fear," Gilmore warns, as a lurching harmonica and a slide guitar caterwaul ominously behind him.

Whereas *"After Awhile"* cohered around the verbal flowering of Gilmore's cosmic consciousness, its successor, *Spinning Around the Sun*, nurtured that sensibility with equally spacious music. Much of it was inspired by the lush pop romanticism of Gilmore's boyhood idol Roy Orbison. The record's cavernous arrangements give the fiddle, piano, and guitars (especially the round, resonant tones of the guitars) ample room to inhabit Gilmore's musings, fleshing them out as opposed to serving merely as garnishes. Most dramatic is the cover of "I'm So Lonesome I Could Cry," where the careening, reverb-steeped guitars lend the song even more of an otherworldly cast than Hank Williams's original. In "Reunion," a shuffling duet with Lucinda Williams, zigzagging guitars conjure images of meteor showers and illuminate otherwise jive pronouncements like, "When Mother Earth and Father Time reunite us one more time / We'll remember that we've never been apart." It is as if Gilmore, the players, and producer Emory Gordy Jr. are mapping the enigmatic geography of the high plains musically here.

Gilmore's next album, *Braver Newer World*, was produced by the ubiquitous T Bone Burnett, whose use of noisy guitars, eerie atmospherics, and arcane instrumentation took the singer's music almost into art-rock territory. The record is not without its share of epiphanies, but too many of its flourishes feel trifling, as if Burnett and his associates thought that they had to make Gilmore's voice and songs seem more unearthly than they already were. Less forced is 2001's *One Endless Night*, an album consisting mainly of covers that Gilmore made with producer and guitarist Buddy Miller, including a willowy version of the Grateful Dead's "Ripple." Here, swathed in fiddle and Dobro, Gilmore intones exquisite lines like, "Rippling, still water / Where there is no pebble tossed or wind to blow," with the equanimity of a sage.

Gilmore's contemplative streak is even more pronounced on the album's cover of Jesse Winchester's "Defying Gravity." With the playful manner of a bodhisattva he warbles, "I live on a big round ball / I never do dream I may fall / But even one day if I do / Well, I'll jump off and smile back at you." The song's title captures the essence of Gilmore's voice, notably the way that on early draughts of post-hillbilly existentialism like "Dallas" and "Tonight I Think I'm Gonna Go Downtown" his ethereal timbre seems to defy gravity and transcend the weightiness of the lyrics. Not that Gilmore glosses over heartache. This is, after all, the lovelorn guy who sang, "She would never see / That this world's just not real to me." Much as Hank Williams often did, Gilmore renders sorrow in a different key, albeit one that springs more from the Buddhist dictum that all life is suffering (and the corollary that all pleasure is but gilded pain) than from anything in Williams's Pentecostal-bred philosophy.

In many ways Gilmore's mysticism is the sagebrush equivalent, much as Van Morrison's is its Gaelic counterpart, of Ralph Ellison's understanding of the blues as the immersion in and lyrical expression of pain and hardship in order to transcend it, if only for the moment.[21] "One of the real strong functions of music is catharsis," Gilmore told me.[22] "It's one of the things that early on I noticed about the blues, how those old guys just blurted out their hurt to the world. Of course back then I didn't give it much thought. But there's something about being able to express that pain that I think is a real aid in dealing with it, in integrating it into the rest of life." It is a matter, as Gilmore put it so indelibly in "Go to Sleep Alone," of "referee[ing] the fight between the being and the seeming."

A negotiation of just this sort takes place in Gilmore's "Another Colorado," yet another metaphysical love song like "Just a Wave." Here, awash in undulating strains of fiddle, Dobro, and Maybelle Carter-style thumb-brush guitar, Gilmore sings of frolicking with his lover along the banks of the Colorado River. He paints an Edenic picture; when in the second stanza he sings, "I took a pillar for a sign / That the salt of the earth was mine," he seems to be laying claim to it as some sort of paradisiacal inheritance. Yet in the chorus that follows we learn that wise men and wise women have told him that there is *another* Colorado, and that it is there, and not amid his current rapture, that he "may find [his] sweet El Dorado," a place, one gathers, of perpetual blessedness. Even more mystifying, these seers tell Gilmore that this blissful state can be found down by the banks of *"one sweet Colorado."* The suggestion here is that the "other" Colorado is not separate from the one in which Gilmore and his lover are reveling—that it is not a separate reality at all, but one that only *seems* to be. The final stanza confirms this impression, casting the entire experience as if it were some sort of koan. "The years flowed softly before my eyes / And the circus joined me in my quest," Gilmore sings, as if awakening from a dream, "And stayed with me throughout my test / Down by the banks of the Colorado."

Gilmore's grasp of the need to hold the being and the seeming in tension, his ability to suffer the tension between tasting transcendence yet not knowing it completely—"There's still time for heaven / Though we're already there," he sings elsewhere—makes him what Van Morrison has called a "Dweller on the Threshold." The two contemplatives might express their thirst for transcendence differently, the Irishman playing Dionysus to the Texan's Apollo. Yet when Morrison, with airy rhythms and seraphic horns bearing him aloft, sings "I'm a dweller on the threshold / And I've crossed some burning ground / And I'll go down to the water / Let the great illusion drown," he could just as easily be searching for Gilmore's "other" Colorado. Or, for that matter, his beloved Veedon Fleece.

## REALITY USED TO BE A FRIEND OF MINE

> "Once more my feelings have succeeded in confusing me, but what's most amusing is I like the way it looks."
>
> —Prince Be, "Beautiful"

> "There is something greater than what we see on the surface."
>
> —Prince Be, *Jesus Wept*

The music of P.M. Dawn is all about refereeing the fight between the being and the seeming. Prince Be, the duo's singer and MC, might not possess Gilmore's serene demeanor, but he plumbs the liminal zone between reality and appearances just as assiduously. Still, whereas Gilmore croons Buddhism-inspired lines like, "This world's just not real to me" with sagelike equipoise, Prince Be, conveying a similar metaphysical insight, raps, "Reality used to be a friend of mine" as if he truly misses what he has relinquished. "I'm grieving with my patient's patience," he intones wearily over the slow funk groove of "My Own Personal Gravity": "No one wants to be down here but everyone was dumb enough to come."

Such pronouncements sound less like those of a mystical adept who has found a measure of peace vis-à-vis his place in the larger scheme of things than those of a novitiate who still is encumbered by the weight of the world. And Prince Be, aka Attrell Cordes, *does* feel that weight, both in terms of his Buddha-like girth and of his assessment of earthly affairs, the subtitle of P.M. Dawn's 1991 debut, *The Utopian Experience*, notwithstanding. Robert Christgau, reviewing the album (the main title of which is *Of the Heart, Of the Soul, and Of the Cross*), called it "Prince Be's deft, thought-out response to a world that bugs him politically, spiritually, existentially, and because he's fat."[23] *Jesus Wept*, P.M. Dawn's third album, contains twenty-one seconds of silence recorded at the gravesite of Martin Luther King, Jr.

Underlying P.M. Dawn's music, however, is affirmation in spite of itself, a will to believe in something—God, certainly, but also beauty, truth, and love (both eros and agape). "There is something greater than what we see on the surface, the crystalline existences, the materialism, the greed," the Prince submits in the "Intro" to *Jesus Wept*. Even the duo's name, which derives from the scripture passage, "In the darkest hour comes the light," hints at the possibility of transcendence. The "P.M." in the appellation, after all, gives way to "Dawn," thus calling attention to the transitional space between being and becoming where people invariably live.

Not that letting go of the desire to exist outside the tension between midnight and dawn, between being and becoming, is easy for Prince Be, whose full *nom de mic* is Prince Be the Nocturnal. "Holding on is like the ways of the wind / The constant search for who you are . . . / Finding you've no place to stand," he sings in "The Ways of the Wind," a bumping, celestial shuffle from 1993. Ultimately, however, it is in these paradoxes, in these disruptions of logic that illuminate the liminal divide between the being and the seeming, that Prince Be glimpses transcendence. "Once more my feelings have succeeded in confusing me / But what's most amusing is / I like the way it looks," he rhymes over a fluttering bass rumble in "Beautiful." "Distorted, isn't it? / But it's beautiful! / Exceptionally beautiful!" he goes on as a choir of background singers, echoing his exultation, chant the line, "How does it feel to be one of the beautiful people" from the Beatles' "Baby You're a Rich Man."

Consisting of Prince Be and his brother Jarrett (aka DJ Minutemix), P.M. Dawn emerged from Jersey City in the late 80s with a mix of psychedelic and socially conscious leanings akin to those of "Daisy Age" hip-hop acts like De La Soul and the Jungle Brothers. In the end, though, P.M. Dawn's lush, contemplative music, which was at once more pop and more ineffable than that of their peers, sounded like it came from another dimension. "Who is Prince Be?" asks the unidentified female announcer in the mock radio spot that opens the duo's second record, *The Bliss Album . . . ? (Vibrations of Love and Anger and the Ponderance of Life and Existence)*. "Maybe a time traveler . . . ? Not an earthbound creature," the woman surmises. With Prince Be "calculat[ing] karma" and mooning lines like "I cry when midnight sighs" in the wistful track that follows, P.M. Dawn certainly sounded like aliens. "Classify me strange," the Prince bids listeners over the beat-down drum-and-bass of 1995's "The Puppet Show," and many did, including the duo's hardcore rap counterparts, who impugned them not only for being soft, but also for being sellouts.

P.M. Dawn's debut single, "Set Adrift on Memory Bliss," indeed was built on a fluffy sample, a passage from Spandau Ballet's creamy synth ballad "True," and to gorgeous effect. And the record did go to No. 1 on the pop chart, quite a feat for a rap act at the time. Either of these things alone would have been enough to attract flack. But then there were the beads, the peace-sign necklaces, and the Day-Glo silk caftans that Prince Be and his brother wore, all of which signified in ways that were anathema to the aggressive precepts of then-ascendant gangsta rap. All of which is to say nothing of the pop-leaning ecumenism of the Prince's musical tastes, or of his duets with the less-than-hard likes of George Michael and Boy George.

Prince Be and his brother defended themselves on record, and not just against general censure, but against the otherwise nonviolent KRS-One, who physically attacked the Prince onstage for questioning his authority as a teacher in the press. "What's hard at first but melts in the heat? They call that plastic," the Prince spits in "Plastic," a scratching, swirling excoriation of the illusion of "hardness" in rap, and especially of the shallow boasting and superficial toughness of his conformist, crotch-grabbing peers. The Prince's sentiment here is reminiscent of the zinger, "Fuck being hard, Posdnuos is complicated,"[24] that Posdnuos, the bespectacled MC from the hip-hop trio De La Soul, threw in the face of his group's critics.

All that P.M. Dawn has ever needed to prove its mettle, in any case, are the Prince's weighty rhymes and the duo's taunt, funky pulse and inspired sampling. "Comatose," a track from *Of the Heart, Of the Soul, and Of the Cross*, for example, contains snatches of the hoodoo blues guitar from Dr. John's "I Walk on Gilded Splinters" and the serrated groove from Sly & the Family Stone's "Thankful n' Thoughtful." And "Shake," which employs the deftly cut beats of house music producer Todd Terry, is body music of the first order. Prince Be's inducement, "Everyone get out of your bodies," might

have fueled charges that his vision was escapist—that is, were it not
for the dance-floor nirvana that his invitation promised, especially
when he exhorts the faithful to "get down and shake" to trigger the
track's irrepressible vamp.

A number of critics originally ascribed an ascetic, even body-hating
subtext to Prince Be's rhymes, especially in lines like, "I think I'm
gonna fly away" from the God-conscious "To Serenade a Rainbow."
Yet even here the Prince sounds grounded when he opines, "I watch
the comedy called intellect / Which wraps the nooses around our
necks / It seems the unreal is becoming more real." This is not anti-
intellectual rhetoric, but rather paradoxical language in the spirit of
"Comatose," a rap in which Prince Be advocates cultivating a counterintuitive way of seeing, a radical looking inward as a way of dis-
cerning appearances from reality and of grasping the fluidity between
the two. "Beyond infinite affections there is nothing / And nothing
understands," he declares, with Sphinx-like relish elsewhere. On
"Why God Loves You" he submits, "We're all more than we can see."

P.M. Dawn's is unquestionably a theistic mysticism, and as album
titles like *Jesus Wept* and the allusion to "Christ consciousness" in the
subtitle of 1995's prayerful "Sometimes I Miss You So Much" attest,
this perspective at times is explicitly Christian. Yet from Prince Be's
frequent nods to Buddhism to less-than-orthodox invocations like
"I'd like to say, 'What's up?' to God" (set off by a swirling Bedouin
melody, no less), there is nothing conventional about the Prince's
strain of contemplation. In "Even After I Die," a meditation, among
other things, on the prospect of incarnation, he could be talking to
his late father or to God, but it likely is the latter, whom he obviously
fears and adores.

Mostly, though, Prince Be just wants to be here now, and to be
there for his own son, to whom he dedicates 1998's gravely titled
*Dearest Christian, I'm So Very Sorry for Bringing You Here. Love,
Dad.* The Prince's biggest concern, as a parent and otherwise, is bal-
ancing appearances and reality as faithfully as he can so as to achieve
a measure of peace with his existence and, with it, some degree of
transcendence. "I'm only human for a lifetime," he muses at one
point, alluding again perhaps to reincarnation, but certainly to eternity and, more pointedly, to looking for the eternal in the now. He
conveys much the same insight by way of a dazzling leap of faith and

imagination in 1995's "Fantasia's Confidential Ghetto," a medley of
radically reimagined versions of Prince's "1999," Talking Heads'
"Once in a Lifetime," and Harry Nilsson's "Coconut."

This triptych ostensibly is an homage, and certainly its update of
"1999" is a paean to the Prince's hero (Prince "A," so to speak).
Closer listen, though, reveals that "Fantasia" is, above all, a statement
of purpose. When to the record's decelerated beat and melancholy
arrangement Prince Be sings, "When I woke up this morning, I could
have sworn it was judgment day," it no longer is the other Prince's
gloriously hedonistic take on the end of the millennium. Nor is it a
case of Prince Be using those lines, and others like "Gotta run from
my destruction," to retrieve some not-so-glorious Biblical vision of
Armageddon. He is expressing a mystical insight here, and an urgent
one. He is saying that each day is one of judgment, not *of* people, but
a chance *for* them to discern the eternal in the everyday. The Prince
is saying that every moment holds the prospect of letting the tangible
mediate the intangible—of living sacramentally, to use religious language. Indeed, after his admonition about not "letting the days go
by" in the medley's trippy revamping of "Once in a Lifetime," his
talk of wine and transubstantiation in "Coconut" sounds positively
Eucharistic. "You put the lime in the coconut, you silly human," he
gently chides, assuming the voice of Nilsson's doctor, recast here as a
loving God. Whether appearance or reality, the reality is that the
Prince and the Lord appear to be on the same wavelength.

# chapter 2

## SEXUAL HEALING, OR SOMETHIN' LIKE SANCTIFIED

### Marvin Gaye, Al Green, Madonna, and PJ Harvey

STANDING ON THE VERGE OF GETTING IT ON

"Life is a paradox between Jesus and pussy."[1]

—Marvin Gaye

"It's you I want, but it's Him that I need."

—Al Green, "Belle"

Marvin Gaye wrestled much of his life with what he perceived to be the irreconcilable tension between his spiritual and sensual impulses. He also spoke vividly about this conflict in interviews, as the above axiom attests. Yet Gaye's struggle to unite the spirit and the flesh inspired him to create music of transporting eroticism. His first sustained outpouring of this sublime sensuality came with 1973's groove-steeped *Let's Get It On*, the last with 1982's *Midnight Love*, the polyrhythmic wonder that proved to be the final album that Gaye would release before his father shot and killed him during an argument in 1984.

The title *Midnight Love* is an allusion to the midnight hour, an image that black preachers invoke to signify the moment of deepest spiritual need, the darkest hour before the dawn. "Baby, I got sick this morning / A sea was storming / Inside of me," Gaye moans, beside himself with desire in "Sexual Healing," the album's centerpiece. Primed by the foreplay of the record's opening track, the bumping funk of "Sexual Healing" offers languorous testimony to the salutary properties of getting it on. Gaye keeps it up for another twenty-five minutes with the steamy likes of "Rockin' After Midnight" and "Turn on Some Music" ("Put three albums on / We gonna make it / Long, long, long"), only to bring the LP to a precipitous, if dissonant, climax with a prayer of thanksgiving to his "Heavenly Father." The record's liner notes underscore this tension, with Gaye professing, "I still believe in Jesus," as if he were trying to convince himself, not so much his audience, as to where, amid all this hedonism, his heart lay.

The surrealistic cover illustration of 1981's widely neglected *In Our Lifetime*, a contrast of sorts between Gaye's socially conscious *What's Going On* and his libidinous *Let's Get It On*, renders this struggle in dualistic detail. Gaye is seated at a table, propped up on a bed of clouds high above the earth. His sanctified self is facing his sinful self, the former depicted as an angel with wings, a white robe, and a halo, the latter as a devil with horns, a black cape, and a serpent as his familiar. A globe, rent in two and burning from within, lies on a black-and-white tablecloth between the twin halves of Gaye's embattled psyche. The world below is a ball of confusion besieged by war, pollution, and, judging by the tawdry hotel at the center of the tableau, lust.

That Gaye would have to fight to integrate these two sides of his persona is hardly surprising. He was raised in a moralistic, Pentecostal home, something that only heightened the guilt that he felt over his prodigious carnal appetites, even though he also believed that sex was a gift from God. Gaye never seemed to reconcile this conflict during his lifetime. Some of the best music that he left behind, though, rapturously married eroticism and piety, bearing witness to the power of sex, as he put it in "Let's Get It On," to give "good feeling, somethin' like sanctified." Prince, his most obvious and gifted heir, also preached sex as salvation, but fusing the flesh and the spirit never posed a mortal dilemma for the Purple One (now, of all things, a Jehovah's Witness) the way that it did for Gaye, who never could take the union of the two for granted. His many affairs and indiscretions notwithstanding, Gaye prized sex as holy, as a sacrament that could mediate the temporal and the eternal, uniting lovers not just with each other but, if only fleetingly, with God.

This reverence accounts for the uncommon tenderness and vulnerability that suffuses many of Gaye's records. Galvanized by his silky, multi-octave tenor, Gaye's gently throbbing music exhibits more of an abiding female sexual impulse than the overriding male urge for climax. At its best and most erotic, his work exudes an intimacy, a mystical urgency that goes beyond the salacious thrill of, say, Prince's records (which rarely integrate the sacred and the sexual as completely as Gaye's do) to reach a higher plane. "The paradox," wrote biographer David Ritz, is that "the sexiest of Marvin Gaye's work is also his most spiritual. That's the paradox of Marvin himself. In his struggle to wed body and soul, in his exploration of sexual passion, he expresses the most human of hungers—the hunger for God."[2]

Mystics through the ages have experienced the holy through eroticism. Angela of Foligno, a fourteenth-century Christian adept, vividly recounted a divine ravishing in which "all her members were unstrung."[3] Teresa of Avila, the sixteenth-century saint and mystic, rankled her Carmelite sisters with graphic details of her "love affair" with God.[4] These women were not actually lusting after God. They were using the language at their disposal, that of sexual intercourse, as a means of speaking of a love that was beyond human ken, and thus knowable only indirectly through the likes of mystical insight and metaphor. A wedding of mysticism and eroticism akin to this is described in the liner notes of the soundtrack to the movie *The Harder They Come*, which claim that people in Jamaica sing praises to God in church until they reach orgasm.[5] Expressions of a sensual and ecstatic variety are common in African American worship, where the convergence of sexual energy and religious fervor renders the two impulses virtually indistinguishable. There also is the ease with which blues, soul, and rock 'n' roll singers have adapted the pressing rhythms and lyrics of black gospel music to "secular" settings, gleaning the likes of "I Got a Woman" from "I Got a Savior" and "Have Mercy Baby" from "Have Mercy Lord."

Much the same mystical affinity, albeit fraught with an at times paralyzing dissonance, was nurtured in Marvin Gaye early on. He began singing in his father's church at age five and is said to have exerted a singular hold over those in the congregation, especially the women. "The ladies in church, they would hug me and bring me to them," he recalled in the liner notes to his 1974 *Anthology*. "Psychologically, sensually, I liked this."[6] Meanwhile, Gaye's father, a harsh disciplinarian with sexual hang-ups of his own, was abusing Marvin and his siblings, administering beatings for which he typically forced the children to strip naked and lay prostrate across their beds.[7] Thus began the outsized sexual conflict that would plague Gaye throughout his life, but that he somehow, and often, managed to transcend through his music. Indeed, it was only through the music that he made—and specifically, in its healing grooves and transporting cries—that Gaye seemed to know, or at least to feel, that life was not reducible to a choice between "Jesus and pussy," but rather involved a dialectical relationship between the two, a relationship grounded in God that transcended such polarities.

Gaye's gift for achieving this higher synthesis—this fusion of soul and body music—became increasingly evident in his "mature" recordings like *Let's Get It On* and *I Want You*, albums that he made after wresting artistic control over his work from Berry Gordy, Jr. in the 1970s. This transcendence, or at least a hunger for it, nevertheless could already be heard back when Gaye was churning out hits as the Prince of Motown in the 1960s. Those early records might have been marketed as the "Sound of *Young* America," but to this day they convey adult concerns that are more sexual and that carry more philosophical-existential freight than aw-shucks titles like "I'll Be Doggone" and "Stubborn Kind of Fellow" suggest. "Can I Get a Witness," a single that nearly broke the pop Top 20 in 1963, employs the call-and-response patterns of black worship and a mile-wide groove to plumb enmity between men and women. "How Sweet It Is (To Be Loved by You)," a Top 10 hit in 1964, uses shelter as a metaphor for a union between lovers that borders on the mystical. "I Heard It through the Grapevine," a harrowing record hooked by incantatory rhythms and desperate lines like "Losin' you would end my life, you see," expresses feelings of betrayal and estrangement as elemental as those depicted in the biblical account of the Fall. And not to be forgotten are Gaye's breathtaking duets with Tammi Terrell, ecstatic, string-saturated declarations of undying love like "Ain't Nothing Like the Real Thing" and "Ain't No Mountain High Enough" whose titles alone portend transcendence.

Gaye's vision of sexual healing did not come into clear focus, however, until the spring of 1973, just as he was separating from his first wife, Anna Gordy, the older sister of Motown's Berry Gordy. Gaye had recently moved from Detroit to Los Angeles and had begun working on the album that would become *Let's Get It On*. He released a terrific funk single called "You're the Man" the previous year, but the record, which found him working in much the same political vein as *What's Going On*, was a commercial disaster. Its failure nevertheless proved fortuitous, convincing Gaye to pursue a different direction. He turned to "Let's Get It On," a song that Ed Townsend, a veteran of the doo-wop and supper club scenes, had written about getting on with his life after undergoing rehab for alcoholism. Gaye cut a serviceable demo of Townsend's song during the first half of March that year. He would not make it his own, though, until he met seventeen-year-old Janis Hunter, who had dropped by the studio with her mother, whom Townsend was dating at the time, while Gaye was tracking his vocals for the song. Inspired by Hunter's beauty (she and Gaye eventually would marry), Marvin promptly retooled the song's lyrics, transforming "Let's Get It On" into one of the most sensual and transcendent pop recordings of all time.

The record's title sounds like a pick-up line, as does its opening entreaty, "We're all sensitive people, with so much to give"; from its lyrics to its slinky rhythmic undertow, everything about "Let's Get It On" smacks of a prelude to casual sex. Or at least it would have were it not for the warmth in Gaye's heavenly tenor and for the record's deep, soul-satisfying pulse, both of which point to something more enduring than a night of carnal fulfillment (not that sex cannot be transcendent in its own right). "Giving yourself to me can never be wrong," Gaye pleads, echoed by the prodding guitar fills of Melvin "Wah Wah" Ragin. "If the spirit moves you, then let me groove you *good* / Let your love come *down*," he shouts. Gaye is not just talking to his partner here; more than just begging her to go to bed with him, he is asking God for a blessing from above. "Do you know the meaning of being sanctified?" he asks, making his intentions explicit as the music begins to fade. This is not just a come-on. "Gaye invokes sanctification . . . as a means to suggest a transcendent purpose to romantic love," the critic Michael Eric Dyson argued.[8] Indeed, Gaye is testifying to how sex can be salvific, how it can become a vehicle for joining two people with each other and, at a more fundamental level, with God, in whose love he believed sex to be grounded.

"The essential simile of 'getting it on' goes beyond sex," observed David Ritz.[9] "It's getting it on with the business of God's love." Nowhere does this conviction find greater purchase than in "Keep Gettin' It On," a recording that at first sounds like a throwaway, a way of padding *Let's Get It On* (at barely thirty minutes, a relatively short LP), by reprising the irresistible groove of the title track. Yet as underscored by lines like, "Wouldn't you rather make love, children / As opposed to war," the message of "Keep Gettin' It On" is hardly an afterthought. The spiritual communion implied in the idea of getting it on assumes larger moral dimensions here. As Gaye exhorts, "Don't just talk about it / Everybody start gettin' it on," the record's percolating rhythms gain sinew and momentum, transforming love into a force with broader social implications. No mere emotion now, love is revealed to have mystical powers that, when shared in a spirit of mutuality and respect, can heal the sorts of social ills that Gaye bemoaned two years earlier in "What's Going On" and "Inner City Blues (Make Me Wanna Holler)."

Gaye's vision of sexual healing rarely was this prophetic, and at times it was muddled by his addictions or otherwise hard to pin down (the critic Mikal Gilmore called it "an interesting if somewhat puzzling way of asserting his religious desires").[10] Gaye's view of sex could also be perverted by his baser instincts, such as the pettiness that marred portions of the musically exquisite *Here, My Dear*, an unflinching, but often self-serving account of the dissolution of his marriage to Anna Gordy. Even worse was *Dream of a Lifetime*, a collection of outtakes released posthumously in which Gaye not only glorifies S&M, but indulges in the misogynistic double standard of demonizing women who flirt with bondage the way that he did. The problem with the likes of "Masochistic Beauty" and "Sanctified Lady" (originally titled "Sanctified Pussy") is not so much their taboo subject matter, much less that they affirm that sex can be transporting or just feel great. They simply lack the intimacy and mutual respect that otherwise make Gaye's grasp of sex as a window to the eternal so sublime.

Gaye is at his transporting best when he sings of sex as what Dyson refers to as "the commerce of a higher spiritual economy" or bridge to the eternal.[11] Witness "If I Should Die Tonight," where, amid an ominous swirl of strings, Gaye haltingly delivers the song's title phrase before pulling himself together and purring, "I won't die blue because I've known you." He has known a love, he goes on to say, that has made his "world stand still," a love that has given him a taste of transcendence that mere sex, or even romantic commitment, could never have afforded him. It certainly is no empty gesture when, toward the end of the record, he thanks God for letting him know what "millions may never know."

Much the same interpenetration of the temporal and the eternal takes place in "Distant Lover" and "Please Stay (Once You Go Away)," both of them from *Let's Get It On*. When in the former, in an unearthly falsetto Gaye sings, "Heaven knows that I long for you every night," he is not just missing the woman who walked out on him. As with "Please Stay," where he sings of dreading to wake up and find her gone, his anguish, heightened by the track's pressing cadences, is born, in equal measure, of his fear of being abandoned by God. In these "songs of loss and lament," wrote David Ritz, "the sense of separation is breathtaking. On one level, the separation is between man and woman. On a deeper level, the separation is between man and God."[12]

Michael Eric Dyson described Gaye as someone who was "genuinely God-intoxicated." As evidence of this obsession, and of Gaye's persistent commingling of "erotic intensity and religious passion," Dyson cites the original version of his 1971 recording, "God Is Love."

> [D]ripping with doo-wop harmonies, ["God Is Love"] is a splendid testimony to Marvin's fusion of sensuous style and spiritual sentiment. Marvin means the song, pure and simple, as a love song to God. It is every bit as delicate, sensuous and, arguably, theologically erotic— which draws from the unapologetic love for God as friend, soul-lover, and caregiver—as any secular song could hope to be.[13]

Even more than the metaphorical expressions of medieval mystics like Angela and Theresa, the theological eroticism that Dyson hears in "God Is Love" is a desire for the divine with an overriding sensual component. It is the counterpart, in many respects, of Gaye's notion of sexual healing, whereby lovers experience immanence so radical that they transcend themselves and glimpse the eternal. Granted,

Gaye uses a simile to describe this feeling, and rightly so, calling it "somethin' *like* sanctified," and thus does not go so far as to make absolute claims for the redemptive power of sex. At the very least, though, he is saying that under the right conditions, "getting it on" offers lovers a means of satisfying their hunger for transcendence like nothing else on earth.

Gaye might not have resolved the conflict between the flesh and the spirit that plagued him during his lifetime, but he certainly left behind a divine body of music that underscored the salutary properties of sex. Al Green, his slightly younger contemporary, has made similarly transporting records, and in similar profusion. Green also has known his share of turmoil over sex and salvation, but unlike Gaye, he ultimately seems to have reconciled body and soul by erasing the line that divides them, subsuming them, at least by the time that he became an ordained minister, under the providence of God.

"Life teaches you that it's difficult to separate 'I love you' from 'I love You,'" is how Green put it, referring to God with the second "You," in an interview that appeared in the *New York Times Magazine* in 2003.[14] Green's belief that spirituality has an erotic dimension, and that sex is inherently spiritual, is not unique to his music any more than it is to Gaye's (or, for that matter, to that of many other pop stars). One would be hard pressed, though, to name a rock or soul singer who has emerged in the last four decades who has integrated these two facets of human experience into his or her music as completely as Al Green. This is the case whether he is singing in concert or in church; when he performs a hymn like "Amazing Grace" as a slow-drag blues, his melismatic vocals and convulsing body suggest both orgasm and possession by the Holy Spirit. Just hearing him sustain his falsetto "aaaah" at the climax of "I'm Still in Love with You," or on the vamp in "Let's Stay Together," is enough to induce the most hedonistic soul to contemplate the eternal, or to awaken carnal urges in the most self-abnegating ascetic.

Green's loyalties might seem divided when, wooing his lover on the title track of *The Belle Album*, he confesses, "It is you I want, but it's Him that I need," the second of these third-person pronouns once again referring to God. Yet love ultimately is not an either/or proposition for Green. It is not a matter of choosing between God and his lover ("Leavin' Him has never ever really

crossed my mind," he makes clear in the first stanza), but rather one
of integrating his devotion to the two. When over an undulating
groove draped in a numinous synth figure he moans, "Let's you and
I let love come down," Green is not just inviting Belle to have sex
with him. Much as Gaye did in "Let's Get It On," he is talking
about undergoing sexual healing, about consecrating their love with
an anointing from on high. "The best thing we could do is to have
Him around," Green tells Belle early on. Punctuating this invoca-
tion with whoops and hollers and shouts about God being his
"drink of water" and his "bright morning star," Green offers heart-
stopping testimony to how the presence of God can enrich and even
sanctify intimacy between two people, making it a manifestation,
however imperfect, of divine love.

   "I'm trying to get to heaven that way," Green explains on the
chorus of "Loving You," the hot mix of sprung backbeats and funky
acoustic guitar that follows "Belle" on *The Belle Album*. Green repeats this line three times, answered in turn by a choir of surging
horns, before he coos the words "Lovin' you" in a silvery falsetto.
He could be referring to his devotion to Belle or to God, but more
than likely it is both, just as the heaven within his reach almost certainly is an allusion to both sex and salvation. In "Chariots of Fire,"
another track on the album, angels swing low to let Green ride, but
the conceit is not so much one of double entendre as a collision of
sanctification and sensuality set to exultant funk that recalls Parlia-
ment trying to land the mothership. "Make it last forever," Green
sings in "Dream," the post-orgasmic—and, like "Chariots," eschatological—ballad that closes the album. Green is not just singing of the
sex suggested by his simile about melting ice cream cones here. He
also is talking about living forever in the presence of God, the one in
whom he, like Gaye, believes love and sex are grounded.

   Green released *The Belle Album* in 1977, four years after he bot-
tomed out spiritually and entered the ministry, a chain of events that
was set in motion when a lover of his, a married woman that he had
spurned, threw scalding grits on him and then killed herself. *Belle*
proved to be Green's most complete fusion of sex and faith to date
and remains the most inspired album (*Call Me* runs a very close second) of a career that until that point had been defined largely by singles. *Belle* also was Green's first self-produced record, and the first

in seven years that he had made without Memphis producer Willie Mitchell.

Galvanized by Al Jackson, Jr.'s metronomic pulse, Teenie Hodges's snaking guitar fills, Mitchell's empathetic string and horn arrangements, and Green's mercurial tenor, the series of hits that Green and Mitchell produced from 1970 to 1976 was as unassailable as any released during that vastly underrated decade. None of these early chart singles references faith or God, yet most express a hunger for transcendence, both sensual and spiritual, as strong as that heard throughout *The Belle Album*. Critic Robert Christgau called it "secular gospel music,"[15] and indeed, many of Green's pop hits from this period invest sex and romantic love with sacramental resonance. In "Tired of Being Alone," for instance, Green's octave-scaling, melisma-steeped glossolalia betrays a hunger for release that goes beyond the physical or emotional. In "Take Me to the River," a roiling sanctified blues, he begs, "Dip me in the water, I want to know / Wash me in the water"; by the time that Green is fully submerged and shouts, "Feelin' good," there is no telling where orgasm ends and baptism begins. Witness, as well, the exhortatory "Love and Happiness," where, amid swirls of churchy organ and the shouts of an "Amen" choir, he gasps, "It's a power," referring to love as if it were a force of healing, much as Gaye did in "Keep Gettin' It On."

"L-O-V-E (Love)," a shuffling Top 20 hit from 1975, begins as a secular exposition of the redemptive properties of that power until Green, doubtless struck by the ineffability of the matter at hand, abandons elucidation for metaphor. "Love is a fire burnin' in my soul / Love is a story that can't be told," he declaims in down-home preacher mode. "I can't explain this feeling / Can't you see that salvation is free / I would give my life for the glory / Just to be able to tell the story," he goes on, his voice enfolded in celestial strings and sultry background voices. All of this testifying aside, the ecstatic "Woo! Hoo! *Hoo!*" that Green unleashes in the wake of these lines is likely the closest he will ever come to unlocking the mysteries that he is trying to expound.

Like his hero Sam Cooke and countless other church-bred singers before him, Green has found it difficult at times to live with the mysteries that attend the relationship between the body and the soul, between sex and salvation. While Green was still in his teens, his father kicked him out of the family gospel quartet for listening to Jackie Wilson, and you can hear a profound sense of rejection, at once spiritual and physical, in any number of his early singles. The desperation in his churning, bluesy take of the Temptations "Can't Get Next to You" is palpable, while the gentle, importunate "Here I Am (Take Me)" could as easily be a plea to God as to a woman. When Green sings, "I'm so tired of being alone / I'm so tired of being on my own," the entreaty that follows might just as well be, "Won't you help me *God* [as opposed to 'girl'] / As soon as you can."

By far the most urgent of Green's early articulations of spiritual and emotional estrangement is his aggrieved reimagining of the Bee Gees' "How Can You Mend a Broken Heart." The first thing that you notice as the record begins is Al Jackson's 4/4 on the high-hat. A forward motion as ineluctable as the rotation of the earth invoked in the song's chorus, Jackson's ticking sets the stage for Green to turn the Bee Gees' lovelorn banalities into a metaphysical rumination on human wholeness. Strings, voices, and a bed of lightly throbbing rhythms soothe him until the third chorus, where, breaking through the self-pity of the lyrics, he moans, "I just wanna, I just wanna, I just wanna, I just wanna, I just wanna *live* again." Green is praying now. No longer just pondering *how* to put together the pieces of his shattered heart, he demands, "*Help* me mend," beseeching heaven to deliver him from what has at this point become his dark night of the soul. We don't know for sure if Green ever sees the morning. He seems on the verge of doing so, though, when, fighting doubt on the vamp, he shouts, "I think I / I know I . . . / I feel like I *got* to . . . live again," twisting the word "live" this way and that as if the effort alone will save him. The lyrics never reveal exactly what is afflicting him, but as the track's six tortured minutes unfold, Green makes it increasingly clear that more than a relationship with a woman is at stake, although that certainly is there as well.

Green seemed to be emerging from not so much a pit of despair as a conflicted period in his life not long after he recorded "How Can You Mend a Broken Heart" in 1971. He became a "born again" Christian two years later, and seemed to find solace in his renewed faith. In interviews he nevertheless admitted that he still struggled with the dissonance that he felt over singing love songs both to women and to God. Then came 1973's infamous "grits incident," shortly after which Green rededicated himself to God, became a preacher, and started the church (of the Full Gospel Tabernacle in Memphis) that he still pastors today. As the *Reverend* Al Green, he continued to sing pop music, albeit with an increasing emphasis on gospel, until 1979, when he fell off the stage during a concert in Cincinnati. Green interpreted the incident as a sign from God and vowed only to sing in church and to make gospel records, which he has done ever since, although he eventually began singing his pop hits at shows again.

Virtually all of Green's gospel albums, many of them released by Myrrh Records, a Christian label, have their glories. Several even qualify as body music on the order of *Let's Get It On*, with 1981's *Higher Plane* and 1983's *I'll Rise Again* being particularly transcendent. Indeed, Green's chant of "more power" to the vamping funk of "Where Love Rules" on *Higher Plane* is a sanctified answer to his shouts of "It's a power" in "Love and Happiness"—and every bit as intense. The trouble is, and despite making Green a perennial favorite in the gospel category at the Grammy Awards, these records have not spoken readily to people outside the pews. This is as much a reflection on Green's pop audience as it as on him, especially since many of his gospel recordings continue to hold sex and salvation in tension, if only implicitly, and largely through the eroticism conveyed in his persona and voice. "[Green] barely missed a beat making his conversion," Robert Christgau observed, referring to this phase of the singer's career. "[H]e remained all personal stamp and driven style, a purely human miracle."[16]

The interplay between the sensual and the sacred might not be as transparent in Green's gospel catalog as it is in his pop hits, or as it is on *The Belle Album*, or even on its febrile disco-gospel successor, *Truth N' Time*. Green has for three decades exalted God above all else, including sex, which even when sanctified can only approximate divine love or serve as a window to the eternal. A commingling of sexuality and sanctification nevertheless still is writ large in his live performances. From his knowing, sexy smile and his heavenly body language to his slip-sliding melisma and the fetching way that he scrunches up his sweat-streamed face, Green really works it, inducing people to shriek and grab hold of him as he sashays up and down the aisles to shake their hands, microphone in tow. Green insists that this electricity or, as he calls it, "fire," has nothing to do with sex, but it is hard, regardless of whether he is giving a concert or leading worship, to take him at his word. It is hard, in fact, to tell what people want to touch more, Green's flesh or the hem of his garment. Or, for that matter, which message the Reverend is sending, or whether it has to be one or the other, instead of some combination of both.

Telling in this regard have been the responses of critics to *I Can't Stop*, the album of love songs that Green made for the jazz-identified Blue Note label in 2003. The record was his first collaboration with Willie Mitchell since their 1986 gospel project, *He Is the Light*, and review upon review of the album describes it as "secular." Such claims, however, ascribe a soul-body dualism to Green's work that, despite some of his comments, which sometimes are contradictory, ultimately is not there. When, over the heartbeat pulse, staccato horns, and tensive strings of the title track, he professes, "I can't quit a love like this from consuming you," Green is talking about a love akin to the ontological force he invokes in "Love and Happiness," a power or "higher love" that is elemental and encompassing enough to embrace both sensuality and spirituality. Witness the album's centerpiece, "My Problem is You," a "Stormy Monday"-inspired slow-burner that gives a lie to the predicament, ostensibly over a woman, stated in the record's title. "The *Answer* Is You" would have been more like it, or at least that is what Teenie Hodges's lowdown guitar solo on the bridge attests—namely, that the *last* thing that the Reverend Green wants to do is get over his "baby." Or maybe it should be "*Baby*." Indeed, it is hard not to hear a love of God—a theological eroticism, to invoke Michael Dyson's wonderful phrase—in Green's profession of love for his partner, especially in light of his confession, in "Belle," that "Leavin' Him has never ever really crossed my mind."

## LIKE A PRAYER

> "Kiss me, I'm dying. Put your hand on my skin, I need to make a connection."
>
> —Madonna, "Skin"

"Is this desire enough? Enough to lift us higher? To lift
above?"

—PJ Harvey, "Is This Desire?"

Early on in her career Madonna proved so adept at manipulating cultural space and reinventing herself within it that it became almost impossible to take anything that she said or did at face value. This
definitely was the case by the mid- to late 1980s. By then Madonna's
megastardom and cultural ubiquity had made her as much a social
construct as anything else, a "person-turned-idea," as Steve Anderson
put it, along the iconic lines of Elvis Presley or Marilyn Monroe.[17] By
the time that Madonna had emerged as this "metaphysic unto herself" it was necessary to treat everything about her, from her mercurial persona to the romantic ideals that she espoused in her songs, not
just at a certain remove, but with a healthy suspension of disbelief.

All of which has made it difficult at times to recognize or appreci-
ate the commingling of sex and spirituality that suffuses and in many
respects defines Madonna's music. Some of this stems from the fact
that while her records are informed by her conflicted Catholic upbringing—and, later, by her embrace of various strains of mysticism—they rarely make the explicit religious or theological
connections that, say, those of Marvin Gaye and Al Green do. There
also of course is Madonna's reputation for licentiousness and her penchant for playing the role of the sexual provocateur, neither of which
inspires visions of sanctification and its like. Madonna's hedonism can
be an enormous stumbling block, prompting many to dismiss her out
of hand. Surely anyone with access to a TV set or a radio during the
last quarter-century has made up their mind one way or another
about her. Yet for all of her signifying and the spectacle that surrounds it, Madonna's music frequently exhibits a yearning for spiritual renewal rooted in sensuality. Through her record's melodies,
grooves, and lyrics—and, to lesser effect, through wardrobe, dance,
and other visuals in concert and onscreen—Madonna conveys a hunger for personal wholeness that hinges on but often transcends sex. It
certainly is no wonder that she has lately—and, as with everything
that she does, controversially—become a student of kabbalah, the
hermetic strain of Judaism that, among other mysteries, speaks to
matters of sexual salvation, of transcendence through immanence.

"Like a Prayer," Madonna's No. 1 pop hit from 1989, was perhaps the first outward expression of the sexually charged urge for transcendence that runs through her music. "God," she utters, a cappella, as the record begins, her appeal tentative, as if she is not sure that God is listening, or is even there. A gospel choir answers her straight away, their fervent "ooh-oohs" followed by the hymnlike strains of an organ. "Life is a mystery / Everyone must stand alone / I hear you call my name / And it feels like home," Madonna intones, after which a transporting disco beat kicks in and, seeming to have made her connection, she starts carrying on about angels, levitation, and being delivered in the midnight hour. It all is very melodramatic, but it also is unmistakably erotic, with lines like, "I'm down on my knees / I wanna take you there," evoking both prayer and fellatio. Things climax on the vamp, with rapturous shrieks, handclaps, and polyrhythms bespeaking possibilities for transcendence that are as carnal as they are sacramental.

The video for "Like a Prayer" is even more over the top, its fusion of Roman Catholic iconography and African American worship styles rendering the record's blend of sex and redemption in vivid detail. With footage of crosses burning, stigmata materializing on Madonna's palms, and a black saint come back to life to save/seduce her, the video is in many ways too explicit, robbing the record of some of its pregnancy and power. It also is a bit of a jumble, including commentary on racism as well as intimations of Madonna's sexual fixation with Jesus and the crucifix. Nevertheless, as the critic Vince Aletti observed, this "more literal dreamscape"—"an allusive tumble of double meaning, a hallucination of surrender to a love at once sacred and profane"—also "tosses more meaty imagery . . . into the song's already suggestive stew."[18] Though hardly without flaws, not the least of which being the way, as the poet and critic bell hooks charges, it "colonizes and appropriates black culture,"[19] the video of "Like a Prayer" testifies evocatively to Madonna's faith in the possibility of experiencing spiritual transformation through sex.

This theme has bubbled at or below the surface of Madonna's music from the beginning. Her early club hits might make the most overt case for the quasi-religious ecstasies of the dance floor—as apt a metaphor for conveying sexual abandon as any. Yet amid the surging rhythms and hooky choruses of these disco reveries also lies a desire for much more than what Prince called "DSMR" ("dance-sex-music-romance"). "Borderline," Madonna's first Top 10 hit, refers not just to the limits to which she will let her lover test her patience, but also—and with erotic allusions to how he makes her "love come down"—to the threshold of intimacy and wholeness to which she aspires. "Open Your Heart," a No. 1 pop single in 1986, is all about mutuality and commitment, its message as emphatic as its propulsive, libidinous grooves. Much the same thing is true of 1989's "Express Yourself," an electro-percussive anthem of sisterly solidarity and uplift.

These early dance hits tend to be more suggestive than explicit, and none of them, taken at face value, is particularly deep. Yet neither are they merely love songs. Through their accretion—together with the likes of "Into the Groove" and "Lucky Star" (the latter a mystically inclined record in which the singer finds her spiritual *and* sexual compass)—these singles establish the transcendental eroticism that forms the backbone of Madonna's music. When she sings, in the ballad "Crazy for You," about time standing still and everything being brand new—"Touch me once and you'll know it's true," she urges— Madonna is not referring merely to ephemeral sensations. Buoyed by the record's soaring melody and throbbing drumbeats, she is concerned with a more enduring transformation, a spiritual renewal that, while not exactly religious, is not unlike the window to glory that Marvin Gaye described with the phrase "somethin' like sanctified."

"Like a Virgin" is a glorious yet routinely disparaged case in point. Madonna has said that she will never perform the song, her first No. 1 pop hit, in concert again, and given the way that some of her critics have scorned it, especially those given to literal mindedness, her decision is understandable. But it also is a shame, because when heard from a mystical standpoint, "Like a Virgin" conveys a sense of awakening and renewal, of wholeness both sexual and spiritual that approximates that expressed by Aretha Franklin in her exquisite recording of "(You Make Me Feel Like) A Natural Woman."

"I made it through the wilderness / Somehow I made it through," Madonna sings to open the record's first verse, alluding to a period of spiritual barrenness akin to the midnight hour that she invokes in "Like a Prayer." "I was beat, incomplete / I'd been had, I was sad and blue / But you made me feel / Yeah, you made me feel / Shiny and new / Like a virgin." Madonna is talking about sex here, of course, but not about virginity in any strict physiological sense. The transfiguration that she is describing, her disarmingly girlish vocals transported by the springy bass line of producer Nile Rodgers, is not limited to the body at all. When on the choruses she gasps, "Hey," her tone is less that of someone experiencing orgasm (although it certainly is that as well) than of someone overcome by the inexpressible joy of having her lover "reach that secret place in her head and heart that she has never surrendered to anyone else."[20] Madonna's "Hey" is the sound of transcendence and rebirth, of someone who has experienced the mutuality or radical immanence of sexual healing.

An urge for spiritual and sexual renewal similar to that expressed in "Like a Virgin" is at work in the music of Polly Jean Harvey, the British singer, guitarist, and provocateur. Harvey's hunger assumes an uncharacteristically religious or theological cast on *To Bring You My Love*, the imperious, blues-steeped album that she made with her band, PJ Harvey, in 1995. In "Teclo," Harvey looks to an eroticized Christ figure for deliverance, much as Madonna does in the video of "Like a Prayer." "Let me ride / Let me ride / Let me ride on his grace for a while," Harvey moans to the track's gently rocking undertow. The sexual connotations of the verb "ride" could just as well be a nod to the double entendre of the blues masters that she holds dear as to the erotized supplications of a medieval mystic like St. Teresa, or likely both.

Harvey appeals to God or Jesus for sexual release at points throughout *To Bring You My Love*. "I was born in the desert / I've been down for years / Jesus come closer / I think my time is near,'" she declaims over the ominous blues progression of the title track, the desert in question reminiscent of the wilderness of which Madonna sings in "Like a Virgin." In "Dancer," a divine emissary dressed in black and wearing a cross bearing Harvey's name sweeps in on a mount, as if out of Brontean mists, to rescue her. "Fly with me, touch the face of the true God / Cry with joy at the depth of my love," he beckons, bathed in "splendor" and "glory," over a pregnant electropulse. Harvey responds with a round of orgasmic shrieks, before pleading, "Oh Lord, be near me tonight . . . / Bring peace to my black and empty heart!" "It's so over the top," wrote Barbara O'Dair in her review of the album in *Rolling Stone*, "that you're not sure her vision of a male savior on a horse isn't a put-on."[21] But that is the point. Harvey's desire is so outsized that nothing short of Rabelaisian proportions can do it justice.

Harvey's gift for mythopoeia is virtually unrivaled in pop music, certainly in the post-punk era. Over the course of a half-dozen albums she has donned myriad personae, from male and female to phantasmal, reinventing herself as everything from a whore and an agent of God to a fertility goddess and a she-Godzilla. Harvey has drawn some of these guises from the Bible and from her native Anglo-Celtic folklore, others from the images of surreal creatures that she gleaned from her parents' blues, Jimi Hendrix, and Captain Beefheart records. All, however, are sensual and mystical to their core. Take, for example, the salacious "Long Snake Moan," a "cock rock" update of the blues that dwarves even that patented by Led Zeppelin, a band whose monumental stomp-and-swagger Harvey's music sometimes evokes. "Hell's door, God above / All drunk on my love / Now won't you hear my long snake *moan*," she roars over a gargantuan guitar riff, before exulting, during the orgiastic maelstrom that closes the track, "It's my voodoo working!"

Harvey's is a music of excess and extremes, of relentless tension and release that turns on heart-stopping screams, caterwauling guitars, and abrupt shifts in volume and tempo. Sometimes these torrents convey the ecstasies of sex. More often, though, they betray pain and discomfort, whether it is born of Harvey's feeling of being trapped in her body (a recurring theme, and likely the root of her perpetual makeovers onstage and in photos) or of her straining against the constraints of a repressed, misogynistic society. "Must be a way that I can dress to please him," she broods in "Dress," her churning debut single. "It's hard to walk in a dress, it's not easy / Spinning over like a heavy-loaded fruit tree / If you put it on / If you put it on," she continues, "investing the act of adornment with both a threat and a dare."[22] Harvey takes the opposite tack on the record's thrashing follow-up, "Sheela-Na-Gig," throwing her paramour's sexism back in his face by spreading her labia at him in scorn. In "Rid of Me," seething at the lover who has spurned her, she warns, "You're not rid of me / I'll make you lick my injuries," before unleashing waves of crashing noise that sound like they could swallow him whole.

Harvey's mystical predilections often enable her to transform pain into a vehicle for transcendence, something that is especially pronounced on her serrated early albums. "I'll make it better / I'll rub it 'til it bleeds," she vows on the quasi-transgressive *Rid of Me*, while on *Dry*, her chafing debut, she sings, "I'm happy and bleeding for you." There is a measured quality to Harvey's vocals, and to the looping guitar figure that she plays here—a serenity even—that belies any irony that her claim might possess. Something similar is at work in "Ecstasy," one of several lacerating blues pieces from this period. "Harvey takes for granted that eroticism hurts, that nothing pretty comes of giving over to love's irrational pull," wrote Ann Powers in "Houses of the Holy," her marvelous essay on *Rid of Me*.[23]

Powers went on to place Harvey and her rapture-induced shape-shifting, most notable in the likes of "Man-Sized" and "50-Ft. Queenie," in the tradition of the female mystics who, trying to break free of their bodies and of their body-reviling societies, underwent startling transfigurations to satisfy their hunger for the divine. "Holy women of the Middle Ages typically experienced their faith in terms of bodily transformation, partly self-induced, but ultimately mysterious," she wrote.[24] "Stigmata, elongation or enlargement of body parts, levitations, and catatonic seizures proved the union with Christ that these women attained, although such symptoms rarely visited men. Accounts of these miracles . . . suggest that women could actually change form, if only momentarily, and so push through the limitations of their traditionally scorned and feared female bodies." Harvey, Powers continued, "cultivates that same shape-changing power."

The object of Harvey's yearning might not be the conventional deity embraced by her medieval foremothers—or, for that matter, by her predecessors Marvin Gaye and Al Green. Harvey's is more of a postmodern quest, much as it is for Madonna, for self-transformation through sensuality—indeed, for sexual liberation—than a striving to be united with a personal deity (or even a transpersonal one). Yet there remains, as large portions of *To Bring You My Love* and its successor, *Is This Desire?* attest, a pronounced spiritual, and at times theological dimension, replete with images of heaven and the divine, to Harvey's eroticized vision of redemption. More than just an end in itself for her, sex possesses the power to transport body *and* soul, temporarily satisfying her transcendental urges and bringing a measure of peace, as she sings in "Dancer," to her "black and empty heart."

*Is This Desire?* is more ruminative than *To Bring You My Love*, its music more ambient and subdued. Harvey's protagonists and their meditations on the question that the record poses, however, are just as obsessive. In "Angelene," employing a virgin-whore dichotomy akin to the one that Madonna has used, Harvey plays a devout prostitute who, with a mix of tranquility and longing, confides, "I see men come and go / But there'll be one who will collect / My soul and come to me." Sounding a more desperate note over the barren title track she wonders, "Is this desire enough / Enough to lift us higher / To lift above?" In the ironically-titled "Joy" she mourns for a solitary woman of thirty who is leading "a life un-wed." This reference is not to marriage per se, but to a life bereft of faith, hope, and joy, a life in which unfilled desire is an abiding and crippling condition.

Harvey has cautioned in interviews against reading details about her love and sex life into her music, but given her career-long obsession with desire and its discontents, it is hard not to hear her talking about herself in the likes of "Joy." Most of her records in fact sound like they were made in the wake of romantic break-ups. Whether or not this is the case, 2001's Manhattan-inspired *Stories from the City, Stories from the Sea* brims with a sense of spiritual and sexual rebirth hitherto unheard from Harvey. Rumor had it that she made the album during the first blush of newfound passion, and from rooftop waltzes at midnight to blissed-out epiphanies like "I can't believe life's so complex / When I just wanna sit here and watch you undress," the feelings of renewal that she conveys here border on wonder. Yet even on this latter track, a throbbing anthem called "This Is Love," there remains a current of doubt. "This is love I'm feeling," Harvey sings. "Does it have to be a life full of dread?"

Dis-ease returns with a vengeance on 2004's *Uh Huh Her*. The music on the record ranges from dirty guitar noise to brooding murk, with an occasional swatch of melody to part the gloom. And the likes of "The Desperate Kingdom of Love" and "The Darker Side of Me and Him" still find Harvey plumbing the meaning of desire, however much it might be in retreat. In "The Slow Drug," its title an allusion to that elemental longing, she seems to view this undertaking, for all its sexual and spiritual worth, as her vocation. "Headlights burning / Looking out for something / Something that we're needing," she muses evocatively to the restless cadences of what sound like a synthesizer and a violin struck with a bow. "Still," she goes on, "the question lingers / I twist it round my fingers / Could you be my calling?"

Madonna's music likewise evinces a preoccupation with the ins and outs of desire, an obsession that has gained focus and grown expressly more spiritual as her career has progressed. "Tell me love isn't true / It's just something that we do," she insists over the urgent folk guitar figure and electronic beats of 2000's "Don't Tell Me." "Tell me everything or not / But don't tell me ever to stop," she continues, equating asking her to quit seeking transcendence through sex to bidding the sun not to shine or the wind not to blow. Madonna's prosaic metaphors aside (she can be the most banal of lyricists), she is expressing much the same commitment to probing the transformative mysteries of desire as Harvey does with her music. It almost is as if the two women are pursuing a vocation, a devotion both mystical and sensual that, again, while not overtly religious, exudes an ardor comparable to that of St. Teresa and other monastic women of the Middle Ages.

Naysayers who have called Madonna everything from an exhibitionist to "a porn queen in heat"[25] would of course maintain that her more transgressive hedonism gainsays or sullies such claims for her music. Certainly 1992's *Sex*, the button-pushing collection of photos in which Madonna acts out her erotic fantasies, did not show her in the best of lights, even if the book was not so much obscene as bad art. That said, dismissing an artist who is as profoundly self-aware and in control of her own self-representation as Madonna is can be dangerous. Her gestures, even those that might offend or otherwise miss the mark, are "credible," argues musicologist Susan McClary, "precisely *because* they engage so provocatively with ongoing cultural conversations about gender, power, and pleasure."[26]

Madonna knows as much, and has acquitted herself and her "pussy-as-power-play feminism"[27] on exactly these grounds. "Express yourself / Don't repress yourself," she urges in "Human Nature," a self-possessed rejoinder released in the wake of *Sex* and its de facto soundtrack album *Erotica*. She goes on, coyly, in an anti-apology of sorts, to say that she is not sorry for dramatizing the things that most people do or fantasize about. "Did I say something true? / Oops, I didn't know I couldn't talk about sex . . . / I didn't know I couldn't talk about *you*," she sings, her jibes awash in sultry beats and futuristic blips and effects. Later, in a pointed whisper, she asks if her sexual frankness would be easier to swallow if she were a man, which, given her outspokenness about sexual reciprocity, particularly as it concerns female pleasure, exposes a chauvinistic double standard and otherwise strikes a nerve.

Madonna had admonished listeners not to underestimate her point of view before this, most notably in "Cherish." And as the emotional nakedness of "Live to Tell" revealed long before that, she certainly is capable of tremendous depth. The trouble is that she has not always shown that depth, something that doubtless explains why some do not take her more seriously. Even more vexing, as McClary points out, is how with Madonna, people subjugate the musical to the visual, thus trivializing her recordings,[28] which not only leave more to the imagination than her videos do, but which buttress the notion that she hardly needed MTV to become a superstar. More to the point here, Madonna's records are where her wedding of spirituality and eroticism is most subtle and evocative.

Madonna's recordings began to speak more explicitly to matters of sexual redemption as the 90s unfolded—and with increasing depth, just as her singing voice deepened and gained in richness. Somewhat paradoxically given its uncharacteristically subdued and glacial veneer, 1993's *Erotica* delves more into the fleshly side of transcendence. "Secret Garden" uses double entendre to speak to spiritual as well as to sexual rebirth, suggesting that for Madonna, the two impulses are but different sides of the same coin. Indeed, in "Nothing Fails," a track from 2003's pensive *American Life*, she confesses, "I'm not religious, but I feel such love / Makes me want to pray." *American Life* also includes songs about "x-static" processes, salvific interventions, and other "profusions" of love (a term that Madonna often uses interchangeably for sex), offering further evidence, as Vince Aletti once put it, of the material girl turned spiritual girl.[29]

Madonna's mystical leanings might not have been evident to some early in her career, but they certainly had moved to the forefront by the mid-90s. Her 1994 single "Bedtime Stories" marked something of a turning point in this regard, rendering the transcendental elements of her eroticism explicit. "Words are useless . . . / How could they explain how I feel . . . / Traveling, traveling—in the arms of unconsciousness / Let's get unconscious," she bids her lover over a strobe-like organ riff. Seeking a similar sort of union and release in "Sanctuary," another numinous track from *Bedtime Stories*, she sings, "It's here in your soul / [That] I want to be married / You are my sanctuary."

Madonna began immersing herself in kabbalah not long after the release of *Bedtime Stories*. She was in Argentina, pregnant with her daughter Lourdes and working on the movie *Evita*, in which she played the lead role of Eva Peron. Madonna has spoken of her study of Jewish mysticism in interviews and donated millions of dollars to kabbalah schools in London and New York. She recently changed her name to Esther, which in Hebrew means "star," and during her 2004 Re-invention Tour, she and her dancers wore black T-shirts that read, "Kabbalists Do It Better." As with virtually everything that she does, Madonna's immersion in kabbalah has caused a furor, especially among those who view it as sacrilegious or as yet another case of celebrity dilettantism. Yet given her mystical-sensual proclivities, it is easy to see how the kabbalah of, say, Rabbi Isaac Luria, according to whom the sum of all things is "copulation and union," would have resonance for Madonna and her pursuit of wholeness and transcendence through sex.[30]

Not surprisingly perhaps, the most sustained expression of this vision came with *Ray of Light*, the first album of new material that Madonna wrote and recorded after she became acquainted with kabbalah. The record's ethereal arrangements and philosophizing, replete with references to gurus and fate fitting karma, at first seem insubstantial—especially its vague, New Agey lyrics. "She's got herself a universe," Madonna sings, depicting herself careening through space, propelled by the kinetic beats and laserlike surges of the title track. It all is very exhilarating, yet also quintessentially Apollonian, almost disembodied, at least until the chorus, when words start to fail her. Sounding a more Dionysian and orgasmic note, she cries, "And I feel / And I *feeeel* / Like I just got home."

Something of an update of "Like a Prayer," in which Madonna also floats on clouds and arrives at an erotico-spiritual destination, "Ray of Light" articulates a sense of connection that encompasses spiritual illumination and carnal ecstasy, in effect erasing distinctions between the two. This is true of a great deal of the *Ray of Light* album, with Madonna scattering aphoristic lines like, "You're frozen when your heart's not open," among the record's heaving strings and muted beats. The track that renders the spiritual intimations of this eroticism explicit, though, is the urgent, obliquely kabbalistic meditation on union and transcendence called "Skin."

"Kiss me I'm dying / Put your hand on my skin / I need to make a connection / I'm walking on a thin line," Madonna implores, transported by a shuffling electro-pulse accented by Middle Eastern overtones. She is burning with desire, to be sure, but the line that she is straddling also suggests a threshold, a portal to more than just the raptures of sex. Indeed, when on the chorus she asks, "Why do you leave me wanting more?" she sounds like she is speaking both to her lover and to her desire—to some personification of the urge for transcendence itself. Knowingly chiding herself on the choruses, Madonna wonders why all of her questions sound like the "stupid" ones that she has asked before. Her self-examination is knowing because, far from stupid, it sounds like a prayer, the erotically charged one that she has been reciting in one form or another for the better part of two decades now.

# chapter 3

## MY LOVE I BRING

### Sinéad O'Connor, Buddy and Julie Miller, and Moby

SHE WHO DWELLS IN THE SECRET PLACE OF THE MOST HIGH

> "My love I bring to you / My heart and soul too / Jah say I must give it to you."
>
> —Pablo Moses, "My Love I Bring"

> "Goddess, I . . . thank you for what you've done and hope I can become just a bit more like you and love the way you do."
>
> —Sinéad O'Connor, "Brigidine Diana"

Sinéad O'Connor's "Three Babies" is a record of uncommon empathy written and sung from the point of view of a woman clinging desperately to her young children. The details of their situation are sketchy. The family appears to be homeless. The little ones are cold and the mother, pressing their bodies to hers, professes her devotion to them. She is talking more to herself, though, than to her babies, but also, at least in her mind, to someone from whom she is estranged yet to whom she still feels connected. It could be the children's father, or even, given her conflicted remark about blasphemy, God.

"Each of these / My babies / Have brought you closer to me," sings O'Connor, playing the part of the mother, on the chorus. Her vocals are more piercing here than they were in the opening two stanzas; the glacial strings and inert rhythms intensify the chill of her lyrics. Yet there also is an eerie calm, an almost dissociative quality, not unlike the numb tranquility that people feel when they are about to drown or freeze to death. Indeed, when the mother vows, "I have wrapped your cold bodies around me / The face on you / The smell of you / Will always be with me," it is as if she is trying to fix her babies in her memory before they die. Or, if their frozen bodies are dead already, before they fade from her consciousness as *she* dies or otherwise loses her hold on reality.

The scene is ominous and unnerving, much like the record's ambient arrangement. It is as if the lives of these four people are slipping away during the five or so minutes that it takes O'Connor to unfurl her impressionistic narrative. Little is revealed about what brought the mother and her babies to this point, or why things had to end in tragedy. Yet there is no mistaking the dignity in O'Connor's brittle quaver. Or in the mother's unwavering commitment to being close to her children and their father (their "Father"?)—in her conviction that nothing, not even the grave, can separate them from each other.

O'Connor's ability to enter into the suffering of another—and to imagine and convey that misery so vividly—is staggering here. It is a display of more than sympathy, which, as a show of fellow-feeling, nevertheless underlines the distance between the self and the other. O'Connor's gesture is one of empathy. It entails a willingness, as the philosopher Emmanuel Levinas so evocatively put it, to be called forth by and "lend oneself" to another.[1] It involves a dwelling within the experience of another that necessitates a transcending of the self that links the responder to the other, illuminating and redeeming the humanity of both. Whereas contemplative and sensual expressions of the urge for transcendence hinge on somehow losing oneself in order to glimpse the eternal, the empathetic path entails *giving* oneself to and participating in the experience of another. Some offering of the self of course is at work in contemplative and erotic pursuits of transcendence, particularly in the latter, which necessitates reciprocity. Empathy, however, involves a more selfless impulse: that of lending oneself to and confronting the mystery of another, even if at considerable historical or imaginative remove.

As is frequently the case with those who open themselves to the hurt of others, O'Connor's capacity for empathy is born of her own suffering, notably the physical abuse that she endured at the hands of her mother while she was growing up in Dublin. "An understanding of sorrow and pain is an important thing to have because if nothing else, it gives you an appreciation for happiness," she said in an interview with *Rolling Stone* in 1991.[2] "People who've been brought up happy and normal often don't have an understanding of what life might be like for other people.... [I]t's important to understand pain and what life is like for other people—and I never take that knowledge for granted."

"Black Boys on Mopeds" is a stirring case in point, a muted yet reverberating indictment of racism and hypocrisy that O'Connor wrote out of the grief and outrage that she felt over a London police killing of an innocent black teenager. "Scorn Not His Simplicity," a piano lament about a mentally disabled boy, is another example. "See the child / With the golden hair / Yet eyes that show the emptiness inside / Do we know / Can we understand just how he feels / Or have we really tried?" O'Connor sings, the compassion in her tearful intonation palpable. O'Connor's outpouring of emotion does not stop with the boy, though. She also burrows inside the hurt of the mother, lifting up and, if just for the moment, redeeming the guilt and helplessness that the woman feels over having brought a child into the world who "looks almost like the others" but "is not the same."

Just as devastating as the way that O'Connor inhabits the suffering of others is the otherworldly soprano with which she relates their sorrows, a voice that is as naked and arresting as her often shorn head. O'Connor's singing can be elfin or cavernous, tender or imperious, chaste or libidinous, yet regardless of mood, it invariably taps a vast reservoir of feeling. In "Jackie," a seething track from her debut album *The Lion & the Cobra*, she dwells within the anguish of a woman whose lover was stolen from her by the sea. In "Troy," an astonishing torrent with Gothic overtones, she plumbs the bereft heart of a woman whose lover has forsaken her for another. "Do you love her? / Is she good for you?" O'Connor shrieks over lacerating strings. "Does she hold you like I do?" she goes on, before unleashing a series of wraithlike wails that echo as if coming from someone falling headlong into an abyss. It all is very over the top, yet undeniably riveting, much like the rock 'n' roll theatrics of, say, Patti Smith or Polly Harvey, two rockers with whom O'Connor shares a penchant for mythopoeia and spectacle. Nurtured in the myths and temperament of her Irish homeland, O'Connor's prodigious sense of drama enables her to transform even the most hackneyed material into something transcendent.

The critic Ann Powers likens O'Connor's gift to method acting, the process by which actors draw on emotions associated with their personal experiences and apply them to the roles that they are playing.[3] As an example Powers cites "Nothing Compares 2 U," a self-pitying castoff written by Prince that O'Connor and co-producer Nellee Hooper refashion as "a gospel of hurt." Much as she did with her gripping, drum-and-bass-inflected revamping of the ballad "I Am Stretching on Your Grave," O'Connor turns the song into a monument to estrangement that is as harrowing as Robert Johnson's "Stones in My Passway" or the Stanley Brothers' "Rank Strangers." The final frames of the video for the record are, if anything, more wrenching. Here, as Mikal Gilmore observed, O'Connor struggles "to make sense out of how she lost the one love she could not afford to lose," only to shed "a solitary [and utterly unscripted] tear of inconsolable loss."[4]

O'Connor's emotional permeability at times has proven her undoing, especially when it has collided with her corresponding, almost infantile inability to suppress her feelings. Most notorious here was the time in 1992 when O'Connor, long an outspoken anti-cleric, tore up a photo of Pope John Paul II while appearing as a guest on *Saturday Night Live*. A few years before that she was censured by the British press for biting the hand that fed her when she publicly denounced her countrymen in the band U2, whose guitarist the Edge had given her career an early break. At one point O'Connor also drew the ire of Frank Sinatra, who vowed that he would "kick her ass" after she threatened not to perform at a concert in New Jersey if the venue played "The Star-Spangled Banner" as planned to open the show.

O'Connor has admitted in interviews that she does not have the best self-control or sense of timing. She nevertheless takes all of this controversy and criticism to heart, just as one might expect from an artist who absorbs things so completely. "It really hurts me when people make me out to be a nasty person," she once said in an interview.[5] When O'Connor uses the word "hurts" here it is easy to imagine her internalizing this pain physically, just as her voice suggests that she does when her heart goes out to someone in song. "They don't care that if they say, 'Sinéad O'Connor is a complete bastard,'

I'm going to sit up all night and think, 'I *am* a complete bastard . . .,'"
she went on to say. "[T]hey don't care about what a person has been
through."

This last comment speaks to perhaps the principal danger that accompanies expressions of empathy: the risk of losing one's sense of
self while immersing oneself in the experiences of others, the risk of
reaching so far beyond oneself so as not to be able to get back. Take
the time that O'Connor ripped up the picture of the pope on *Saturday Night Live*. Presumably she made the gesture out of fellow-feeling for those who have been oppressed by the Roman Catholic
Church. The act clearly meant a great deal to her, and she must have
anticipated the virulent backlash that would greet it. Yet the connection between her symbolic display and the feelings of empathy that
likely motivated it never was self-evident, perhaps not even to her,
thus making her appear rash and foolish—wholly unsympathetic—to
millions of people. By failing to hold onto a sense of who she was as
she lent her heart to others, O'Connor not only lost herself, she
undercut the spiritual generosity that prompted her gesture in the
first place. It almost was as if she had conflated her own feelings of
victimization, especially those related to growing up Irish and Catholic, with her stirrings of compassion and outrage on behalf of those
who have in some way suffered at the hands of Rome and the Pope.

Themes of abuse and victimization, both social and interpersonal,
lie at the heart of O'Connor's message, and they frequently are inter-
woven with commentary about Ireland and the Catholic Church. All
of these things—abuse, mother country, and mother church (motherhood, in every respect)—converge in "Famine," a heavy-hearted yet
ultimately hopeful jeremiad from 1994, all of it spoken, in which
O'Connor recites a litany of social ills that have grown out of centuries of strife in Ireland. "We used to worship God as a mother / Now
look at what we're doing to each other / We've even made killers of
ourselves," she mourns to a cadence of marching hip-hop beats. Moving from rebuke to exhortation on the chorus, she proclaims, "If
there ever is gonna be healing / There has to be remembering / And
then grieving / So that there then can be forgiving."

O'Connor offers her heart seemingly to all within hearing in
"Famine," a song that nevertheless is something of a muddle, and perhaps of questionable historicity. (She contends, among other things,

that the Irish Potato Famine never happened.) Yet what makes the recording so stirring, besides its fundament-seizing groove, is that O'Connor does not lose her sense of self here the way that she sometimes does when she reaches out to others in empathy. In contrast to her attention-grabbing appearance on *Saturday Night Live*, she enters into the well of pain and thirst at the heart of the Irish experience and does so with a clear sense of her place within it. "She's never lost that unmistakably Irish mix of transcendent desire and tragic fatalism," wrote Ann Powers, "that urge to forever circle back to the root—of history or of personal experience—if not to repair what can't be mended, then at least to understand and grieve. Like U2, O'Connor has always made music that's in some essential way about the terrible hunger for a home that can only really be reached internally, through faith and imagination."[6]

O'Connor makes just such a spiritual homecoming on 2000's *Faith and Courage*, a stirring album steeped in Rastafarianism and dub-style production[7] in which she sings of having a "healing room" inside her. On the confessional likes of "What Doesn't Belong to Me" and "The Lamb's Book of Life" she reckons with both her tangled Irish roots and her conflicted decade-plus in and out of the limelight. "Out of Ireland I did run / Great hatred and little room / Aimed to break my heart / Wreck me up and tear me all apart," she sings over the rat-a-tat reggae of the latter. "I know that I have done many things / To give you reason not to listen to me . . . / I just hope that you can show compassion / And love me enough to just please listen," she goes on. "I bring these blessings with me / A strong heart full of hope and a feeling . . . / [That] out of hopelessness we can come."

A trio of successive covers born of faith and imagination on 2003's *She Who Dwells . . .*, a career-capping double album released in conjunction with the announcement of her retirement, casts O'Connor's empathetic resolve in similar relief.[8] The first of the three songs is a spongy update of reggae singer Pablo Moses's "My Love I Bring." "My love I bring to you / My heart and soul too / Jah say I must give it to you," O'Connor sings on the chorus, making explicit the theological imperative implied in the album's full title: *She Who Dwells in the Secret Place of the Most High Shall Abide Under the Shadow of the Almighty*. A creaky, Celtic-inflected version of the

Southern soul standard "Do Right Woman" follows, with O'Connor leaning hard on the lines, "Take me for granted," before plumbing the reciprocity that forms the backbone of the chorus. Rounding out this triptych is a Spectorian remake of the old Every Brothers hit "Love Hurts" in which O'Connor's ravaged performance underscores just what is at stake when one lends one's heart to another and risks losing oneself in the process.

These last two songs might have been written about romance and heartache. Yet here, recontextualized in the wake of the Rastafarian "My Love I Bring," they invest love with broader moral and social connotations, with a redemptive power much like that of Marvin Gaye's "Keep Gettin' It On" or Al Green's "Love and Happiness." Confirming this impression several tracks further into the album is "Brigidine Diana," a paean to the late Princess of Wales and the solidarity that she achieved with people suffering with AIDS and people who otherwise were on the margins. "Your love and your compassion were Christ-like," O'Connor sings to the track's hymnlike arrangement, lifting up Princess Diana, a conflicted soul with whom she clearly identifies, as a role model, an avatar of empathy. "Goddess, I . . . thank you for what you've done / And hope I can become / Just a bit more like you / And love the way you do."

All of which raises the question, broached most explicitly by recordings like "Three Babies" and "Black Boys on Mopeds," as to whether O'Connor's dwelling within the suffering of others, particularly those cases where she does not lose herself there, ultimately is more prophetic than empathetic. This question is easier to answer when applied to figures like Johnny Cash or Curtis Mayfield, artists whose expressions of empathy persistently open outward, giving voice to the silent cries of entire classes of people and calling all who hear them into account. A prophetic dimension similar to this certainly attends some of O'Connor's work. Her primary impulse, nevertheless, is not so much to call attention to the hurt of others as to participate in it imaginatively or interpersonally, as opposed to, say, politically or socially. Finer phenomenological distinctions notwithstanding, O'Connor typically seeks transcendence more through entering into the pain of others and, by means of this indwelling, redeeming it, rather than by promoting social change.

## My Love Will Follow You

> "You can have my heart, though it isn't new. It's been used and broken and only comes in blue."
>
> —Julie Miller, "Broken Things"

> "If you should go so far that you cannot get back, you may not remember but my heart will not lose track."
>
> —Buddy Miller, "My Love Will Follow You"

Singer-songwriters Buddy and Julie Miller create an ardent mix of country, blues, rock, and soul music that, despite winning the devotion of the famous likes of Emmylou Harris and the Dixie Chicks, should be much better known than it is. Some of this is due to the Millers' self-effacing, even reclusive tendencies, and perhaps to the fact that they sometimes work from an expressly Christian perspective. The couple, however, does not make gospel or even religious music so much as records that suggest possibilities for human communion that cut across lines of faith and dogma. At the heart of their music, which only occasionally invokes Jesus or God, is an attunement to the suffering of others born of the Millers' belief that there exists a spark of the divine within all people. In one particularly uplifting song they assert, "Our love will hold up the sky / When the rain comes down too hard." This claim is neither sentimental nor grandiose. It bears witness to the couple's conviction that people not only can enter into the pain of others, but that the act of doing so somehow can redeem that suffering, if only by memorializing or otherwise lifting it up.

Empathy pervades the Millers' music, yet nowhere is it as explicit as in Julie's narratives, stories that invariably become vehicles by which she lends her heart to others. She wrote the song "Rachel," for example, after reading a book based on the journal of Rachel Scott, an exceedingly kindhearted student at Columbine High School in Colorado who anticipated the violence that claimed her life there in 1999. "There is a life no one can take / There is a chain of love no one can break," the Millers sing to swelling choruses of harmonium, electric guitar, and organ, their interlocking voices testifying to their faith in the indestructibility of the human spirit. "She was just so kind to the kids who were rejected at her school," Julie said, talking about Scott in an interview in the summer of 2001.[9] "She also knew that something terrible was going to happen, because in her journal she referred to her school as 'these halls of tragedy.' I can't believe I could miss someone so much that I'd never even met."

Julie's capacity to step outside herself and into the hurt of others, even that of a stranger like Rachel Scott, is one of the hallmarks of the Millers' records, which typically are issued under one or the other's name (even though both write and perform the bulk of the material for each other's projects). "Quecreek," a fiddle-sweetened ballad from Buddy's fourth record, was written out of the stirrings of empathy that Julie felt for the Pennsylvania miners who were rescued after being trapped in a flooded coal shaft for three days in 2002. "100 Million Little Bombs," a keening lament that the couple wrote for Buddy's second solo album, bemoans the fields of still active landmines that claim the lives of thousands around the world each year, many of them children. The title track of Julie's 1999 album *Broken Things* is dedicated to the families of the twenty-nine people who were killed when terrorists bombed the village of Omagh in Northern Ireland in 1998, as well as to "all whose hearts are broken things."

"Broken Things" encapsulates Julie's posture of openness toward the world. "You can have my heart, though it isn't new / It's been used and broken / And only comes in blue," she sings, her choked prayer enfolded in the diaphanous figure that Buddy plays on acoustic guitar. "I heard that you make old things new / So I give these pieces all to you / If you want it you can have my heart," she goes on, backed by the sighing of a bowed cello and the hushed harmonies of singer Emmylou Harris. Julie is seeking renewal here, but not merely for herself. She wants her heart to be mended so that she can again lend it to others, a self-transcending impulse that doubtless accounts for why her heart is in tatters in the first place. "I need something like a cure for my soul," she blurts, sounding a much more desperate note to the throbbing blues-rock of "I Need You": "I need something bad and I need it now / I got something wrong with me / You better fix it 'cause I don't know how."

Julie's solo albums, which lean more toward rock than Buddy's country-soul recordings, contain expressions of empathy for a sexually-abused child ("Dancing Girl"), a homeless woman who is mentally ill ("All the Pieces of Mary"), and a friend's mother who was orphaned as a child ("Maggie"). Julie even revives the old battlefield requiem "The Boston Boy," not only taking it to heart, but adapting it to a new context and transforming it, transported again by the exquisite harmonies of Emmylou Harris, into a wrenching study in empathy. "In my [Nashville] neighborhood are many historical markers where Civil War battles were fought," Miller wrote, explaining the evolution of the song in the liner notes to her album *Broken Things*. "I drive down a street called Warfield to go to the grocery. I think of [the soldiers'] blood under my feet when I walk in my yard."

As with Sinéad O'Connor, Miller's participation in the anguish of others is grounded in the agony that she has known—everything from having grown up with an abusive father to living with fibromyalgia, a condition that afflicts her with chronic, debilitating pain. Yet in contrast to O'Connor, who sometimes loses a sense of who she is when she dwells within the suffering of another, Miller consistently retains a sense of herself when she empathizes with others. The way that Miller's porous heart goes out to apparently all who are broken or hurting is less an act of volition than a consequence of who she seems called to be. This is not to suggest that all suffering is redemptive, or that Miller had to go through hell to become the profoundly empathetic soul that she is. Sometimes misery just makes people bitter or otherwise consumes them. Yet as the theologian John Mogabgab wrote, there remains the possibility "that our hearts, wounded by the boundlessness of human agony, grow tender and alert to the wounds of others. Then our wounds become portals of vulnerability through which the pain of others can enter our lives, awakening us to a more generous sense of our common humanity and discovering in turn refuge, consolation and healing."[10]

The transformation that Mogabgab describes certainly is what happens with Julie Miller. "When I look at the world I see a painful planet," she told me in a 1999 interview.[11] "[I see] a place full of people who are orphaned in their heart and souls. Which is just how I felt, orphaned, before I came to know God, [who] put this deep concern for people in my heart." And not just for people, but for all manner of animals, including her ten or so cats, all of whom she picked up as strays. In Miller's eyes *all* living things are God's creatures, even the possum that she used to harbor under the bed in the Millers' attic, much to the chagrin of their friend and former tenant, singer-song-writer Jim Lauderdale.

Steve Earle, another of the Millers' collaborators, tells of the time that he met Buddy, Julie, Emmylou Harris, and others at the Nashville airport. They were on their way to Washington, DC, where they were scheduled to appear together at a benefit concert, when a bird became trapped in the glass terminal. The group was late, but Julie refused to go to their gate until the creature was whisked safely back outside. "There absolutely wasn't any way in her mind that we were going to get on the airplane until that bird was taken care of," Earle recalled.[12] "Animals gravitate toward Julie, especially wounded ones and those that are lost. And I think there's a reason for that. She has a connection to things that are intimidated by their surroundings and she relates to that. She responds to that."

Buddy is much more reserved than Julie, but he, too, is deeply empathetic, a quality that is most apparent when he is singing or playing guitar. His at times brooding, at times stabbing guitar lines often echo his wife's outpourings, while during other passages he will dispatch a series of notes that seem to lunge forward as if reaching to catch her should she fall. Likewise, his voice often anticipates and embraces his wife's, especially when, during a flurry of gospel-style call-and-response, his shouts and moans play off hers, communicating things that the words alone could not possibly convey.

Something similar happens when Buddy performs love songs previously recorded by others, particularly when he reimagines them as declarations of spiritual and vocational intent. His hurtling remake of Roger Miller's and George Jones's "Nothing Can Stop Me," for example, invests the song's vow of fidelity with much greater depth than the love-struck ditty it doubtless was meant to be. More sublime, though, are his ravaged updates of the Otis Redding hit, "That's How Strong My Love Is," and of Percy Mayfield's signature song, "Please Send Me Someone to Love." Both transcend the outwardly romantic content of their lyrics to become soul music of a more universal sort, the former a statement of empathetic resolve, the latter a reason for being. Miller's 2004 album of re-contextualized gospel music is another matter altogether, a veiled expression of grief and anger over the US invasion of Afghanistan and Iraq, including an epic update of Bob Dylan's "With God on Our Side."

"That's Just How She Cries," a simmering soul ballad from the only album that the Millers have released as a duo, offers further evidence of Buddy's enormous emotional reserves, in this case his ability to enter into the heartache of his wife. "She is silent / Without words she speaks / So listen to her eyes / 'Cause that's how she cries," he sings in a murmured croon, his words echoed by braided strains of harmonica and electric guitar. Julie wrote these lines for a friend who was going through some sort of ordeal, but here, with Buddy singing them, they become a testament to how *Julie* holds the hurt of others in her heart. A stunning turnabout, Buddy's reimagining of "That's Just How She Cries" is a heartrending and heartening display of spiritual generosity in which he participates empathetically in his wife's feelings of empathy for another.

This implicit, often unspoken communion is a hallmark of the musical idioms in which the Millers work—distinctly American genres like country, soul, and blues that are steeped in themes of struggle, hope, loss, and redemption. Foremost perhaps is the influence of the Louvin Brothers and their tragic songs of life and the Staple Singers and their beacons to freedom, recordings that typically speak to temporal *and* eternal concerns. The Millers perform items from the catalogs of both, and it is telling that both were also family acts. Whether it is the urgent exchanges in the couple's update of the Staples' "It's Been a Change," or the strikingly close intervals of their harmonies in their covers of the Louvins' material, the intimacy that the Millers achieve (doubtless an outgrowth of their capacity for empathy) is that typically heard only among kin.

"We know each other so well that we have a kind of telepathy going," Buddy has said, referring to this affinity. "Whenever we do something together, it becomes something else. It's kind of like a third thing."[13] So thoroughly do the Millers' penetrate each other's minds and hearts while performing together that it has become second nature to them. When they sing together, their voices—Julie's aspirated and girlish, Buddy's reedy and stout—modulate not only the way that partners do when anticipating each other's moves on the dance floor, but also in much the same way that longtime lovers do in bed. Some of this comes, as Buddy has observed, from the fact that he and Julie have lived and sung together for years—for more than a quarter-century at this point. Yet also underlying this deeper commu-

nion is the way that the Millers have oriented themselves empathetically toward each other and toward the rest of the world: their
unwavering commitment to entering into each other's experiences
and, as often as possible, into the suffering of others.

This commitment, along with the spiritual transparency that attends it, redeems any clichés about nature mirroring human misery
that recur in Julie's otherwise nonpareil songwriting. "Time and space
are relative," she sings in "The Speed of Light," and in the Millers'
case, much the same thing is true about what constitutes stale or hackneyed verse. When Buddy and Julie sing about the sky crying, the
wind howling, or a river flowing like tears, the conviction in their
voices suggests that they are not merely trading in images, but invoking metaphysical truths that transcend notions of what is shopworn
and what is not. They are testifying to their belief in the interconnectedness—the interpenetration—of all experience, including God's, and
thus suggesting that God shares empathetically in suffering.

Nothing that the Millers' have recorded, not even Julie's definitive
supplication, "Broken Things," expresses this conviction better than
"My Love Will Follow You." The song is yet another that the couple
wrote together, and its seemingly boundless outpouring of steadfastness remains the highpoint of Buddy's first solo album, if not of the
Millers' entire catalog. More than just a testament to the couple's
commitment to each other, "My Love Will Follow You" is redolent
of the Apostle Paul's assertion, in The Epistle to the Romans, that
nothing—not principalities, nor powers, nor anything on earth—can
separate people from the love of God. "If you should go so far / That
you cannot get back / You may not remember / But my heart will not
lose track," Buddy vows as heaving strains of steel guitar and piano
transport him from the song's second-to-last chorus to the bridge.

Musically and emotionally, this passage could hardly be more expansive, bridging not just whatever might separate the two lovers in
the song—or, for that matter, the Millers from each other—but also
it seems, any gulf that might exist between heaven and earth as well.
"My Love Will Follow You" might as well be giving voice to the all-
encompassing heart of a God who, far from distant, is the embodiment of empathy, a God who suffers with and is very much present
in the world, *especially* amid unspeakable loss. At the very least, "My
Love Will Follow You" bears witness to a larger force that binds all

things together, a force that makes empathy and healing possible in the first place. A force that might be able, as the Millers claim, to hold up the sky when hard rains fall.

## Every Time You Touch Me

> "Why does my heart feel so bad? / Why does my soul feel so sad?"
>
> —Unidentified member of the Shining Light Gospel Choir

> "Until he extends the circle of his compassion to all living things, man will not himself find peace."
>
> —Albert Schweitzer

Moby uses his immense capacity for empathy to create rhapsodies that evoke what the Millers are talking about when they sing of love being able to hold up the sky. Like the Millers, Moby—a descendant of Herman Melville (hence the nickname)—is a Christian who, while having little use for institutional religion, embraces the more radical implications of Jesus' teachings about tolerance and mercy. Moby also is a vegan and an environmentalist who opposes anything that might harm the earth or living beings. Reports are that he even catches and sets free the cockroaches that overrun his Manhattan apartment. "I think that all cellular life has its own kind of consciousness and its own character," he told an interviewer for *Spin* magazine in 1995. "You can't say that human consciousness is somehow inherently better than buttercup consciousness."[14]

Moby lines the booklets that accompany his albums with quotations and essays that witness to the interdependence and sanctity of all life. "Until he extends the circle of his compassion to all living things, man will not himself find peace" goes the passage from Albert Schweitzer that appears, along with likeminded sentiments from Thoreau, Einstein, and St. Francis, on the back of Moby's 1995 album, *Everything Is Wrong*. "God is angry, I think," is how he begins the second of the two short essays that he wrote for the record's liner notes. From there he launches into a diatribe about the way that many politicians and religious leaders in the United States "are masquerad-

ing hate, racism, sexism, and ignorance under the banner of conservative Christian values."

Moby is nothing if not persistent with his exhortations and entreat-
ies. His sincerity certainly is a tonic for the terminal irony and indifference that came to define Generation X, the demographic group,
ironically enough, that has most readily embraced his music. Yet for
all of his pamphleteering, much of it righteous, Moby expresses himself most eloquently through music, employing a dappled sonic palette that comprises everything from thrash-metal and techno to disco
and ambient tone poems. It is tempting to call his recordings cine-
matic, in part because he has written so much music for film. Moby
is less an animator of the work and ideas of others, though, than a
visionary who is intent on proving that dance music can have much
the same emotional and conceptual reach as classical composition, as
well as much the same grandeur. At his best, as on several early singles
and on omnivorous opuses like *Everything Is Wrong* and *Play*, Moby
fashions a deeply affecting symphonic language that greatly expands
the vernacular of techno music and electronica. A language that in
many cases is the sound of one heart going out to another—and, quite
often, to the entire universe.

*Play* is Moby's most sublime outpouring to date, a groove-steeped,
multi-platinum-selling song cycle from 1999 that is galvanized by
samples of field recordings of old blues and gospel singers made by
the late Alan Lomax. Titles like "The Sky Is Broken" and "If Things
Were Perfect" chart the album's emotional compass, but the devastating laments "Why Does My Heart Feel So Bad?" and "Natural
Blues" lay bare its throbbing heart. On both tracks Moby suppresses
his own voice in order to create space for the anguished cries of others—in each case, those of an African American gospel singer from
the early to mid-twentieth century. These gestures are not acts of cultural appropriation, but of self-emptying; through music that cradles
and lifts up these "dead" voices, Moby pours himself into the sorrow
that they convey, reanimating and dwelling within it, preserving the
humanity in each.

The first of these two tracks begins with a reverberating, melisma-
rich male voice moaning, "Why does my heart feel so bad? / Why
does my soul feel so sad?" A bed of gently shuffling rhythms props

up the nameless singer—the album's notes just credit the Shining Light Gospel Choir—as descending figures played on piano and synthesizer usher in the second chorus. The music suggests the image of a stairway unfolding from above, as if from the sky, while an ecstatic female voice chants, "These open doors." It is not clear whether the woman is using the word "open" as a verb or an adjective here, but it makes no difference. Repeated over and over, her pronouncement only deepens the sense of imminent deliverance, as well as the impression that in lifting up the voice of the disconsolate male singer, Moby is presenting the man's weary heart as an offering to heaven, a candidate for healing.

Moby traverses considerable historical, cultural, and spiritual distance here, stepping out of his experience as a white DJ-turned-rock star and into that of an anonymous black church singer who lived under the pall of Jim Crow. Moby's act of self-transcendence does not erase the cultural or historical expanse that separates him from his haggard counterpart, which, despite his immense spiritual generosity, will always remain. Yet it does bear witness to his belief in the possibility, if only by dint of faith and imagination, of entering the pain of another, in the process reclaiming some portion of the humanity within it.

Redemption of this sort also is evident in "Natural Blues." Here Moby resurrects a lamentation called "Trouble So Hard," a recording that Alan Lomax made with a Depression-era singer named Vera Hall. "Oh Lordy, trouble so hard / Oh Lordy, trouble so hard / Don't nobody know my trouble but God / Don't nobody know my trouble but God," Hall begins, her mournful tenor backed by the celestial sustains of a lone synthesizer. Skittering drum beats and rumbling bass and piano set a loop of Hall's refrain in motion, a wounded litany borne aloft by keyboards and untethered voices that testify that someone outside heaven knows and is willing to share in the trouble of which she sings.

"Natural Blues" and "Why Does My Heart Feel So Bad?" are not the only tracks on *Play* that have this transporting effect. Taken as a whole, the album, which ranges from jungle grooves to orchestral reveries to gutbucket blues, evinces a liturgical cohesion and sweep, mixing rousing proclamation ("Run On") with hushed offertories

("Guitar Flute & String"), surging choral anthems ("South Side") with confessional meditations ("My Weakness"). Elegiac soundscapes like "Everloving" serve as a balm for the suffering that courses through the album, while propulsive rave-ups like "Bodyrock," which samples "Lover's Rap" by Spoonie Gee & the Treacherous Three, provide catharsis that all but obliterates the pain. Over the course of *Play*'s seventy-seven minutes, Moby presides over what amounts to a club-friendly Mass, a service of healing and renewal in which he lifts up the world's hurt and points beyond it, inviting dancers to participate in and redeem it with him.

Moby's music has not always sounded so lofty a note. His first real band was a hardcore punk outfit called the Vatican Commandos, with which he played guitar. Remnants of this period still can be heard in his live shows and on portions of *Everything Is Wrong* and the mostly pummeling *Animal Rights*. Moby also was interim lead singer for the San Francisco dadaist band Flipper and, in the late 80s, worked as a DJ with acts ranging from Run-D.M.C. to Cher. His tenure as a turntablist in the clubs of New York City is what crystallized his vision of the transcendental possibilities of electronic music.

This vision was already apparent by the time Moby released his 1991 single "Go," a frenetic remix of the trippy theme from the TV series *Twin Peaks* and a major hit in the UK. Working under various guises during this period, Moby released a flurry of singles and mixes to the dance market, most of them heavy on samples, synthesizers, and tricked-out, hyper-kinetic beats. Typical of this phase is "Thousand," an early B-side that, as its title suggests, registers at least 1,000 beats per minute (the *Guinness Book of Records* listed it as the fastest single ever). Even amid the putative hedonism of dance culture, though, Moby's records—all of them inscribed with thanks to Jesus— convey an array of anxiety, torture, and ecstasy, much of it overtly spiritual and spilling over with concern for a broken world. Fittingly, most exude a tactile, emotionally expansive quality that usually is not associated with techno, an idiom that often is thought of as icy or brittle. "Techno with a spirit-feel" is how the critic Robert Christgau described Moby's early singles, "modest and luxuriant, compelling and humane."[15]

*Move*, a thirty-one-minute EP from 1993, brought together the hallmarks of Moby's formative output—speed, tangibility, humanity—in an extended format for the first time, foreshadowing the liturgical arc of *Play*. The record opens with the ecstatic title track, a piano-driven recording better known as "You Make Me Feel So Good" that is galvanized by the soaring hosannas of club divas Carole Sylvan and Rozz Morehead. In jarring contrast, the ravaged supplication that follows finds Moby frantically shouting variants of the song's title, "All That I Need Is to Be Loved," over a nightmarish rattle and hum. The disc concludes, three tracks later, with "Unloved Symphony," a foreboding yet exhilarating techno anthem that bleeds into "The Rain Falls and the Sky Shudders," a muted piano benediction that reaches out in empathy to the sobbing firmament.

*Everything Is Wrong*, Moby's commercial breakthrough from 1995, picks up where the final notes of *Move* leave off, with a hymn to the heavens. In this case the "Hymn" is a numinous duet featuring waves of piano arpeggios and heaving synthesizer echoed by the wordless chanting of a choir. It sounds a portentous opening note, one befitting an album interspersed with cautionary essays and statistics that works as something of a manifesto. And not just as an empathetic or theological statement, but as a musical one as well, with Moby testifying to the limitless promise of electronica via dazzling shifts back and forth from astral ballads, atavistic blues, and menacing industrial clamor to glacial ambience, disco rapture, and dub-inflected drum-and-bass.

One of the two centerpieces of *Everything Is Wrong* is an overhauling of "All That I Need Is to Be Loved" that is even more desperate than its techno precursor. The updated version of the song is less a case of Moby being estranged from a lover than from the ground of his being. "All that I need is to be loved / Can't you take this out of me?" he howls over an implacable din cauterized by buzz-sawing guitars. "All that I want is to be near you / Oh my God, how can I love Thee?" he goes on in despair, his use of the archaic pronoun "Thee" suggesting that he is indeed pleading his case before God.

Moby grew up the child of a single parent and has often spoken in interviews about his feelings of inadequacy, about feeling unloved and even unlovable. These themes are writ large in tracks like "All That I Need" and "Unloved Symphony." The intense hunger that

these recordings convey, a burning for communion with another, is
the desire from which Moby craves release when he screams, "Can't
you take this out of me?" in "All That I Need." Moby is seeking
more than just deliverance here. He is searching for insight into the
meaning of self-emptying love. He wants to love the way that God
loves, a love that, when approximated by human beings, Moby believes has the power to draw people nearer to each other and to God.

Moby's vision encompasses more than just expressions of theologically grounded empathy. There is sexual transcendence, for example,
on *Animal Rights*, as well as meditations on romance and betrayal on
2002's *18* and elsewhere. And many of Moby's early house and
techno singles achieve transcendence more in keeping with the sensual release of the dance floor than anything else. Surely at some level,
"Every Time You Touch Me," the other centerpiece of *Everything Is
Wrong*, is about the transformative power of love and sex. Yet given
the primacy of empathy and the divine in so much of Moby's work,
it is hard not to hear "Every Time You Touch Me" as the God-intoxicated flipside of the fear and trembling of "All That I Need." It even
follows "All That I Need" on the album, as if in answer to it (albeit
after a brief interlude of chopped-up beats and voices pointedly titled
"Let's Go Free").

"Oh, come and take me away / Oh, 'cause everything is wrong
today," implores one of the divas who appears on "Every Time You
Touch Me," her urgent vocals agitated by the strobe-like beats of a
drum machine. No sooner than she sings of looking to the east (the
horizon where each new day dawns), a crescendo of strings sweeps
her headlong into the chorus. "Every time you touch me I feel like
I'm being born," belts out the other woman who sings on the record.
The ecstasy in her voice is that of one who has made the connection
for which Moby yearns in "All That I Need." This is a physical bond,
to be sure, but also one that penetrates the spirit, an interpenetration
that, for Moby, is grounded in divine love.

"God Moving Over the Face of the Waters," the piano blessing that
appears toward the end of *Everything Is Wrong*, all but confirms as
much. Here Moby's playing does not evoke the roiling images associated with the primordial chaos of the ancient creation myths from
which the track's title comes. Instead, his bruised notes are more

those of tender, brooding concern, a feeling for and with the world, especially the suffering within it. "God Moving Over the Face of the Waters" is a reflection, however imperfect, of the divine empathy in which Moby longs to participate. It is the sound of one heart lending itself to a world of others.

# SECTION II

# NAYSAYERS
Dystopians and "Idiots"

## chapter 4

# THE GREAT WRONG PLACE
# IN WHICH WE LIVE

## Nine Inch Nails, Tricky,
## Joy Division, and New Order

Musicians who express the urge for transcendence through negation are not as transparently spiritual as contemplatives, sensualists, or empaths are. Unlike those artists, whose response to the world is largely mystical, those who express their restlessness negatively do not exhibit a pull toward anything, much less a striving for some higher union or state of consciousness. They certainly do not feel drawn to the likes of God or the holy. Naysayers tend not to believe that anything, human or divine, can satisfy their hunger for transcendence, if they recognize the presence of such a hunger at all. Their overriding impulse is one of aversion, typically to a world that makes no sense to them and that holds out little hope of transcendence. The uncompromising, often cacophonous music that they make reflects this antipathy—a din that frequently conveys nothing so much as a yearning for oblivion.

Naysayers nevertheless are not nihilists, no matter how bleak their outlook might seem. Whereas nihilism involves the inability to see beyond one's antipathy and ultimately is narcissistic, negation is motivated by the desire, as the critic Greil Marcus put it, to "destroy the world *and* to survive it."[1] Naysayers might not be able to envision what the aftermath of such a process might look like, yet just by giving voice to their dissatisfaction, they point beyond it and betray a hunger for something better. Expressions of negation are in this way political. They involve acknowledging not only the possibility, however remote, of transcending one's circumstances, but also the ability to look beyond oneself to others, even if only to see other people as targets at which to hurl invective.

Punks, thug rappers, and heavy metal and industrial noise bands are perhaps the most prevalent subspecies of popular musicians who express negation. Wary of anything that promises transcendence lest it prove false, these naysayers tend to be of two main types. The first are dystopians, artists who make discordant, at times assaulting music that evokes the hostile, even hellish worlds that they know. The second group consists, for lack of a better term, of idiots, albeit knowing ones. These are artists who go beyond evoking the chaos in their midst. They seek to unmask and, in some cases, to obliterate the "non-sense" around them by embodying or becoming it, often going to ridiculous, shocking, or dangerous extremes to do so. The music that naysayers in either camp create can be off-putting, but it also can be exhilarating, as in Johnny Rotten's excoriating yowls of "No future" during the final, unhinged bars of the Sex Pistols' "God Save the Queen." It even can be beautiful, as in the cascading melody of Joy Division's sublimely gloomy post-punk anthem, "Love Will Tear Us Apart."

Gestures of negation doubtless will strike some as counterintuitive to the pursuit of transcendence; they certainly run counter to popular understandings of spirituality. Though rarely religious, these gestures nevertheless are spiritual, if only as evidence of the restlessness at the root of all human experience, as testimony to how people channel the fire that burns within them. Throwing alienation in the face of whatever breeds it can afford some naysayers a qualified or fractured sort of uplift. Venting antipathy also can be a decisive moment in the "dark night of the soul" through which some must pass if they are to come out on the other side and affirm anything. Negation often is a fitting response to inhumanity and oppression. Above all it serves as a corrective to false claims to transcendence, to the merest hint that anything finite might be able to satisfy the human taste for the eternal. Naysayers refuse heaven, so to speak, because everything that they have experienced has taught them that no rumor of glory can be true. Yet even this rejection of the prospect of transcendence is, paradoxically, an expression of the urge for it insofar as it points beyond the mundane or the everyday.

Negation of course is not unique to musical subgenres like punk or rap. Philosophies and faith systems from Marxism to Christianity steadfastly utter emphatic "No's" to cheap or illusory claims to transcendence. Negation is the impulse at work in the concept of idolatry expressed in the first of the Ten Commandments and in the cries of many of the Hebrew prophets. Negation is inherent in Buddhism's First Noble Truth, which recognizes that existence is suffering because nothing on earth can satisfy human desire. Clearing away finite claims to transcendence in order to affirm the possibility of achieving it, if only in part, also is the founding principle of Protestantism, as well as the source of its name. Negation is essential to any dialectical pursuit of truth, a process of refinement by which every affirmation or "Yes" is hardened, as the theologian Paul Tillich put it, in the fire of a thousand "No's."[2]

## I Do Not Want This

"My head is filled with disease . . . I really don't know who I am in this world of piss."

—Trent Reznor, "Terrible Lie"

"Gray would be the color if I had a heart."

—Trent Reznor, "Something I Can Never Have"

In recent years, maybe the most clarion voice to articulate a vision of a world gone horribly wrong is that of Trent Reznor, the auteur behind the industrial rock group Nine Inch Nails. Reznor's lyrics are not especially deep, and they certainly do not give explicit voice to anything that overtly resembles spirituality. At times they even sound like sophomoric diary entries, at others like the cartoonish ranting of a provocateur aiming for maximum shock value. Hooked by rat-a-tatting lines like, "I'm hard as fucking steel and I've got the power," "Big Man with a Gun" is an anti-authoritarian screed and meditation on the eroticism of power that is both cartoonish and sophomoric. Yet just because Reznor's outpourings are broken or distorted does not necessarily make them less spiritual. Expressions of the urge for transcendence in fact are often more pronounced when they are born of the sort of anger and anguish that Reznor vents. What makes the recordings of Nine Inch Nails signify most, though, and what grounds their naysaying spirituality, is the alienation that seethes from the harrowing soundscapes that Reznor creates: ear-piercing barrages rife with unhinged screaming, grinding guitars, pulverizing beats, and nightmarish walls of abrading synthesizer noise. Nirvana's "Smells Like Teen Spirit" might have been the anthem of the flannel-flying rank-and-file of Generation X, but for its Goth-leaning, "blanker-than-thou" contingent, NIN's digital maelstroms proved the high-tech soundtrack to the millenarian angst of the 1990s.[3] The name Nine Inch Nails even calls to mind instruments of torture. NIN, the acronym for it, has a ring of negation as well.

Underlying the musical mayhem of Nine Inch Nails is Reznor's overriding sense of himself as a solitary individual pitted against God and the world. "Head like a hole / Black as your soul / I'd rather die than give you control," he vows amid the grating buzz and lashing electro-beats of "Head Like a Hole," NIN's debut single. "Piggy" and "March of the Pigs" are just as strident in their opposition to principalities and powers, with Reznor using the term "pig" after the fashion of the mass murderer Charles Manson to refer to anyone in authority. "Mr. Self Destruct" and "Heresy," meanwhile, express revulsion over complacency and conformity.

Reznor appears, on first blush, to be anti-everything. A classically trained pianist who sees his jarring, computer- and keyboard-generated music as a challenge to the hegemony of traditional rock music, he even is anti-guitar. Despite selling millions of copies, the records of Nine Inch Nails also are defiantly anti-commercial. Ultimately, though, Reznor's antipathy is less a function of any pose or polemic that he has embraced than an outgrowth of his pervasive feelings of spiritual and emotional emptiness, a cavity like that evoked in "Head Like a Hole" that he is unable to fill and does not trust any worldly thing to fill either. "I'm the one without a soul / I'm the one with this big fucking hole," he rages, his howling buried beneath the throttling clamor of "Wish," from NIN's 1992 EP, *Broken*. "I know what's coming to me is never going to arrive," he roars in "Last," the track that comes next, echoing this sense of spiritual abandonment, this sense that the deliverance for which he waits will never come.[4]

*Pretty Hate Machine*, NIN's 1989 debut, is an album of dance-oriented rock co-produced by studio mavens Flood, Adrian Sherwood, and Keith LeBlanc that scarcely hinted at the forbidding clangor that would follow. Reznor has attributed the angst that courses through the record to romantic dissolution, and undoubtedly that is the case. Yet much like Moby's desolate cries in "All That I Need Is to Be Loved," the ripples of Reznor's despair have wider spiritual and existential implications. "I'm down to just one thing and I'm starting to scare myself," he moans over the uncharacteristically subdued tones of "Something I Can Never Have," before adding, "Gray would be the color if I had a heart." Above the brittle funk of "Terrible Lie" he admits, "My head is filled with disease . . . I really don't know who I am in this world of piss." Later, to the acrid disco of "Sin" he owns, "I'm just an effigy to be defaced / To be disgraced," as a curtain of surging beats and menacing noise overtakes him, much as his self-loathing does by the track's end.

As the self-loathing that serves as the leitmotif of *Broken* attests, such extreme despondency cuts deeper than romantic disaffection. Reznor even admitted as much in an interview that he did with *Spin* magazine in 1995. "On *Pretty Hate Machine* I'm depressed by everything around me, but I still like myself; I've still got myself," he told writer Eric Weisbard.[5] "On *Broken*, I've lost myself; nothing's better and I want to die." The album indeed verges on nihilism at points, and it might have succumbed utterly to it were it not for Reznor's determination to voice his dis-ease and, by doing so, to point beyond it, whether he meant to do so or not. Despite the anguish it conveys, "Last" is not the final word on anything, if only because Reznor persists in order to utter it.

Even so, apart from "Help Me I'm in Hell," an ambient instrumental that builds in tension but, not surprisingly, never achieves release, *Broken* consists entirely of lacerating noise. All of it converges on "Happiness in Slavery," an anti-anthem in which pile-driving rhythms, scourging synthesizers, and stinging guitars provide a grisly backdrop for images of torture and self-abuse. The video for the record depicts these scenes in brutally explicit detail, with sadomasochistic performance artist Bob Flanagan submitting to being violated sexually by a machine and then to being crushed to a pulp. All of this

takes place while Reznor screeches the sardonic precept of the record's title.

"Happiness in Slavery" speaks to another theme that colors Rezn-
or's disaffected worldview: the conflict between people and machines.
The "group" Nine Inch Nails, which apart from live performances is
essentially a one-man synthesizer band, embodies this tension, albeit
ironically, since much of the music that Reznor creates in the studio
could not have been made without the technological advances of the
late twentieth century. Still, the alienation that arises not just from
people being superseded by machines, but from the authoritarianism
for which machines are such a fitting metaphor, is never far from the
surface of NIN's music. Reznor might cast the feelings born of this
dehumanization in exaggeratedly violent terms, yet he does so not to
cure people of their uglier emotions. He does it to get them to confront this ugliness, the effect of which, whether intended or not, is to
underscore the essential, if shattered, humanity that lies at its core.

Here again, many of the transgressive scenes that Reznor paints
would be shrill and melodramatic were the recordings of Nine Inch
Nails not so consistently and palpably chilling. Even with the benefit
of gripping sonics, however, Reznor's images often smack of histrion-
ics—or worse, of caricature, although nothing compared to the shtick
of his former protégé Marilyn Manson. Considering Reznor's cultural reference points, which include typically over-the-top vehicles
like comic books and horror movies, as well as grandiloquent rock
allegories like Pink Floyd's *The Wall*, this is hardly surprising. Growing up in rural Western Pennsylvania, the epicenter of nowhere, Reznor did not listen to "hip" music like punk or hip-hop, but to the
by turns bloated and cheesy likes of progressive rock and synthesizer
pop. One of his earliest inspirations was the rock 'n' roll big top of
arch-parodists KISS. All of these things, along with the computer en-
gineering that he studied in college, contribute to the geekiness that
fuels the at times quotidian alienation that NIN's records convey.

Reznor's banal cultural touchstones and surroundings also nurtured in him the misfit self-concept and penchant for spectacle that
begat his persona as the Dark Lord of industrial music. Something of
a post-punk answer to the Lizard King nonsense of the Doors' Jim
Morrison, Reznor's dissolute image made him a lightning rod for
controversy, especially among proponents of American "family val-

ues" like William Bennett and C. Delores Tucker. Both made Reznor a poster child for their censorious crusades and both played right into his hands, as did then-presidential candidate Bob Dole. All three of them gave the outsize violator fantasy "Big Man with a Gun" much wider exposure than it otherwise might have received. (Depending on how one hears it, the record is either a satiric dig at police brutality or a burlesque of the sexual degradation and violence glorified by gangsta rap.)

Reznor doubtless intended "Big Man" to be a joke, albeit a biting one. ("The point is . . . to bring people out of complacency," he said at the time. "Socially, lyrically—your parents should hate it. Bob Dole *should* have a fucking problem with it."[6]) Truly dangerous, though—and Reznor has acknowledged as much in interviews—is "The Downward Spiral," the title track from the multi-platinum album that, predictably enough, Nine Inch Nails recorded in the house where Charles Manson and his followers murdered Sharon Tate and several of her friends. "He couldn't believe how easy it was / He put the gun into his face / Bang! / (So much blood for such a tiny little hole)," Reznor begins in a subliminal whisper, seemingly advocating suicide as a means of escaping the hellish reality that NIN's music evokes. These opening lines come well past the halfway point of the four-minute track, as if to dramatize the victim's struggle to work up the nerve to kill himself. Muffled screams are embedded in the record's arrangement, which sounds more like musique concrète than any traditional songform, and more like oblivion than reality. "Problems have solutions," Reznor later declares, with glacial equanimity. "A lifetime of fucking things up fixed in one determined flash."

"The Downward Spiral" is perhaps the most explicit and bleak evocation of oblivion in the catalog of Nine Inch Nails, and a hunger for something like it, yet subtly different, is also evident in the elegiac "The Day the World Went Away" from the group's 1999 album, *The Fragile*. Here when Reznor muses, "There is a place that still remains / It eats the fear, it eats the pain / The sweetest price he'll have to pay / The day the whole world went away," he seems to be talking not about opting out of existence, but about something more akin to dying to oneself and to earthly desire. Similarly, in "The Great Below" and "La Mer," an ambient pair of back-to-back tracks from *The Fragile*, Reznor speaks of the ocean making him "disappear," of

"becom[ing] the sea" and "going home." "Nothing [no *thing*?] can
stop me now," he insists as "La Mer" draws to a close, not so much
as one who wishes to drown himself, but as one who seeks to drown
the desire that he knows will only betray him.

It might be a stretch to suggest that there is something akin to Zen
Buddhism at work in *The Fragile*, particularly given the rancor that
Reznor expresses at points throughout the album (which, tellingly
enough, was released on NIN's Nothing imprint). Yet just as Noah
Levine, in his memoir *Dharma Punx*, called attention to the "fierce
wisdom" of punk's anti-establishment ethic[7]—to punk's urge to annihilate what cannot bring satisfaction in the first place—the transcendental undercurrents in tracks like "La Mer" and "The Day the World
Went Away" are strong. Even at Reznor's most self-loathing, such as
in "I Do Not Want This" from *The Downward Spiral*, his resistance
to seemingly every source of suffering, including himself, issues from
an impulse both to destroy the world and to survive it.

Indeed, even though Reznor flirts with self-annihilation in his lyrics, he has yet to exercise that option. Instead he continues to exist in
order to make records, and this will to survive, this impulse to live
and to speak his piece, however aggrieved that it might be, reveals a
hunger for something better, something beyond malice and self-
loathing. "I want to do something that matters," he shouts at the
close of "I Do Not Want This," while in the groove-steeped yet otherwise menacing "Closer" he begs, "Help me get away from myself."
In both cases Reznor betrays an urge for transcendence, however dim
his hope of attaining it might be. "Come come come on / You've gotta
fill me up . . . / Come come come on / You've gotta fix me up," he
pleads over the thrashing racket of 1992's "Last." Seven years later,
amid the swirling haze of "The Way Is Through," he swears, "All I've
undergone / I will keep on," before heading, as the title of the track
that follows it reveals, "Into the Void," even if he does not know
where that passage might lead.

Reznor embarks on just such a negative, yet paradoxically affirming—or at least purgative—journey in "Hurt," a song that Johnny
Cash transformed into a monument to his lifelong struggle to subdue
the beast within. "I hurt myself today / To see if I still feel," Reznor
begins, backed by gusts of squalling synthesizer and, as the track un-
folds, an increasingly throbbing pulse. "I focus on the pain / The only

thing that's real." The allusion to drug abuse that follows—"The needle tears a hole / The old familiar sting / Try to kill it all away"—is especially pointed in the video of Cash's recording of the song, which eloquently confronts his battle with addiction. Yet ultimately "Hurt" testifies to how *all* finite things—not just narcotics (as Cash well knew)—"will let you down" and "make you hurt," to how nothing on earth can satisfy the human urge for transcendence. Despite knowing this, Reznor hungers to feel something, if only the pain that affirms his existence. "If I could start again / I would keep myself / I would find a way," he asserts as waves of noise batter him at the end of his recording of "Hurt." Merely by articulating this urge, this will not just to annihilate everything but to begin anew, he has.

## I Don't Like This Century

"Do you know what it's like to struggle? / Do you? / Do you? / Have you ever had to struggle?"

—Tricky, "Strugglin'"

"We're hungry / Beware of our appetite / Distant drums bring the news of a kill tonight."

—Tricky, "Hell Is Around the Corner"

Tricky employs what he calls a "hip-hop blues," a heady admixture of punk, rap, blues, and reggae, to expel his dyspepsia: a dis-ease born of growing up poor and black in postindustrial, post-welfare England. "Can't stand to feel / Hate to feel," he gasps on "Vent," the opening track on his 1996 album, *Pre-Millennium Tension*. "Gone insane / Hijack a plane / Don't push me 'cause I'm close to the edge." This last line, as well as the one that comes after it, is taken from "The Message," Grandmaster Flash & the Furious Five's soul-on-ice cry from the American ghetto. Tricky's voice never gets louder than a whisper here, yet it has the force of a shout, which it likely would have been were he able to get more air through the thrumming guitar loop and throttling beats that stifle him. "Can't hardly breathe," he wheezes on the closing vamp. The overwhelming mood is that of being trapped, of walls closing in and oxygen running out, with no door or window—no vent whatsoever—in sight.

Such is the claustrophobic, at times paranoiac world that Tricky inhabits, a hostile realm in which the prospect of transcendence is so remote that it scarcely seems worth pursuing. An unsettling mix of menace and lethargy pervades Tricky's evocation of these nether reaches, a place where intimacy and trust between people are all but impossible, and where institutions and authority are indifferent at best, and typically oppressive. Tricky's is a city of perpetual night out of *Blade Runner* where survival spells vigilance and where every turn must be met with resistance, lest it get the better of you. Even readiness, though, is no guarantee. In "The Moment I Feared," a harrowing, polyrhythmic fantasy from Tricky's *Angels with Dirty Faces*, a gang of thugs hunts him down, kicks in his door and rapes him.

Violation of another sort visits Tricky's collaborator Martina Topley-Bird in their stunning revamping of Public Enemy's "Black Steel in the Hour of Chaos." "Here is a land that never gave a damn about a brother like myself," raps Topley-Bird, aka Martine, as a swirl of helter-skelter beats and dirty guitar buzz envelops her. Martine, who is of African, Salvadoran, and Seminole Indian descent, is objecting to being put in prison, presumably in the US, for failing to register for the military draft. Casting her as a "public enemy" for refusing to be part of the war machinery that bullied her forebears makes for a disarming conceit, one that underscores some of the crucial differences between Tricky's vision and that of Trent Reznor, his fellow millenarian noise-sculptor. Whereas Reznor's often private hell is shot through with humdrum angst and at times verges on narcissism, Tricky's disenfranchisement and thirst for transcendence are rooted in a tangle of ethnicity and poverty that has global ramifications. Tricky's antipathy betrays no whiff of KISS camp or B-movie melodrama either. "I wanna take my clothes off / Tear my mouth and nose off and take out my eyes," he announces at one point. "I don't like this century," he proclaims at another. Though rarely as emphatic or transgressive as the horrorscapes of Nine Inch Nails (and not nearly as popular), Tricky's dystopian take on his surroundings is scarier and more relevant. "I wanna demonstrate hate / I wanna rattle," he vows in "Tear Out My Eyes," and with assassin-like cool that is what, through words but especially through music, he does.

Evidence of this unsettling intent, of Tricky's desperate, if dissipated, urge to shake off his social and historical inheritance, could be heard as early as 1994's "Karmacoma," a ghostly bit of hooky word-play set to dub rhythms and Middle Eastern modalities that he made with the British trip-hop collective Massive Attack. The record's title evokes the sense of stuckness that later would come to define Tricky's music, particularly the suggestion that a karmic world in which moral conduct shapes personal destiny no longer has currency, or at least is in need of life support. The anomie that such feelings beget accounts for the entropic cast of much of Tricky's music, as well as for provoca-tive, at times sociopathic gibes like "I fight evil with evil" and "I'll fuck you in the ass / Just for a laugh."

This lack of a moral compass, or at least the lack of any compulsion to heed one, was bred in Tricky, who was born Adrian Thaws, early on. The child of a Jamaican father and a mother who was half-Welsh and half-African, he grew up in Knowle West, a predominantly white ghetto near Bristol, a city that once was a port for the British slave trade. Tricky's mother committed suicide when he was four. After that he and his kid sister went to live with their grandmother. He eventually adopted the persona of Tricky Kid while running with local street gangs, later using it as his *nom de microphone* when he teamed up with the production team the Wild Bunch in Massive Attack.

Just as formative as this early scuffling was the commingling of dig-nity, eroticism, and resilience that Tricky heard in his grandmother's Nina Simone and Billie Holiday records, echoes of which suffuse his music, particularly its languid grooves and Martine's humid phrasing. Hip-hop nevertheless is what "opened up [Tricky's] head," as the critic Charles Aaron put it, "and forever changed the way he thought about music and identity."[8] Rap, Aaron observed, asserted Tricky's blackness in a positive way, affirming something that his largely white peers in Britain's electronic music scene tended to downplay or ig-nore. Tricky confirmed as much in an interview that he did with *Op-tion* magazine in 1996.[9] "With Chuck D [of the rap group Public Enemy]," he recalled, "that was the first time I ever thought, 'Yeah, I'm black and I'm proud,' instead of 'I'll fuck you up to survive.'"

*Maxinquaye*, Tricky's enthralling solo debut, gives voice to this dignity and resistance like a tumbledown answer to Public Enemy's *It Takes a Nation of Millions to Hold Us Back*. The creaky cadences of "Strugglin'" evoke the marching of a chain gang, replete with distant siren cries and a loop of what sounds like rifles cocking, as Tricky rasps, "They label me insane / But I think I'm more noble than most . . . / Roll with the bullets to survive." As Martine wails the word "strugglin'," Tricky, gunning for every false claim to transcendence he can hit, chides, "Do you know what it's like to struggle? / Do you? / Do you? / Have you ever had to struggle?"

Sounding a less confrontational note on "Pumpkin," Tricky, who suffers from asthma, coughs, "I can't see / And I can't breathe." Later he bemoans his "Suffocated Love," while in the knotty yet seductive "Aftermath" he transforms the romantic unrest of the oldies radio staple "How Can I Be Sure" ("in a world that is constantly changing") into a presentiment of existential paralysis. Dread gives way to a yearning for oblivion in the woozy "Ponderosa," or in any case to a hunger for numbness, as Tricky and Martine slur, "I drink till I'm drunk / And I smoke till I'm senseless," to the clatter of ramshackle beats.

Resistance, though, ultimately trumps resignation on *Maxinquaye*, where Tricky's naysaying, no less than Reznor's compulsion to live to tell, conveys an urge for transcendence, negatively expressed though it might be. "With the quick speed / I'll make your nose bleed," Tricky boasts on "Abbaon Fat Track," and to the ominous melody of "Hell Is Around the Corner" he warns, "We're hungry / Beware of our appetite / Distant drums bring the news of a kill tonight." Several lines later, amid the disembodied groans of male and female voices, he adds, "My brain thinks bomb-like," while on "Feed Me" Martine purrs, "Together we'll destroy." These are not merely expressions of resistance, or of destruction for its own sake. Martine's subsequent profession, "And together we can build what we are when we dream the spirit free," makes this plain enough. She and Tricky are exhibiting a negationist as opposed to a nihilistic impulse here. They are seeking not just to destroy the world but to survive it. Indeed, to remake it and, in doing so, to transcend it by doing more than outlasting it, even though that, in itself, would constitute a sort of transcendence (as would the act of articulating one's alienation in the first place).

This constructive urge extends to the way that Tricky builds the tracks on *Maxinquaye*: evocative collages of beats, voices, samples, and newly recorded instrumental parts that lend warmth and swatches of exotica even to the album's most forbidding moments. The grooves dry up considerably on Tricky's subsequent records, which, though still imperious, are flintier and more austere—more "industrial" in their evocation of urban clangor, from the groaning of cranes and bulldozers to the honking of car horns and the rattle and hum of subway trains. Tricky's later records also are less expansive emotionally than *Maxinquaye*. *Pre-Millennium Tension*, for example, is confined largely to musings about celebrity and its discontents. "They used to call me Tricky Kid / I live the life they wish to live," he raps to the stubborn beats and roiling drone of the "Tricky Kid." Martine, heaping further abuse in "Makes Me Wanna Die," taunts, "Who do you think you are? / You're insignificant / A small piece, an -ism." Tricky's overweening self-concept on the album borders on messianic. Yet as braggadocio like "My evil is strong" suggests, this persona is more in the tradition of antiheroes like Staggerlee and Railroad Bill than of more conventional liberators like Gandhi and Malcolm X. Antihero or not, Tricky's hubris is as naked an expression of the urge for transcendence as any. "They got me like Jesus," he gripes at one point, echoing Chuck D's beleaguered barb from "Welcome to the Terrordome."

Less hostile and more resigned, at least on the surface, is 1998's *Angels with Dirty Faces*, where the tyranny of corporate culture serves as the album's subtext. On "6 Minutes," a blistering fusion of funk and rock seared by Taser-like guitar barbs, Tricky deplores "this industry full of vomit" and warrants that his "voodoo [will] make 'em sick." Guest singer Polly Harvey takes up the refrain in "Broken Homes." "Those men will break your bones / Don't know how to build stable homes," she warns, her chilly alto alluding both to record executives and to the media. "You trample on my soul," Tricky charges amid the beat maelstrom of "Money Greedy." He later recut the track using a sample from Public Enemy's "You're Gonna Get Yours" after a high-ranking official at his record label alleged that all black people working in the music business were felons. "Every black man in the music industry has a criminal conviction / How can you say that with conviction," Tricky spits on the remake, which he titled "Divine Comedy" and released on his own Durban Poison label.

It might be hard to sympathize with Tricky's malaise about multi-national entertainment conglomerates, particularly given the relish with which he boasts about being a "superstar" with a record deal in "Tricky Kid." The fact that these corporations are rarely multi*cultural*, though, justifiably fuels his rancor. Indeed, not to be denied is the fundamental dis-ease that Tricky expresses in "Divine Comedy," the source of which, like so much of his music, is a convergence of racism and poverty and his fierce desire to transcend them, if not to annihilate them outright. This mix of striving and angst certainly helps explain Tricky's commitment to lifting up "angels" with "dirty faces." The faces of these angels do not have to be black; as the African, Latin, and Asian inflections heard throughout *Angels* prove, many also are red, brown, and yellow, and no doubt some of them are white. And most belong to women. Regardless, however, of gender or race, all of them bear the smudge of disenfranchisement and all, even with that ignominious mark, are invisible or "disappear without traces," as Tricky puts it in the album's title track.

In "Singing the Blues," an embattled woman who could be modeled after Tricky's mother (for whom *Maxinquaye* is named), returns home after a soul-sucking week on the job only to discover that she has been robbed even before her mounting bills can fleece her of her paycheck. Hounded by a guitar figure as relentless as her creditors she insists, "But I need my ten dollars *today!*" Picking up the besieged woman's plaint in "Talk to Me," Martine moans, "Cry me a bayou," and time and again, Tricky obliges, elevating not just besmirched angels like the one in "Singing the Blues," but also Martine, with whom he has made records as well as had a child. "My baby-mama kick it like Billie Holiday," Tricky crows hoarsely amid the murk of "Record Companies." On "Carriage for Two" he rasps, "I've got me a little black girl / And this little black girl's beautiful," as Martine croons, "God bless the child whose got her own," Holiday's pregnant line about the kinship between self-determination and self-worth.

Ultimately, Tricky's impulse to move beyond negation and to affirm the nobility of the struggle of another sets him apart from his dystopian counterpart Trent Reznor. Granted, any affirmation or any articulation of a yearning for transcendence in Tricky's music typically is muted or submerged. It would be a stretch to say that his records convey hope, so consumed is he with dyspepsia. The dissonance that suffuses his music nevertheless is expansive enough to embrace this tension between antipathy and sympathy, between the urge to tear down and to lift up. No matter how grim Tricky's vision, his sickness—his "voodoo," as he calls it—charts a way out, even if just through a profusion of asthmatic "No's."

Tricky has released any number of records since the epochal *Maxinquaye* came out in 1995. These include projects with street-level rappers, from the mentoring exercise billed as *Tricky Presents Grassroots* to a corrosive summit with DJ Muggs of Cypress Hill called *Juxtapose*. Tricky even paid slantwise tribute to his grandmother's record collection in 1995 with *Nearly God*, an album of deconstructed torch songs that featured singers like Björk and Neneh Cherry. His best work, though, remains the recordings that he has made with the unassailable Martine out front, singing and rapping with a lyricism, verve, and will to "get over" that indeed would have made Billie Holiday proud. A winning exception is 2001's *Blowback*, an album of funk-rock by way of dancehall reggae that relies on unlikely cameos from Cyndi Lauper, Alanis Morissette, and members of the Red Hot Chili Peppers. Even surrounded by these mainstream rock acts, and as tracks like "Give It to 'Em" and "Diss Never (Dig Up We History)" attest, Tricky does not forego incisiveness for accessibility, resistance for appeasement.

Much the same can be said of *Vulnerable*, 2003's slightly less galvanic successor to *Blowback*. Costanza, the Italian ingénue that Tricky introduces here, is no Martine (nor Alanis, for that matter). Yet even when she sighs putatively slight lines like, "I'm needy / I'm greedy / Feed me," or, "You leave me hungry / Wanting more," she taps the restlessness that permeates Tricky's music, an underlying striving that runs deeper than the eroticism conveyed here. "I drink your blood and I'm still thirsty / I wait for God and it's very hard," Tricky raps, deepening this impression over the hip-hop blues of "Wait for God." On the album's pressing closing track he whispers, "Search search *survive*." Given Tricky's self-professed goal to "demonstrate hate," we might have expected the final word in this progression to have been "destroy." Yet as the album's title suggests, even an inveterate naysayer can flash glimmers of vulnerability, if not of qualified affirmation. Indeed, when Tricky urges, "Say you're lucky alive," his exhortation, underlined by the music's tight, arid groove, betrays a thirst for transcendence that can contend with his desire to "rattle" or "demonstrate hate."

## WHERE WILL IT END?

> "You'll see the horrors of a faraway place, meet the architects of law face to face."
>
> —Ian Curtis, "Atrocity Exhibition"

The music of England's Joy Division is among the gloomiest and most influential of the post-punk era, anticipating everything from industrial noise and dance-oriented rock to death metal and grunge. The group's dystopian brooding might not be as transgressive as the digital barrages of Nine Inch Nails, or as suffocating as the thrumming beatdown of Tricky, yet if anything, Joy Division's unremitting urban Gothic is darker than either, and a precursor to both. The band issued only a handful of singles, an EP, and a pair of bracingly grim LPs during its three years together. This body of work turned on the doomed romanticism of lead singer and lyricist, Ian Curtis, a depressive soul who suffered from epilepsy and ultimately hanged himself, presumably over his failing marriage, just as Joy Division was on the verge of achieving wider acclaim. It would be a mistake, though, to attribute the band's doleful, ominous droning solely to Curtis's emotional malaise. To do so would not only reduce the group's music to personal psychology, it would divorce it from the larger economic and cultural morass from which it emerged. "Coming from the industrial desolation of Manchester," wrote Steven Grant in the first edition of the *Trouser Press Record Guide*, "Joy Division expressed, in uncompromising terms, the angst of the great wrong place in which we live."[10]

Personal and societal miseries were linked inextricably in Joy Division's universe, each informing and illuminating the other and contributing to a vision of the world as a cruel, chaotic place in which isolated individuals entertained scant hope of transcendence. The name Joy Division itself—a ghastly phrase that the Nazis used to describe the female prisoners whom they forced to work as prostitutes in the death camps—conjures so bleak and dehumanizing a picture as to suggest that Curtis's resignation and despair just might qualify as nihilism. Allusions to fascism and totalitarianism crop up elsewhere in the group's music and iconography, yet as the critic Mikal Gilmore has suggested, the band's name also could be giving voice to the conviction "that no horror, no matter how terrible, is unendurable. Maybe that sounds as joyless and morose as everything else about Joy Division's music, but it shouldn't. In this case, it's nothing less than a surpassing testament to the life force itself."[11]

This is not to say that the negation that reverberates throughout Joy Division's monuments to isolation and estrangement—throbbing "No's" to intimacy, trust, safety, and perhaps redemption itself—is not so intense at times as to be overwhelming. Abandoning himself to the free-falling rush of "Disorder," the opening track on 1979's *Unknown Pleasures*, Curtis sings of things being all but hopelessly out of hand. To the menacing lurch of the song that comes after it, he paints one forbidding scene after another, only to howl, "Where will it end?" in an aggrieved monotone. "I don't care anymore / I've lost the will to want more," Curtis concedes to the flogging beats of "Insight," before adding, "I'm not afraid anymore / I keep my eyes on the door." An oblivion-like din of squalling guitar and synthesizer closes the track, suggesting that the door for which he watches, and the insight to which he aspires, is death, likely as not by his own hand.

Monolithic titles like "Wilderness," "Interzone," and "Shadowplay" chart the desolate spiritual and emotional terrain of *Unknown Pleasures*, evoking a subterranean region in which souls are adrift, or are lost or in limbo, and never benignly so. Martin Hannett's glacial production heightens this sense of being cut off and in danger, his stark settings clarifying Bernard Albrecht's scraping guitar figures, Peter Hook's cascading bass lines, and Stephen Morris's scourge-like, often grooveless drumming to chilling, though gripping effect. The sound of glass shattering or the occasional siren going off only makes the perils portended by the music seem that much more real.

Things take an even more forbidding turn on *Closer*, Joy Division's second and final album. The ruinous proceedings begin with "Atrocity Exhibition," a macabre sideshow named after J. G. Ballard's dystopian novel about the dissolution of the planet earth. "This is the way, step inside," Curtis beckons, herding a crowd of spectators into an asylum to gawk at a man who is being tortured. "You'll see the

horrors of a faraway place / Meet the architects of law face to face,"
he goes on, hawking the carnage over noxious guitars and tribal
drumming, before adding, "Take my hand and I'll show you what
was and will be." As Morris's heart-of-darkness beat mounts, it is
clear that the mayhem that Curtis promises is much closer to home
than advertised, and that it has been wrought not by alien hands but
by those within the sound of his voice.

This air of apocalypse pervades *Closer*, where dogs and vultures
feed on carcasses that symbolize decaying relationships, where
swarms of screeching guitar noise evoke clouds of locust, and where
dirge-like cadences invariably grind to a lifeless halt. "It all falls apart
after it's touched," Curtis utters ominously to the inexorable march
of one track. In another he proclaims, "The present is well out of
hand," and, amid the relentless pounding of "Twenty Four Hours,"
he moans, "Just for one moment / I thought I'd found my way / Destiny unfolded / I watched it slip away." "Decades," the dissipated,
almost static track that closes the album, evokes Curtis's interminable
sentence in this moral and spiritual gulag.

"Why bother . . . with music so seemingly dead-end and depressing?" Mikal Gilmore asked, writing in *Rolling Stone* during the early
post-punk era.[12] Gilmore's is a valid question, and one that applies
not just to the music of Joy Division, but to the work of any artist
who conveys negation in uncompromising and often repugnant
terms. "Maybe," Gilmore went on, "because in the midst of a movement overrun by studied nihilism and faddish despair it is somehow
affecting to hear someone whose convictions range beyond mere tru-
isms. Maybe because Ian Curtis' descent into despair leaves us with a
deeper feeling of our own frailty."

These intimations of a shared experience, and the promise of community, no matter how broken, that they hold are not the only salutary by-products of Curtis's despair. His struggle also witnesses to
the dangers of false claims to transcendence—to the lure of easy paths
out of the pit—as well as to the persistence of a desire for something
beyond degradation and despondency. At one point Gilmore even asserted that the group's most transporting music "seemed almost spir-
ited enough to dispel the gloom it so doggedly invoked," only to back
off that claim and conclude that "Joy Division never really aspire to
transcendence." And yet, as lines like "I tried to get to you" and "I

was a fool to ask for so much" attest, it is not so much that Curtis and the rest of the band do not express an urge for transcendence.[13] It is more that their striving for it has been eclipsed, a frustration, Curtis's suicide notwithstanding, that does not make their hunger for release less real.

Joy Division's recordings often confirm as much. From the rocket propulsion of "Interzone" to the ecstatic chants of "Dance, dance, dance to the radio" in "Transmission," the band's music frequently conveys a qualified, if gallows-bred, sort of uplift. Just the "expression of [these] feelings is a victory over obliteration," wrote Evelyn McDonnell in 1995.[14] "Joy Division aspired to heaven even when trapped in hell," she went on, and nowhere is this more evident than in "Love Will Tear Us Apart," the band's biggest and final single. Issued just two months before Curtis hanged himself in 1980, the record might lament love's inevitable dissolution, but its churning dance rhythms and intoxicating, if dissonant, synthesizer lines bespeak transcendence in spite of themselves, seeming, as McDonnell wrote, "to hurl the burden conveyed by Curtis' voice and lyrics heavenward."[15] Even at its most dour, "Love Will Tear Us Apart" bears witness to an aspiration, however much it might be thwarted, that endures as much in Curtis's haunted droning as it does in the record's indomitable grooves.

New Order, the band that Hook, Morris, and Albrecht formed after Curtis's death, turned this transcendental urge into a mantra by rendering the dance grooves that were latent in Joy Division's most kinetic recordings explicit. New Order's music was still dark and chilling, its programmed beats lending it an increasingly techno or industrial sheen. The band's lyrics also continued to speak of forbidding things like the casualties of war and romance. The words, however, do not matter so much with New Order, even when it is possible to make out what Albrecht, who had become the group's lead singer (and had started using the surname Sumner), is muttering deep in the mix. A sort of electrodisco in excelsis, the music now is paramount, as well as gloriously expansive in a way that Joy Division's only rarely is. Not only that, New Order's sound proved historic in that it bridged the punk-disco divide during the ascendancy of rockism, the tendency, among other things, of fans of rock music to devalue dance music, much of which is associated with gay, black, and Latin subcultures.

Beyond the addition of beats and sequencers, the crucial difference between the sounds of Joy Division and New Order was the addition of Gillian Gilbert on keyboards. Gilbert's stately flourishes of synthesizer not only gave the group's music greater depth and texture, they opened up its sonic horizons and cast the always melodic playing of bassist Hook in sharper relief. The group's 1983 hit "Blue Monday," a record with maybe the most indelible drum break since "Be My Baby," may have had the greatest impact, for a time becoming the best-selling twelve-inch single ever. But 1982's "Temptation," with its chugging beats, surging riffs, and rapturous vocals, had already crystallized this transformation. When Sumner beams, "I've never met anyone like you before," his euphoria likely is due to finding a new lover, but it could just as easily have been born of the thrill of happening on a new technology and an epiphanic new sound.

A series of enchanting yet tensive singles followed "Temptation" and "Blue Monday," with critics heaping modifiers like cathartic and transcendent on everything from the strobelike, Arthur Baker-produced "Confusion" to the scintillating likes of "Thieves Like Us," "Love Vigilantes," and "Bizarre Love Triangle." It was no wonder. Single after single—and New Order is quintessentially a singles band—delivers on the yearning for transcendence that in the music of Joy Division, and especially in the singing and lyrics of Ian Curtis, was habitually thwarted. The lyrics, again, are of little consequence. It is the bracing sweep and reach of New Order's music, the sheer release brimming from its grooves that signifies most.

Ironic perhaps, though not entirely surprising, were the charges of fascism that followed the band, much as they did Joy Division. Foremost here was the group's choice of a name, which came from that of Pol Pot's genocidal Army. The iconic, high-tech dust jackets of New Order's singles and albums, which for years contained no photos of the band or information about the packages' contents, likewise added to the vaguely fascistic mystique, as did the group's refusal to grant interviews or to perform encores in concert. Sumner contends that these gestures were made with little forethought, particularly the choice of the band's name. Yet they doubtless were an extension of the willful inscrutability that the group had been cultivating since the days of Joy Division.

Whatever the case, and even if New Order made these gestures in service of the alienation that to some extent persisted in their recordings, the band's sublime, catchy music told a different story. New Order fulfilled the negationist impulse and promise of Joy Division by destroying and surviving its previous incarnation and going on to create something new and transcendent. To many the band's arrival just meant heavenly dance music, which in itself is a gift. As a flourish of affirmation in the wake of the sepulchral gloom of Joy Division, though, New Order's emergence qualified as something of a resurrection—a new order indeed.

# chapter 5

## LICENSE TO ILL

### The Stooges, the Sex Pistols, PiL, and Eminem

I WANNA BE YOUR DOG

> "Woo-oo, I've been *dirt* . . . , woo-oo, I've been *hurt*, and I don't care."
>
> —Iggy Pop, "Dirt"

> "Gimme danger, little stranger, and I'll feel your disease."
>
> —Iggy Pop, "Gimme Danger"

I Wanna Be Your Dog," the Stooges' thudding monument to lubricity and self-loathing, is at once a proposition and a statement of purpose. Over a ramrod beat lifted from the Velvet Underground's "I'm Waiting for the Man," Iggy Stooge (not yet Pop) invites the object of his lust over to his place to have sex with him. Iggy's is a crude come-on, yet in the end it is more self-abasing and more complex than those of other lurid 60s fantasies like "Midnight Rambler" and "96 Tears." Unlike the protagonists of those records, who tend to be more of the stalker/rapist variety, Iggy is not exactly being a sexual predator here. If anything, the song's title suggests that he wants to submit to the whims of the person that he is fantasizing about. "[I'm] so messed up, I want you here / In my room, I want you here," he grunts to the implacable thrusting of the rhythm section and to what sounds, rather incongruously, like sleigh bells. "And now I wanna be your dog / And now I wanna be your dog," he glowers, repeating the line one more time, before barking, "Well, come on!"

Iggy's ham-fisted proposition might seem clear enough;[1] less obvious perhaps is the way that it serves as a statement of purpose. Like so much of the Stooges' brutish, putatively mindless music, "I Wanna Be Your Dog" reflects the group's desire not just to evoke the blue-collar tedium and alienation that they knew, but to move beyond evocation to embody those conditions and the revulsion that they breed. Thus we have Iggy mugging as a stooge and a dog and generally playing the idiot, yet not mainly to gain attention or to achieve catharsis. Iggy acts the fool as a way of confronting the degradation that surrounds him in hopes of divesting it of its power and, if not annihilating it, then at least prevailing over it by proving that he can survive it. "I am the world's forgotten boy / The one who's searchin', searchin' to destroy," he snarls in "Search and Destroy," propounding his misfit-cum-violator ethic amid a firestorm of metallic guitar. On the track that follows it on *Raw Power* he urges, "Gimme danger, little stranger / And I'll feel your disease / There's nothing in my dreams / Just some ugly memories." Much as he is in "I Wanna Be Your Dog," Iggy is on the prowl and bound for the gutter here. He is opening himself to infection and harm in hopes of becoming immune to them and, by means of that resistance, transcending them.

Iggy, who was born James Jewel Osterberg, first exhibited this proto-punk embodiment of the adage, "What doesn't kill you makes you stronger," at the Stooges' hometown concert debut in Ann Arbor, Michigan, on Halloween 1967. With the band hacking out pummeling three-chord rock behind him, a strutting, yowling Iggy reportedly smeared peanut butter over his naked torso, rolled in shards of glass, screwed his body into agonizing positions, and hurled himself into the crowd so that people could stomp all over him. "Woo-oo, I've been *dirt* . . . / Woo-oo, I've been *hurt* / And I don't care," he would sing three years later, as if explaining this penchant for sadomasochism. "Do you feel it? / Do you feel it when you *pop* me?" he goes on, feeding off the abuse, before screaming, "There's a fire! / There's a fire! / Ow!" as the stiletto fills of guitarist Ron Asheton give way to a stabbing solo.

This ethic of self-abasement is idiotic, and often inane ("Now I'm gonna be twenty-two / I say, 'Oh my' and, uh, 'Boo-hoo,'" Iggy once sang), but it hardly is stupid. Iggy and the Stooges were avatars of "non-sense" who went out of their way to internalize and *become* the soul-sucking chaos that engulfed them in order to express their repugnance for it, thereby pointing beyond it and betraying a hunger for something better. *I Need More*, trumpeted the title of Iggy's 1982 autobiography. No matter how frustrated or beaten down that hunger might have been, the Stooges' imperious caterwauling witnesses to their overriding urge to satisfy it, even if they had no clue as to what might be able to bring that satisfaction about.

The mayhem that the Stooges personified is, on the face of things, more profane than anything else. At a more fundamental level, though, it testifies to a desire, a hunger that, while fueled by negation (though not its sometime lookalike nihilism), is spiritual or transcendental in nature. "The Stooges carry a strong element of sickness in their music, a crazed quaking uncertainty, an errant foolishness that effectively mirrors the absurdity and desperation of the times," wrote Lester Bangs in the unforgettable piece that he did on the band for *Creem* magazine in 1970.[2] "[B]ut I believe that they also carry a strong element of cure, a post-derangement sanity."

The times that gave rise to the Stooges' "errant foolishness" certainly called for extreme measures, especially in Detroit, where the inner city had been reduced to ashes during the race riots that took place there in July of 1967, just as the so-called Summer of Love was in full flower. This also was only three months before the Stooges played their first gig in neighboring Ann Arbor. By the time the group released their self-titled debut album in 1969, conflict over the Vietnam War would reach fever pitch, Martin Luther King and Bobby Kennedy would be assassinated, and the galvanizing riot over gay rights would have taken place at the Stonewall Inn in New York. Add to this malaise the social and economic stagnation of Iggy's trailer park upbringing—as well as the cloud of post-adolescent angst that clung to the band—and conditions were ripe for the Stooges' ID-driven assault on middle-American respectability and taste.

Iggy and the Stooges, of course, were not political in the sense that countercultural visionaries like Bob Dylan and Curtis Mayfield were. The Stooges were too busy staving off working-class ennui by getting high, getting laid, and getting out of having to get jobs to give much thought to idealism or insurrection. This might make them seem trifling compared to, say, the MC5, their revolutionary Motor City contemporaries. Not, however, according to the late Craig Lee, or at least not by extension of his defense of LA's middle-class surf punks against charges that they lacked the moral authority of their prole-leaning British counterparts. "Facing a sterile, anonymous life in suburbia is as depressing to some kids as facing a life of dull labor and low wages," Lee wrote in the *L.A. Weekly*.[3]

The Stooges likely would have scorned the notion that there was anything prophetic about their music, yet with "1969," the fuzz-toned, wah-wah-steeped totem that opened their debut album, they anticipated Lee's insight—and, for that matter, much of punk. "It's 1969, OK / All across the USA / It's another year for me and you / Another year with nothing to do." Iggy crassly pronounces these lines over the cretin bop that opens the record, fully aware of the irony of his complaint, and of how much indeed needed to be done. Here the Stooges not only tapped the anomie of a nation rent by war, rising unemployment, lingering segregation, and pervasive bad faith, they shattered the complacency that attended those things as acutely as any of the era's fist-pumping rockers.

The troglodyte stomp of "No Fun" sounds much the same knowingly monotonous note, albeit one that, coming from a band schooled on Motown and Motor City R&B, swings in ways that few of their metal-leaning peers could have imagined. "Maybe go out / Maybe stay home / Maybe call my mom on the telephone," Iggy ruminates blankly on the song's bridge. The Stooges' senses might have been dulled by tedium and drugs, but they were paying attention to what was happening around them, and with the likes of "No Fun" and "1969," they embodied that non-sense as a way of calling attention to just how stupid it was. So exaggerated is Iggy's thickened delivery on these tracks that it constitutes a "stoopid" new dialect, one that would become the argot of knowing dolts from glam-rock numskulls Slade and gabba-hey punks the Ramones to rap brats the Beastie Boys and purveyors of metalloid sludge like the Melvins. Writing thirty-five years ago, Lester Bangs claimed that the Stooges' uncouth music was "what rock 'n' roll at heart is and always has been."[4] And what it always would be, or so it seems now, at least as far as regression and iconoclasm in rock, and some rap, is concerned.

Much of the Stooges' debut album consists of pubescent scowling and rude mating rituals on the order of "I Wanna Be Your Dog" and "Real Cool Time." Maladroitly hitting on a woman in the latter, Iggy

leers, "Can I, uh, come over / To-*night*? / We could have a real cool
time / To-*night*." What began as sullenness and prurience, though,
turns to menace on *Fun House*, the record's successor. Here Iggy
rants about being treated like dirt, having sadistic sex, and phoning
from the twisted precincts alluded to in the album's title. "A scarify-
ing trip through the All-American freak show" is how Mark Coleman described the record for *Rolling Stone*, and from Iggy's feral and
often incomprehensible yelping, to the squalling proto-skronk of
guest saxophonist Steve Mackay, that summation fairly captures the
album's transgressive heart.[5]

*Fun House* was produced by Don Gallucci, the former organist for
the Kingsmen, the garage-rock combo best known for their 1963 hit
version of "Louie, Louie," a song that the Stooges routinely demol-
ished in concert. The thrashing, atavistic racket that Iggy, who now
was using the surname Pop, and the band make on *Fun House*, however, goes well beyond the rousing three-chord crunch that any association with Gallucci might suggest. Witness especially the second
half of the record, where, with the players engaging in primal assaults
on rhythm, tone, and texture, the proceedings more resemble the "energy music" of avant-garde jazz saxophonists Albert Ayler and Ar-
chie Shepp than anything discernible as rock 'n' roll. Much like such
in-your-face antecedents as the Velvet Underground's *White Light/
White Heat* and Captain Beefheart's *Trout Mask Replica*, *Fun House*
overthrew notions of what rock music was and how it could mean.
That is, if the nomenclature of rock 'n' roll could be applied to the
record at all.

*Fun House* constituted a subversion so radical—not just musically,
but also socially and culturally—that it all but stood negation on its
head. Whether it was Iggy gleefully submitting to being treated like
shit or the band's anarchic playing on the set-closing "L.A. Blues,"
the negation for which the Stooges became a repository practically
affirmed its opposite, or at least pointed to the possibility of creating
an alternative from the debris that they had scattered. Under the guise
of idiocy, the Stooges *became* the chaos or non-sense that dogged
them so as to dispel and get beyond it, even if they did not know
where that search to transcend it might lead. Gestures like theirs
might seem counterintuitive or make no sense. They certainly do not
conform to popular understandings of spirituality or transcendence.

Yet what else, short of surrendering to nihilism, is a soul to do when things are broken irreparably, other than to cast them aside and start over? For Iggy this meant taking things to the extreme. It meant rolling around in the shards of what he and the Stooges had shattered, picking out the pieces and pressing on, thus affirming not only his existence, but also the possibility that something worth surviving for lay beyond it. Apocalyptic and transcendent, *No Fun* was Iggy and the Stooges inventing punk a good half-decade before its time.

Flirting with annihilation by embodying it or becoming a repository for it, even in the service of transcendence (and even if such naysaying is largely symbolic), nevertheless involves risking not surviving the process of doing so. This process certainly got the better of the Stooges, who after flogging away for three years to considerable derision (this, after all, is the group whose singer coated himself with peanut butter and bid his audience to lick it off) disbanded in 1971. Drugs and alcohol were major factors, with Iggy entering rehab for addiction to heroin and bass player Dave Alexander eventually drinking himself to death in 1975, after the Stooges had broken up the second and final time. Before that, though, they regrouped, minus Alexander, long enough to make *Raw Power*. That they did qualified as a sort of affirmation, particularly given how they had watched lesser bands like Alice Cooper and Grand Funk Railroad succeed with watered-down versions of their act.

*Raw Power* found the Stooges forging their metallic thudding into something more in keeping with the sleek glam-rock of the record's producer, David Bowie, with Ron Asheton shifting to bass to make room for newcomer James Williamson, who plays the guitar hero, à la Mick Ronson, to Iggy's Bowie. Some of the ferocity of the *Raw Power* sessions was lost in Bowie's mix of the record, a remastered version of which surfaced commercially only in 1997. Still, from "Search and Destroy," with its searing opening guitar solo and vocal couplet—"I'm a streetwalking cheetah with a heart full of napalm / A runaway son of the nuclear A-bomb"—to "Gimme Danger," "Death Trip," and the title track, the original has its share of bracing moments. It even is arguable that the murky sonics of Bowie's mix better serve the Stooges' uncouth vision. The album's best tracks are, in any case, as emblematic of that idiotic, sadomasochistic ethic as early touchstones like "No Fun" and "I Wanna Be Your Dog."

The Stooges split up for good in 1974, and Iggy, who went through drug treatment a second time, would not record again until he made his first solo album in 1977. With Bowie returning as producer, the record, which was aptly titled *The Idiot*, saw Iggy foregoing his misfit persona for that of a droll hedonist after the fashion of Brian Ferry, although much less elegantly than that allusion might suggest. Iggy's vocal range had always been limited, but now he was singing punk-cabaret anthems like "Nightclubbing" and "Dum Dum Boys" in a vampiric croon befitting someone who had lived the ravages of "Gimme Danger" and "Death Trip" and survived them.

*Lust for Life*, another collaboration with Bowie, came out the same year, its title rendering explicit Iggy's will not just to survive, but to live life to the fullest. Iggy's productivity also spoke to this newfound vigor; he made only three albums in his seven years with the Stooges, and now here were two in 1977 alone. "No more beatin' my brains / With liquor and drugs," he sings to the tambourine-spanked, neo-Motown bop of the title track. Even here, however, he cannot resist slipping in the waggish jab, "I'm just a modern guy / Of course I've had it in the ear before," to remind listeners that he once had done it all, or had it done to him.

The "new" Iggy still retained plenty of his "lizard charisma,"[6] this reptilian designation a nod to his nickname, which came from the moniker of his pre-Stooges band, the Iguanas. Iggy was by this time being embraced as the harbinger of punk that he was, and he has enjoyed the rank of elder ever since, even if his solo recordings have rarely lived up to that reputation. A mixed bag of attitude, ham-handed social commentary, and hard-rock clichés, most of the music that Iggy has released since his creative surge in 1977 has not challenged listeners in the way that the outsized idiocy of the Stooges once did.

The only place that any real confrontation has persisted is onstage, where, even after turning fifty in the late 90s, Iggy has continued to put on shows as frenzied and demanding as any in rock.[7] Sure, his act was still larded with shtick, but it always has been something of a put-on, albeit one with serious intent. Iggy's commitment to embodying and feeding off chaos and danger—and to forcing his audience to deal with the antipathy that they breed—remains unassailable. There remains a fire, as he roars in "Dirt"—a "post-derangement sanity" or "element of cure," as Bangs put it—that enables Iggy to obliterate non-sense, whether staged or real, by personifying it so as to gain a measure of transcendence over it.

## I *Is* ANARCHY

"I wanna be an anarchist, get pissed, destroy."

—Johnny Rotten, "Anarchy in the UK"

"We like noise, it's our choice. It's what we wanna do."

—Johnny Rotten, "Seventeen"

The Sex Pistols seized on the search-and-destroy ethic of the Stooges, embraced it as ideology, and sparked a revolution. "Rrright! Now!" cackles Johnny Rotten to detonate "Anarchy in the UK," the group's imperious debut single. Rotten sounds like he is declaring an end to history as anyone knew it, and coming on the eve of 1977, year one of punk, he was: a world-historical rift that challenged certainties both about rock 'n' roll and popular culture, and about the humanity of modern society itself. "I am an antichrist / I am an anarchist," Rotten proclaims over Steve Jones's Tommy-gun guitar riff, rolling his "r's" demonically as he anoints himself the enemy of all that is good and holy—the incarnation, per his adopted surname, of its putrid opposite. The definitive naysayers of punk, Rotten and the Sex Pistols did more than just assail the cultural and economic stagnation of post-industrial England; bent on total destruction, they set out to annihilate absolutely everything, even "passersby." "I *is* anarchy," Rotten jeers, making it clear that no one would be a bystander, much less innocent, in the new world dis-order.

As with the Stooges, such extreme gestures of negation doubtless seem more profane than anything else. They certainly have induced writer upon writer, even those who have championed the Sex Pistols, to chalk up the band's rage for chaos to nihilism. The impetus for this rage, however, is not rooted in a nihilistic longing for oblivion, but in a restlessness—a deep-seated hunger, to borrow from the title of Iggy's autobiography, for something more. As Rotten yowls in "Anarchy," the Sex Pistols might not have known what they wanted, but they knew how to get it, and the fact that they wanted *anything*, even utter bollocks, was evidence of this urge for transcendence.

The Sex Pistols express this urge negatively, by striking back at whatever thwarts it, but the last thing to which "Anarchy" gives voice is resignation. From the feral relish in Rotten's maniacal yawp to the implacable advance of the band's yawning barrage, the record is proof that the group believed fiercely in themselves and in what they had to say—and, as Rotten warned, that they knew how to get it. When over the track's crashing final bars he screams, "I wanna be an anarchist / Get pissed, destroy," it is the clarion call of a band that, though they would be together just fourteen months, was intent on making history rather than on becoming a footnote to it. A band determined to transcend history by pointing beyond it. Beyond the past and the present, but most emphatically, beyond a future that they knew was no future at all.

"Anarchy in the UK" was the Sex Pistols' manifesto, a blanket "No" to all false claims to transcendence, and nothing if not a desire for the real thing. Yet it was only with the group's second single, "God Save the Queen," that they expressly applied the search-and-destroy ethic of "Anarchy" to the particulars of their asphyxiating surroundings. Upward of a million people were out of work in Great Britain at the time, and many of them were on welfare and crammed into government housing. Racial tensions born of social and economic injustice also ran high. All of which made the hypocrisy of British notions of civility more glaring and oppressive than ever. The Sex Pistols responded by taking aim at the one person who exemplified England and its bourgeois society more than anyone else, Queen Elizabeth II.

"God save the queen, her fascist regime / It made you moron, a potential H-bomb," Rotten seethes, his invective buttressed by the fractured, sped-up rockabilly hacked out by Jones, drummer Paul Cook, and bassist Glen Matlock. As social commentary, the opening lines of "God Save the Queen" are contemptuous and strident, but they by no means fall outside the bounds of acceptable protest. They certainly are no patch, for example, on the biting satire of Aristophanes or Jonathan Swift. Not so with the record's second stanza, where, in one of the most extreme acts of negation imaginable, Rotten rants, "She ain't no human being," denying the undeniable, the very humanity of Elizabeth II. "Our figurehead is not what she seems," he goes on, and neither is the nation for which she stands. "There is no future in England's dreaming."

"God Save the Queen" is in many ways the British punk counterpart to the Stooges' calendar-conscious "1969"—the Sex Pistols' "1977," so to speak. Or maybe their update of the Stooges' "No Fun," especially if the word "fun" is substituted for "future," which is pretty much what "No Fun," a song that the Sex Pistols often did in concert, was saying anyway. "Oh, Lord God, have mercy / All crimes are paid . . . God *save*," Rotten brays, his prayer not one of concern for the souls of England and its Queen but a sardonic pretense that barely conceals the singer's real wish—their consignment to hell. "God Save the Queen" was banned from the radio upon its release, in the coup of coups, in May of 1977, just in time for the Silver Jubilee marking Elizabeth's twenty-fifth anniversary on the throne. The record reached No. 2 on the British pop hit parade and No. 1 on the independent chart and was listed on both, appropriately enough, as a blank, the epitome of negation itself. Along with "Anarchy in the UK," it also became one of the galvanizing singles of punk, a record that gave birth to dozens, if not hundreds, of kindred bands. A record that testified to the possibility of transcending, by sheer force of will, one's social and cultural inheritance, and of mapping a new future, however trackless a wilderness that future might prove to be.

"Punk, like some great scabby legged buzzard, came soaring over the drab British horizon to fix us all with its crazy polarizing stare," wrote the Mekons' Jon Langford, reflecting, with his painterly eye, on the cultural fallout triggered by Glen Matlock's use of the word "fuck" in a nationally televised interview. "In a country with three TV channels (one of which mostly showed a potter's wheel or occasionally a windmill going 'round and 'round and 'round), punk became instantly inescapable for both the kids on the street and their parents back indoors. The former, with pants suddenly caught on fire, commenced spitting and pogoing and severing all links with the past, to fumble ungratefully for control of their own culture and entertainment, while the latter huffed and puffed, sniffing Armageddon in every Oxfam shirt or safety pin, and kicked their nine-inch black-and-white steam-powered TV sets around the living room floor."[8]

The story of how the Sex Pistols came together under the scheming ministrations of impresario Malcolm McLaren, of how they pissed away a series of record deals and were banished from the radio and just about everywhere else, has been told often and does not bear re-hashing here.[9] The Sex Pistols were not exactly idiots in the Stooges' mold, but they set themselves up, in much the same misfit way, as repositories of chaos and discord. And they sought transcendence by aiming just as low, declaring themselves "vacant" in one single and elsewhere professing that they had "No Feelings" and were "lazy sods" who had no intention of getting jobs. "We like noise / It's our choice / It's what we wanna do," Rotten scoffs in "Seventeen," setting the Pistols, like cockney Stooges, against all that was deemed good and decent by polite English society.

More of an affront than anything that the band said or did, though, was their decision to bill themselves as "Sex Pistols," a signifier so transparently transgressive, and doubly so, as to guarantee that spectacle would surround them at every turn. The appellation was McLaren's coinage, after the fashion of Marshall McLuhan, for whom packaging was the message, and the name did more than just offend. It assured the group a regular thrashing, much like what happened when Iggy baited his audience from the stage. Rotten got himself knifed on one occasion, and all of the Sex Pistols were attacked, spit on, or otherwise assailed just about every time they walked down the street or appeared in public. And not just for the way they looked—the spiked hair, the safety pins, the torn and ratty clothing—or for how they acted—the sneering, the insolence, the "gobbing." But also for the music they made: a rude, venomous din that challenged virtually every convention of British rock.

Rock music basically meant one of two things in England during the mid-70s. There was the bloat, on the one hand, of progressive bands like Genesis and Yes with their concept albums and orchestral pretensions, but also the profusion, among rock royalty like Led Zeppelin and Rod Stewart, of drugs, groupies, and general excess on the other. Enter nineteen-year-old John Lydon, who turned up at Sex, McLaren's "anti-fashion" boutique in London's King's Road, in late 1975 wearing a tattered Pink Floyd T-shirt with the words "I Hate" scribbled above the logo. Lydon had never been in a band, but Glen Matlock, who worked at Sex, and his mates Steve Jones and Paul

Cook, had, and they were looking for a singer for the new group that they were putting together. McLaren suggested that they give Lydon, who lacked experience but looked the part, a try. Jones christened him "Johnny Rotten," a nod to Lydon's poor personal hygiene, and the original lineup of the Sex Pistols was set. Sid Vicious later was recruited to play bass after Matlock was expelled from the group for professing his not-so-punk fondness for the Beatles.

The music that the Sex Pistols made during their brief time together is often referred to as artless, but it was hardly unaccomplished—and if artless, then only willfully so. (Jones, Matlock, and Cook, after all, were veterans of England's "pub-" or roots-rock scene.) Like their image and name, the Sex Pistols *meant* to make crude, offensive records, but also, and perhaps more importantly, music that shattered and went beyond what came before it. "The *musical* center of what the Sex Pistols spawned is so far removed from even the most radical rhythm and blues," argued Dave Marsh in his book, *The Heart of Rock & Soul.*[10]

> There's a difference between a transformation and a fracture, between a breakthrough and a breakdown. The revolts of "Papa's Got a Brand New Bag" and "Dance to the Music" never severed the connective tissue that "Anarchy" shreds from start to finish. . . . [T]he Sex Pistols were not only sincere in their desire to make rock that smashed rock . . . they were absolutely equal to the task.

Marsh's claims for just how radical a departure the Sex Pistols' music was might smack of overstatement, especially listening now, more than a quarter-century on. Compared with, say, the ultra-compressed blitzes of hardcore bands like Bad Brains and the Angry Samoans, the Sex Pistols' records sound merely like accelerated, dirtied-up hardrock with a metallic sheen. Punk's archetypal forcebeat nevertheless powers their playing—very little of the Pistols' rock "rolls" or swings, and this likely is what Marsh was driving at. The Ramones employed the forcebeat first, and to better effect, but the Pistols, as more than one writer has put it, "fired the shot heard 'round the world," defining a sound and a sensibility that paved the way for hardcore punk and a host of other things. At their best, the Sex Pistols made music that was exhilarating and noxious enough to back up their effrontery and ideology.

"To call this band dangerous is more than a suave existentialist compliment. They mean no good," wrote Robert Christgau in his review of the band's only studio album, *Never Mind the Bollocks, Here's the Sex Pistols*, in 1977.[11]

> It won't do to pass off Rotten's hate and disgust as role-playing—the gusto of the performance is too convincing. . . . The forbidden ideas from which Rotten makes his songs take on undeniable truth value, whether one is sympathetic ("Holidays in the Sun" is a hysterically frightening vision of global economics) or filled with loathing ("Bodies," an indictment from which Rotten doesn't altogether exclude himself, is effectively anti-abortion, anti-woman, and anti-sex). These ideas must be dealt with, and can be expected to affect the way fans think and behave.

"Bodies" is everything that Christgau claims for it, an expression of negation and disgust that borders on the absolute. Rotten's denunciations here might even have been enough to warrant the charges of nihilism that some have leveled against the Sex Pistols, were it not for the suggestion, as Mark Coleman has observed, that Rotten "sensed something basic about the sanctity of human life, as well as the rotten ways human beings have come to live it."[12] This sense of "something basic" is rooted in the human capacity for self-transcendence, in a connection—spiritual though certainly not religious—to something larger and more enduring than the everyday. In the case of "Bodies" it had to do with the lines that people invariably cross, the sorts of transgressions, born of a basic flaw or brokenness, that the Sex Pistols routinely met by heaping even nastier abuse on those who perpetrated them.

Much the same sort of confrontation, born of the sense that a line had been crossed, takes place in "Holidays in the Sun," the band's inscrutable final single of 1977, and arguably their masterstroke. It is almost impossible to make linear sense of "Holidays"; as Rotten sings, even *he* is baffled by the urge that has overcome him and by what surely will happen when he acts upon it. He seems bent on getting as far away as he can from modern consumerist society, with its vacations at the beach for the well-heeled and either low-wage drudgery or the dole—utter vacancy—for everyone else. So repulsed is Rotten by this state of affairs that he would rather chuck it all and go, of all places, over the Berlin Wall (which in 1977 of course was still standing) and be a tourist at Belsen, the site of one of the Nazi death camps during World War II.

Rotten's is an appalling pronouncement, an assault, as Dave Marsh wrote, on "the very concept of culture in a society that endures the reality of Belsen through the desensitizing apparatus of liberal moralism."[13] Yet "Holidays" also expresses a ferocious desire for transcendence, albeit by way of negation, a "No" so radical that it makes no sense, at least not when met with accepted values or logic. With the rest of the band grinding away behind him, Rotten roars about scaling a wall that has been designed to thwart any such attempt, an impasse, like the Holocaust, that symbolizes a cultural and historical chasm that seemingly cannot be breached. "I gotta go over the wall," he screams, knowing that doing so likely will have grave consequences. Indeed, "they're staring all night . . . and day" at him from the other side, a standoff that he outrageously yet persuasively claims could lead to World War III. Rotten nevertheless has to go through with his act of sedition. He is bound to go against the grain in order to subvert what passes for common sense and morality, even if he has to dig under it and die trying. Nothing less than the welfare of his soul, as well as that of modern society, seems to depend on it.

"We're the future, *your* future," Rotten taunted wickedly in "God Save the Queen" and, for a brief season, history bore him out. This certainly was true in the UK, where, in the late 70s, bands like the Buzzcocks, Wire, Essential Logic, X-Ray Spex, the Clash, the Mekons, the Adverts, the Slits, the Raincoats, the Au Pairs, and Gang of Four became variations of that anarchic future as well. Yet like everything else—and perhaps inevitably—punk soon became codified and commodified and had to be toppled, which for the Sex Pistols came when Rotten dissolved the group, in what was perhaps an act of euthanasia, the morning after they played the Winterland Ballroom in San Francisco on January 14, 1978. True to naysaying form, Rotten, who soon went back to using the surname Lydon, would go on to denounce the band as a farce and, by the year's end, start an "anti-rock 'n' roll" collective called Public Image, Ltd. (aka PiL).

Built around the cavernous soundings of bass player Jah Wobble, PiL made droning, dub-reggae-inspired art-rock—"Death Disco" is how the title of one of their early tracks put it—that subverted conventional notions of rhythm, melody, and songwriting. "Public Image," their first single, spoke directly to this anti-rockist agenda, taking a swipe at McLaren's McLuhanesque marketing of the Sex Pistols, and at his manipulation of Rotten's misfit persona in particular. "The name means just that: Our image *is* limited," Lydon said in an interview at the time.[14] He could have been talking not just about PiL but about the limitations inherent in all popular music—indeed, in all finite forms of expression.

PiL made a lot of indulgent, tedious music, and maybe that was the point, or at least part of it: to create bollocks of an entirely different yet more or less disorienting sort. At least one of the band's albums, though, fulfilled the promise of Lydon's anti-rockist vision. The record was first released in 1979 in the UK as *Metal Box*, a three-disc set of 45-rpm vinyl packaged in a film canister and one of the most visceral-sounding "rock" records ever. Subsequently streamlined as a double-LP called *Second Edition* and issued in the US, the album was galvanized by Wobble's echoing bass and Lydon's by turns apocalyptic and dissociative pronouncements. The record is thoroughly gripping. The nightmarish yet oddly hooky "Poptones" dramatizes a rape from the point of view of the victim, while "Swan Lake" confronts the recent death of Lydon's mother. The death of former Sex Pistol Sid Vicious, who died of a heroin overdose in February of 1979 while awaiting trial for the murder of his girlfriend Nancy Spungeon, casts a pall over the proceedings as well.

The music, more than the lyrics, though, is paramount on *Second Edition*, a sound born of an intense striving to go beyond what preceded it. Indeed, the music seemed as antithetical to rock 'n' roll as anything remotely connected with pop music, yet it was oddly of a piece with the naysaying ethos of the Sex Pistols to which it was meant to be a rejoinder. As Mikal Gilmore put it, writing in the early 80s, "Lydon and PiL rerouted the Pistols' much vaunted anarchism, applying it to song structure, and in the process, authored the first major attempt to transmogrify rock parlance since Captain Beefheart's *Trout Mask Replica*."[15]

Gilmore just as easily could have cited the Stooges' *Fun House*, a record that, like *Second Edition*, so thoroughly subverted negation that it had the effect of affirming its opposite, thereby giving emphatic, if indirect voice to a hunger for transcendence. The fact that Lydon and PiL did not, and perhaps could not, articulate what might have been able to satisfy that hunger makes no difference. Like that of the Stooges and the Sex Pistols before them, their music betrays a striving for meaning that goes well beyond the mundane, an overriding urge for transcendence, no matter how negatively or even profanely it might be expressed.

## My Name Is . . .

> "On this earth and since birth I've been cursed with this curse just to curse and just blurt; it's berserk."
>
> —Eminem, "The Way I Am"

Much as the Sex Pistols deployed the search-and-destroy tactics of the Stooges, Eminem makes use of something akin to the Pistols' anarchic will to power, and maybe with even more force and malevolence than they did. There is no explicit link between Johnny Rotten and Eminem, at least not like there was between the Stooges and the Sex Pistols, who used to play Iggy's "No Fun" in concert and clearly were heirs to his misfit-violator legacy. Yet on "Public Service Announcement 2000," the set piece that triggers *The Marshall Mathers LP*, Eminem's longtime producer Jeff Bass makes a claim for the rapper, or rather for his Slim Shady persona, that echoes Rotten's maniacal vow to destroy passersby. "Slim Shady does not give a fuck what you think," Bass begins, aiming his comment at anyone who hears the album. "Slim Shady is fed up with your shit, and he's going to kill you."

On "Kill You," the track that follows, Eminem (in the guise of Slim Shady) threatens to rape and murder his mother, the person whom he blames most for his degrading, unstable childhood. It is an unabashedly transgressive move, one that even the most gratuitously violent black rapper would have avoided, if only given the prevalence of "mother love" in African American culture. Yet Eminem does not stop here. He goes on, later in the album, to rhyme about slitting the throat of his estranged wife Kim. "I *invented* violence," he boasts midway through "Kill You," before cranking up his chainsaw and turning it on everyone who crosses his path. "You don't wanna fuck with Shady / 'cause Shady will fuckin' kill you," his posse chants each time the insanely hooky chorus comes around, and they mean it. So does Eminem, but not exactly the way it sounds. "I'm just playin', ladies," he snickers, in a trickster-like flourish, as the track fades, "You know I love you."

With much the same wicked relish that Johnny Rotten displayed in "Anarchy in the UK," Eminem, whose real name is Marshall Mathers, sets out to bewilder and offend, and he dishes out plenty of lethal rhymes, even when he is just "playin'," which is often. "God sent me to piss the world off," he announces in "My Name Is," a self-mythologizing statement of purpose from 1999's *Slim Shady LP.* Eminem's noxious alter ego, of course, is just that, a fill-in-the-blank public image that he adopted as a vehicle for venting his anger, a license to "ill" that permits him to hurl his rage at every person or thing that ever has humiliated or kept him down. "I don't do white music / I do don't black music / I make fight music," he asserts, in 2000's "Who Knew." Such an avowal hardly is surprising coming from someone who grew up on the margins of black and white Detroit and was bullied on both sides of the tracks—that is, from someone who has never experienced the world as a safe place.

In the tradition of mayhem-scattering naysayers like Iggy Pop and Johnny Rotten before him, Eminem devised Slim Shady to serve as a repository of the sickness and non-sense that have plagued him so that he could unmask and overthrow them. Yet even more than those forebears—or, for that matter, than Trent Reznor or Madonna—Eminem poses a stumbling block for many people, especially when claims to the likes of spirituality and transcendence are made for his music. Such assertions are not to been taken lightly, particularly when they minimize the violence and hatred to which Eminem routinely, although rarely heedlessly, gives voice. Yet just because artists like Eminem express brokenness and rancor, as opposed to uplift and redemption, does not necessarily mean that what they have to say is any less spiritual. What, after all, is Eminem's relentless drive to succeed, his fight to overcome his soul-crushing childhood, other than an expression of deep-seated spiritual restlessness? And what, his enormous ego notwithstanding, does his striving and unrelenting obsession with telling his story betray if not an urge for transcendence? Even at their most naysaying and profane Eminem's rhymes point beyond the dis-ease from which he suffers, even if what they point to seldom comes into clear focus.

This is not to say that all of Eminem's lyrics should be taken at face value, much less as words to live by. "Stan," the centerpiece of *The Marshall Mathers LP*, dramatizes the dangers of what can happen when someone does so—in this case, a naïve and troubled fan. "What's this shit you said about you like to cut your wrists, too?" Eminem asks, letting his listeners overhear his answer to the fan mail of his fictitious admirer. "I say that shit just clownin', dawg, c'mon, how fucked up is you? / You got some issues, Stan. I think you need some counselin' / To help your ass from bouncin' off the walls when you get down some." Even more explicit is the "PSA" that opens *The Slim Shady LP*. "This is a public service announcement brought to you in part by Slim Shady," booms the stentorian baritone of Jeff Bass. "The views and the events expressed here are totally fucked and are not necessarily the views of anyone. However, the events and suggestions that appear on this album are not to be taken lightly. . . . Slim Shady is not responsible for your actions. Upon purchasing this album you have agreed not to try this at home."

These disclaimers, especially the words "not to be taken lightly" and "brought to you *in part by* Slim Shady," strike at the heart of Eminem's unruly genius. They point not only beyond the dramatic construct Slim Shady to Eminem the artist and Marshall Mathers the man—that is, to how Shady is but one "totally fucked" aspect of Eminem/Mathers—but also to the sophistication and self-awareness at work in the MC's multivalent agenda. "Too often in hop-hop, rage, especially against women, is merely a convention," wrote Robert Christgau.

> It's unexamined, and thus brutal. When Eminem rhymes about raping his mother or murdering his wife, it's not. Eminem unpacks rage, and the conventionalizing of rage; he's deeply frightening, yet at the same time devastatingly funny. . . . Does every one of his seven million [fans] understand that he's representing rather than advocating? Of course not—but the percentage that doesn't is lower by a factor of 100 than the percentage of pundits who never listen to hip-hop yet assume Eminem is destroying America's moral fiber.[16]

Eminem, in other words, does not want to kill anyone. More than anything else he wants to get inside people's heads and, from misogyny to self-loathing, to eradicate the dis-ease that has taken root there, or at least to alert people to the dangers of it. When on the chorus of "Kill You" his crew sings, "You don't wanna fuck with Shady / 'cause Shady will fuck with you," they are not just warning listeners to steer clear of the ruinous Slim Shady. Articulating something akin to the doctrine of original sin, they also are referring to the sickness or shadiness that lies within the conflicted psyches of all people, and to how, if this contagion is not approached with caution, it can get the better of a person—and of those around them. "My name is Marshall Mathers, I'm an alcoholic / I have a disease and they don't know what to call it," Eminem declares in "Just Don't Give A." Others might not know how to identify what ails him, but Eminem has a name for it: Slim Shady, the alter ego that he assumes in order to confront and build up his immunity to it, much as Iggy turned sickness into strength with his Stooge persona, and in that way transcended it.

To be sure, Eminem's vision of what might enable him to "get over" or rise above his circumstances consists mostly of the banal likes of fame and fortune. Yet it also hinges on gaining respect, on having, as he rhymes in "My Name Is," "an ass big enough for the world to kiss." No less than that of any sharecropping "hillbilly" or blues singer—or even a punk like Iggy, who grew up in as asphyxiating a part of greater Detroit as Mathers did—Eminem's music expresses a fierce urge to transcend the humiliation that he has known. Witness "If I Had A," where over a sleek, gangsta bump supplied by producer Dr. Dre, Eminem spits a litany of soul-sucking things that he, as Marshall Mathers, is tired of. The list includes everything from pumping gas for $5.50 an hour and not being able to afford a telephone, to "committing too many sins" and "not being able to get to sleep without [taking] a Tylenol PM."

It all adds up to being sick of being "white trash" and "always poor" and of being tired of living with a "guilty conscience," all of which were hallmarks of Eminem's nomadic, trailer park childhood with his drug-addicted mother, who herself is a survivor of abuse. Eminem was still living that degrading, peripatetic life in 1999, the year that he released *The Slim Shady LP,* his multi-platinum breakthrough album. "Free Slim Shady" trumpets the cartoon at the center of the booklet that accompanies the CD, calling not just for the liberation of Eminem/Marshall Mathers from the prisonlike trailer depicted in the comic. It also expresses Eminem's need to break free of Shady, the misfit-monster, likened in "Brain Damage" to Frankenstein, to which that squalor gave birth.

Eminem's raging desire to overcome and ultimately annihilate his past is the reason why he raps, once again figuratively, about killing his mother, his (now ex-)wife, and even himself. "Well, since age twelve I felt like I'm someone else / Because I hung my original self from the top bunk with a belt," he rhymes to the head-bopping lurch of "My Name Is." Even the name of the company under which Eminem conducts his business, "Aftermath Entertainment," conveys this impulse—his will to raze the world that he has known and everything in it and yet also to survive the aftermath of that destruction.

It is telling perhaps that hip-hop, an idiom identified with disenfranchised African Americans, has afforded Eminem with the means to articulate this restlessness. The result is an inimitable jabberwocky that flows as freely as it signifies, an obsession with words turned reason for living that makes Eminem worth listing to in the first place. "When Eminem's rhymes click," Sasha Frere-Jones wrote in *The New Yorker*, "they feel both musically calibrated and lexically tuned, the careful work of someone who loves language and has crumpled up a lot of paper trying to figure out how, and where, words fit together."[17] Or, as Eminem puts it, by way of apology and vocation, in "The Way I Am": "On this earth and since birth I've been cursed with this curse just to curse and just blurt; it's berserk and bizarre, this shit works / And it sells, and it helps in itself to relieve all this tension, dispensin' these sentences, gettin' the stress that's been eatin' me recently off of this chest and I rest again peacefully."

There are plenty of items in Eminem's catalog that are neither salutary nor therapeutic, notably the humorless self-pity that mars some of 2002's rock move *The Eminem Show*, as well as the pro forma hate that he demonstrates when he baits gay people. The latter cannot be excused or explained away, not even as the by-product of degradation and self-loathing. Still, there remains a hermeneutic of disruption in Eminem's music, an ill intentionality that, even at his most egregious, is hard to dismiss. Take "Criminal," where over a rubbery beat Eminem vows to murder "a fag or a lez" but never delivers on the threat.

"Explicitly and unmistakably, there for any person with a 90 IQ to understand, the song is about *words'* power to cause pain," argued Robert Christgau, who has written about Eminem with as much insight and humanity as anyone.[18] The song, as Christgau went on to observe, even "comes with a statement of principle, uttered by Eminem himself. It's about how 'stupid' it is to think he'd kill anyone 'in real life.' It concludes: 'Well shit, if you believe that, then I'll kill *you.*'"

Such jabs are disarming, and in some cases, wickedly funny. And evidenced by lines like, "[There are] so many motherfuckin' people who feel like me" (from "White America"), Eminem knows that legions of his suburban white followers get the joke. Nevertheless, in 2002's "My Dad's Gone Crazy," a mad brilliant track hooked by a loop of his then-six-year-old daughter Hailie chirping, "I think my dad's gone cra-zee," even Eminem feels compelled to spell things out. "My songs can make you cry, take you by surprise at the same time," he begins rather prosaically, before delivering the knockout punch. "See what you're seeing is a genius at work, which to me isn't work, so it's easy to misinterpret me at first / 'Cause when I speak, it's tongue-in-cheek, I'd yank my fuckin' teeth before I'd ever bite my tongue."

"My Dad's Gone Crazy" marked a turning point of sorts for Eminem: the arrival of Marshall Mathers the grownup, an adult who increasingly has distanced himself from the ill-bent Slim Shady. Eminem had by this time won joint custody of his daughter in a divorce settlement and was working hard at being a good father. He also would star in the Hollywood blockbuster *8 Mile*, a semi-autobiographical redaction of his hard-knock childhood that sought to clean up his image and airbrush his rise to fame. (The movie functions as an underdog narrative of uplift, as something of hip-hop's answer to *Rocky.*) Eminem even reflected apologetically in print and on record about rap and race, right down to confronting his naïve appropriation and exploitation of black culture, particularly after *The Source* got hold of some tapes from his teenage years that found him thoughtlessly using the word "nigger."

Eminem's newfound maturity might not signify as seditiously as the Iggy-like stupidity and regression of his Shady-ness. Yet as Frere-Jones pointed out in *The New Yorker*, it was about time that Eminem picked on someone his own size and stopped beating up on his mother and his ex-wife, both of whom have suffered—and, at least figuratively, died—enough.[19] In an uncharacteristic flurry of social analysis, Eminem does exactly that in 2004's "Mosh," an excoriating diatribe aimed at the Bush Administration and the war in Iraq. "Strap him with an AK-47 / Let him go fight his own war let him impress daddy that way," Eminem jibes to a doomsday beat, alluding to the President and the elder Bush. "No more blood for oil, we got our own battles to fight on our soil / No more psychological warfare to trick us to thinking that we ain't loyal."

More than just righteous anger, the line in "Mosh" that contrasts battles waged on foreign and domestic soil evinces vision, even to the point of articulating an enlightened understanding of the meaning of national security. Analytic sophistication, though, is hardly Eminem's stock-in-trade, and in the conceit around which he builds *Encore*, the album on which "Mosh" appears, he seems to own as much, if not to foreshadow his retirement. He stages his exit, first by committing artistic suicide with an album that consists in part of willfully stilted beats and rhymes punctuated by the sounds of belching, vomiting, and flatulence, and then by turning the gun, at least in song, on himself. And yet not before, in still another "gotcha" move, spraying the audience with bullets and leaving scores of bodies in his wake. This dramatization, which is also depicted in the CD booklet that accompanies *Encore*, might have been the perfect exit for Eminem, especially since it hinges on the ultimate variation of the lethal joke that he has led with since he invented Shady. That said, it is not likely that this will be the last the world hears from Eminem, not given his all-consuming urge to outdo and reinvent himself.

# SECTION III

# PROPHETS
## Voices of Uplift, Resistance, and Possibility

# chapter 6

## KEEP ON PUSHING

### Curtis Mayfield, Johnny Cash, and U2

WE PEOPLE WHO ARE DARKER THAN BLUE

> "You don't need no baggage, you just get on board."
> —Curtis Mayfield, "People Get Ready"

> "I know we've come a long way, but let us not be so satisfied, for tomorrow can be an even brighter day."
> —Curtis Mayfield, "We People Who Are Darker Than Blue"

The hit records that Curtis Mayfield made with the Impressions are among the most inspired and inspiring of the 1960s. All are sung in sweet, gospel-infused harmony and set to buoyant melodies and rhythms, and most, from "It's All Right" and "I'm So Proud" to "Keep on Pushing" and "People Get Ready," were written by Mayfield as barely masked paeans to black uplift and pride. In fact, the veil that surrounded "We're a Winner," the Impressions irrepressible ode to transcendence from late 1967, was so thin that many radio programmers saw right through it.[1] Some, including those at Chicago's WLS, the powerhouse AM station in the group's hometown, boycotted the single for fear that it might heighten racial tensions that already were gravely strained at the time.

Whether it was due to his disappointment over this embargo (the single nevertheless reached the pop Top 20) or to witnessing the Civil Rights Act's promise of equality fade, Mayfield decided to drop the mask. With the Impressions' 1968 single "This Is My Country" he confronted slavery and the ongoing disinheritance of African Americans in the United States, ominously posing the question, "Shall we perish unjust, or live unequal as a nation?" With the lyrics to 1969's "Choice of Colors" he rejected hatred and intolerance of every stripe: "How long have you hated your white teacher? / Who told you to love your black preacher?" Mayfield's fellow Impressions Sam Gooden and Fred Cash issue this challenge, trading lines before Curtis admonishes, "Can you respect your brother's woman friend / And share with black folks not of kin?" Such chiding might not seem radical today. Yet after the race riots in Detroit in 1967, the assassination of Martin Luther King in 1968, and the conflagration at the Democratic National Convention later that year, "Choice of Colors" spoke with urgency to its historical moment, especially with Mayfield's bluesy guitar barbs pricking consciences right in line.

Mayfield left the Impressions to pursue a solo career in 1970 and, if anything, the records that he started releasing then were more prophetic. The A- and B-sides of his first single testify to the scope of this vision, from the affirmation of "The Makings of You" to the foreboding of "(Don't Worry) If There's Hell Below We're All Going to Go." With "We People Who are Darker Than Blue" he weds lamentation and uplift to articulate a uniquely black ontology and ethic, a view of black humanity and praxis as indelible in its way as that expressed in Ralph Ellison's *Invisible Man* or Lorraine Hansberry's *A Raisin in the Sun*. "We people who are darker than blue / Don't let us hang around this town / And let what others say come true," Mayfield implores in the opening chorus, his bittersweet falsetto accentuated by the bruised string and horn arrangement of co-producer Johnny Pate. "We're just good for nothing, they all figure," Mayfield goes on, before insisting, a couple of lines later, "Now we can't hardly stand for that." From here he leads his band into an extended, polyrhythmic break, rallying the faithful with congas and tumbas and the syncopated riffing of wah-wah and chicken-scratch guitar. "Get yourself together / Learn to know your side," he raps. "Shall we commit our own genocide / Before you check out your mind?" Then the horns blow, issuing a call to action before the tumult subsides and Mayfield, by way of benediction, sings, "I know we've come a long way / But let us not be so satisfied / For tomorrow can be an even brighter day."

Mayfield utters a prophetic word here, not one predictive of the future, but a word of judgment and encouragement born of his outrage over the oppression that he witnessed in his midst. This is a word that takes listeners not uptown, at least not at first, but, as the title of one of Mayfield's most devastating originals puts it, to "The Other Side of Town"—through the broken-spirited slums of the ghetto. His is a word that is meant to stir people up, moving those with "ears to hear" to work for change, while making those whose hearts are hardened squirm. Like those spoken by the Hebrew prophets, Mayfield's is a word that shatters indifference, a word in relation to which no one can remain neutral.[2]

The voice of some prophets is primarily one of resistance, an unwavering stand against forces of injustice inspired by a vision of what it might take to overcome them.[3] Other prophets model what transcendence might look like, and certainly Mayfield, with his embrace of people of all races and the premium that he placed on black self-determination and entrepreneurship, did that. Yet mainly his message was one of uplift. Mayfield stood in solidarity with and gave voice to the aspirations of everyday people who struggled in silence, bidding all who were able to do so to "Move On Up," as one inexorable funk workout put it, but also to offer a hand up to those "whose hopes grow thinner."[4] Always more of a motivator and bridge-builder than a revolutionary or separatist, Mayfield, who died in 1999 of complications from diabetes, was concerned more with bringing a word of encouragement to those who had been beaten down than with opposing those who might be standing in the way.

Uplift, resistance, and embodiment are but three moments in the prophetic life, different emphases that often overlap and seek the same end. Namely, to confront that which thwarts transcendence and to point to what might be able to bring it about—and to do so for the many, not just for the lucky few. All prophetic expressions in this sense are social as well as eschatological. They are attempts to represent what is and what can be, not in some far-off beyond, but in the *near* future ("Soon and very soon," as one gospel favorite puts it), if not in the present. "Why wait? / Why don't you look around? / Haven't you found that the judgment day is already in play?" Mayfield presses in 1971's "I Plan to Stay a Believer." "We're over twenty million strong / And it wouldn't take long to save the ghetto, child," he urges deep into the track, before adding, "If we'd get off our ass."

Mayfield had been intimating this vision with the Impressions all along, albeit always, at least until "This Is My Country" came out in 1968, from behind the veil. Socially-encoded beacons like "Keep On Pushing" and "People Get Ready" (the former staring down the "great big stone wall" of racism, the latter hooked by the summons, "You don't need no baggage, you just get on board"), did more than just echo the hard-fought victories of the freedom movement; they inspired them. "Keep On Pushing" was on the radio, climbing as high as the pop Top 10 and stamping its pressing melody and exhortatory chorus onto the nation's zeitgeist just months before Congress passed the Civil Rights Act. Mayfield wrote "People Get Ready," in what he called "a deep mood, a spiritual state of mind," on the eve of Martin Luther King's 1964 march on the Impressions' hometown of Chicago.[5] A year earlier, over the ebullient groove of "It's All Right," Mayfield urged his black brothers and sisters—and, presumably, anyone who would stand with them—to "listen to the beat" and "pat your feet." That is, to get in step and march for freedom.

It was not only Mayfield's barely masked encomiums to equality that carried his message of uplift and transcendence. Even a putative love song like "I'm So Proud," the Impressions' swooning Top 20 pop hit from 1964, is a paean to black pride—in this case to black womanhood—much as Chuck Berry's "Brown-Eyed Handsome Man" celebrated African American masculinity the previous decade. The word "soul" in the Impressions' 1965 single "Woman's Got Soul" likewise is code for blackness (and righteousness), just as it is in "Talking About My Baby" from the year before. "Need to Belong," a 1963 hit that Mayfield wrote for former Impressions lead singer Jerry Butler, turns on the line, "It hurts to be known as no one." Here, in a brooding baritone, Butler pines not just for a soulmate. He longs for the day when he can claim his place as a first-class citizen in the nation that his forebears did so much to build. Butler is aching to do what Mayfield would do in "This Is My Country," where, over one of the bluest chord changes ever, he avers, "I paid three hundred years or more of slave-driving sweat and welts on my back," before asserting, that blue chord modulating right in time, "This is *my* country."

Virtually everything in the Impressions' catalog can be decoded in this way, all of it steeped in Mayfield's roots in the church yet all of it very much of its historical moment. A record like "Meeting Over

Yonder" might sound like an old tent revival hymn, but it does not paint a picture of some sweet hereafter so much as speak to things in the here and now. In the tradition of the best black spirituals and preaching, it concerns hope for the future and for the present. Whatever its theological import, when the horns resound and the Impressions sing, "The best thing for you, you, and me / Is going to the meeting up yonder," it doubles as an inducement for people to organize and to march, much as similarly transparent calls from the era like Martha & the Vandellas' "Dancing in the Street" did. Similarly with Mayfield's allusions to the River Jordan in "Amen," its horns paraphrasing the melody of "Swing Low, Sweet Chariot," and in "People Get Ready," references that serve as much as metaphors for historical freedom as they do for some otherworldly afterlife. Thus does Mayfield's multivalent message, his blurring of the lines between the sacred and the secular, speak, as the writer Ernest Hardy put it, "both to the avid churchgoer and the person whose faith is drawn solely from what he or she has seen in the 'real' world."[6]

Nevertheless, it was in church, at the Traveling Soul Spiritualist Church where his grandmother Annabelle served as pastor, that Mayfield first witnessed how the gospel tradition of call and response could inflame and unite people. It was also in church that he learned to sing (he adored Sam Cooke) and where he met Jerry Butler, with whom he would form the Impressions. Mayfield's grandmother's congregation was located on the South Side of Chicago, the focal point for Southern blacks who migrated to the North during the 30s and 40s in search of a better life. The Impressions' music spoke chiefly to this audience, certainly at first, and mainly of hope and encouragement, even though to many, the North's promise of social and economic freedom increasingly felt, as Langston Hughes so indelibly put it, like a dream deferred. The Impressions' records were born of this tension and predicament. Still, as Ernest Hardy observed, "there's never even the suggestion of defeat [in their music], though there's frequently sadness and between-the-lines admissions of heavy prices paid."[7]

"Faith is the key," the Impressions exhort, in three-part harmony, in "People Get Ready," and harmony *was* key, as much to the trio's social ideals as it was to how their vocal arrangements came together. "There's hope for all," they go on to sing, and by "all," they mean everyone, even white people. As Craig Werner observed, writing in his wonderful book, *A Change Is Gonna Come: Music, Race and the Soul of America*, Mayfield articulated "a deeply held vision of redemption that accepted white presence while insisting on the beauty of blackness. . . . Amid the rapidly polarizing racial climate of the late 60s, [records like] "Choice of Colors" and "This Is My Country" held out that hope that Black Power and democratic brotherhood were, however unlikely it sometimes seemed, profoundly compatible."[8]

By the late 60s, however, with Martin Luther King dead and the civil rights movement beginning to fragment, the glory-bound train of "People Get Ready" had begun to derail. Mayfield continued to resist separatism, and his vision of community remained as open and inclusive as ever. Yet increasingly—and much as Marvin Gaye did with *What's Going On* and *Trouble Man*—Mayfield painted a darker, more turbulent picture of America. "Sisters! Niggers! Whiteys! Jews! Crackers! Don't worry! If there's hell below, we're all gonna go!" he shouts sardonically to open his 1970 solo debut. The seismic rumble of bass guitar that follows conjures images of an abyss yawning beneath the nation's feet. Much of the music on Mayfield's early and mid-70s albums sounded a similarly tumultuous note. There were exceptions, notably the bromidic—and, if saccharine, then at least earned—likes of "Miss Black America" and "The Makings of You." Predominately, though—even on visionary, uplifting tracks like "Beautiful Brother of Mine"—Mayfield's arrangements were built around fuzz-toned bass, wah-wah guitar, and aggressive, percussive rhythms. And they often were driven by pungent horns and strings. His music reflected the malaise of a country stuck in a war that it could not see its way out of, and of deteriorating race relations at home, where for many in the inner city, "moving on up" had devolved into a venal distortion of the gospel impulse to "get over."

*Superfly*, the 1972 movie for which Mayfield provided the soundtrack, was all about getting over, and not by way of Jordan or the mountain top, but by means of a treacherous underworld of greed, drugs, and betrayal. Gordon Parks Jr. directed the film, which sensationally depicted the very real desperation of ghetto life and became, along with the likes of *Shaft* and *Sweet Sweetback's Badaaass Song*, a touchstone of the then-emerging subgenre of "blaxploitation" movies. Mayfield, however, would have none of Parks's proto-gangsta glamorization of sex, guns, and cocaine, no matter how much the "Pusherman" might have served as an archetype of black male ascendancy after the fashion of Staggerlee or Railroad Bill. Yet true to dialogic form, and much as he had been doing since his earliest days with the Impressions, Mayfield did not attack the premise of Parks's story outright, but instead created an album's worth of music that functions as a "masked dialogue" with it.[9] With the sobering, string-washed disco of "Freddie's Dead" and "Little Child Runnin' Wild," Mayfield exposes the pusher's false promise of transcendence and speaks, as Robert Christgau wrote, "for (and to) the ghetto's victims rather than its achievers."[10]

Not that moviegoers heard words of judgment like "His hope was a rope / And he should have known," which Mayfield leveled at the murdered drug dealer Freddie. Mayfield included just an instrumental version of "Freddie's Dead" with the music that he submitted for the movie, only later releasing the take with the lyrics on the soundtrack album that he put out on his Curtom record label. Yet in a move as streetwise as that of any pusher, he released the record three months *before* the film opened, the upshot of which was that audiences had internalized Mayfield's anti-drug message long before they saw Parks's sympathetic portrayal of the dealer's underworld on screen.

"Freddie's Dead" went to No. 4 on the pop chart in 1972, enabling Mayfield's message to get over like never before. Not only that, on the closing vamp of the album's title track, which also made the pop Top 10 that year (the *Superfly* soundtrack reached No. 1), Mayfield reclaims the gospel notion of getting over, vindicating the movie's protagonist, who, despite his season in hell, stays true to himself and gets out alive. Even this, though, was but a qualified sort of uplift. Getting out alive certainly was a long way from the train to glory of "People Get Ready," but with the idealism of the civil rights and Black Power movements giving way to cynicism, materialism, and fatigue, survival seemed like all that anyone struggling to get over could hope for. Mayfield drank more deeply of the blues, where transcendence has more to do with keeping on, with just living to see another day, than with the gospel promise of getting over. With *Back to the World*, the album that he released after *Superfly*, he took a hard look at the black experience in Vietnam. On his soundtrack to the 1977 movie *Short Eyes*, a record that was anchored by the chilling "Doo

Doo Wop Is Strong in Here," he ventured into the depths of prison life, which increasingly had become an alternate ghetto for the urban black males who populated *Superfly*. That is, at least for those whose number did not come up in the lottery for the draft.

Soundtrack recordings, including ill-advised returns to the blax-ploitation genre like *Sweet Exorcist*, dominated Mayfield's work as the 70s wore on, just as attempts to cash in on the disco and Quiet Storm trends would in the late 70s and early 80s. These creative doldrums suggested that if Mayfield had not lost his faith (and 1980's sublime "Something to Believe In" alone confirmed that was not the case), then he at least had lost his compass. His voice, as Craig Werner pointed out, sounded more and more isolated, a development that co-incided with the disintegration of the civil rights movement and that was dramatized by Mayfield's late 70s remake of the Impressions' "It's All Right."

"The Impressions' 60s version of the song radiates an energy of connection, especially when the three voices come together at the ends of lines," Werner wrote in *A Change Is Gonna Come*.[11] "The 70s remake accentuates the distance between Mayfield and the female backup singers, who sound like they're located in a different room. You can feel the call and response fundamental to what Cornell West called the 'audacious hope' of the gospel vision falling apart. . . . [W]hatever the remake of 'It's All Right' might have claimed, the underlying message came through clearly: *Nothing* was going to be all right."

Mayfield spent much of the 80s trying to figure out how and where his voice fit into the increasingly fragmented pop landscape, especially with the rise of gangsta rap, much of which gave voice to values and attitudes that were antithetical to his message of peace, uplift, and re-spect. Then tragedy struck in 1990, when, during a performance in Brooklyn, some scaffolding fell on Mayfield and left him paralyzed from the neck down. A series of albums paying tribute to his music and vision followed, along with accolades like his induction, along with the Impressions, into the Rock and Roll Hall of Fame. Mayfield kept the faith, exuding positivity while becoming a godfather to a new generation of soul singers and rappers from Erykah Badu to the Fu-gees. He also released an album, the final studio project of his life, that marked the resurgence of his prophetic voice.

The songs on the album, *New World Order*, uttered words of judgment about lives forfeited to crack ("Here But I'm Gone") and about the troubled state of global affairs ("The Got Dang Song"). True to form, however, they also offered words of affirmation ("I Believe in You") and uplift ("Back to Living Again"). Mayfield effectively updated his sound as well, working with programmed beats and contemporary rap and R&B acts. Spike Lee even used the album's title track, with its reflections on the Million Man March, in his movie *Get on the Bus*, which also included the Impressions' "Keep On Pushing," "People Get Ready," and "We're a Winner."

*New World Order* also saw Mayfield updating "We People Who are Darker Than Blue" as a latter-day slow jam, a track that testified more eloquently than anything else on the record to the steadfastness and resilience of his vision. He reworked the rap from the song's extended mid-section, interpolating the ominous roll call and bass line from "(Don't Worry) If There's Hell Below We're All Going to Go." Other than that, though, he left the lyrics much as they were a quarter-century before, making just one small change to the final stanza, where he repeated and extended the word "long" in the third-to-last line as if in recognition of his weariness and that of his beloved community. "Pardon me, brother," Mayfield sings, as hungry as ever for change, heading into the second half of that stanza, "I know we've come a long, *long* way / But let us not be so satisfied / For tomorrow can be an even brighter day."

## THE MAN IN BLACK

> "I keep the ends out for the tie that binds."
>
> —Johnny Cash, "I Walk the Line"

> " 'Til things are brighter, I'm the Man in Black."
>
> —Johnny Cash, "Man in Black"

Like Curtis Mayfield, Johnny Cash was in it for the long haul. Until his death in 2003, he stood resolutely with people on society's margins, giving voice to their often silent cries and struggles and witnessing to the need for justice, tolerance, and decency on their behalf.

Cash expressly recognized this path of solidarity as his calling in
1971, the year that he reinvented himself as the Man in Black. Yet this
sensibility, which was at its core prophetic, already was evident at
least as far back as 1956, when he wrote and recorded "Folsom Prison
Blues" for Sun Records. Best known for its thuggish, head-turning
admission, "I shot a man in Reno just to watch him die," the record
hinges on the way that Cash connects the dots between poverty and
incarceration, transforming the song's putative boast into a meditation on the spiritual and emotional prison that privation often becomes. Cash's protagonist here is not bedeviled so much by the
thought of the murder that he has committed. It is the idea of being
stuck in his cell while rich people puff on cigars in the trains that chug
along outside the prison's bars that tortures him. Even more than the
walls that hold him—and with the locomotive, boom-chicka of the
rhythm section rubbing it in—what makes him hang his head and cry
is the opportunity that is ever beyond his reach.

Something similar is at work with respect to racism and disenfranchisement in Cash's 1964 recording of "The Ballad of Ira Hayes." The
song recounts how its namesake, a Pima Indian who was among the
twenty-seven soldiers who planted the US flag at Iwo Jima, returns
home from World War II only to find himself ignored and without
prospects, before eventually turning to liquor. "Call him drunken Ira
Hayes / He won't answer anymore / Not the whiskey drinkin'
Indian / Nor the marine that went to war," Cash intones to the tune
of some old outlaw ballad (certainly no hero's fanfare). Images of
thirst tie the narrative together, linking Hayes's craving for whiskey
with the parched land of the Pima, whose fields had been fertile until
the US government rescinded the tribe's water rights. The story ends
with Hayes passing out drunk and lying dead in two inches of water
on the reservation. The coroner listed the cause of death as alcohol
poisoning, but Cash's snarling rejoinder, "His ghost is lyin' thirsty,"
tells a different story. It was the patriot's thirst for his inheritance as a
citizen of the nation that he helped defend that ultimately did him in.

Johnny Cash spent much of his life standing in solidarity with the
suffering, forgotten likes of Ira Hayes and the inmate in "Folsom
Prison Blues." And not just at arm's length, but by visiting people in
penitentiaries, hospital wards, and on battlefields and reservations, as
well as through spontaneous acts of kindness and generosity. Cash's

brother Tommy often tells the story of when, before a show at a high school gymnasium back in the 60s, he found his brother alone in the boys' locker room, peering into the mesh-wire lockers and holding a rolled up one-hundred-dollar bill between his thumb and forefinger. He was looking for the "dirtiest, rattiest" pair of sneakers, figuring that the owner of the locker in question could use the money the most.

Another time Cash is said to have stopped his car to help an old man with a crutch who was hobbling along the shoulder of the road in Nashville. Without telling the man who he was, Cash put the stranger, who was homeless, up in a hotel and arranged for a car to take him to the hospital the next morning so that he could be fitted for a prosthetic leg.[12] "Those are my heroes: the poor, the downtrodden, the sick, the disenfranchised," Cash told me in an interview, his own health failing, a year before his death.[13] "I just heard a new song by Guy Clark called 'Homeless,'" he went on. "It's really a good song. I'm going to record it. 'Homeless, get out of here / Don't give 'em no money, they just spend it on beer.'"

"Ain't no end to street people," Cash continued, short of breath, his eyesight fading from the effects of glaucoma brought on by diabetes. "There's no end to the people on the margins. There's no end to the people who can relate to that, people on the margins of economic situations, and of the law. How many people have we got in prison in the USA now, 1.3 million?" The figure at the time was closer to two million, but numbers aside, Cash knew that it was vastly larger than it should have been and, just as urgently, he knew that whatever the number was, it certainly would grow.

Johnny Cash's attunement to such things—his identification with the lonely and the oppressed, as well as the stubbornness with which he took their side—is the very thing that made him the "Man in Black." In the comments that he made to me the day that we spoke, he might as well have been paraphrasing his hit single of that name, a statement of vocation that, besides citing all of the classes of people that he mentioned during our interview, includes those going through crises of faith, those who are aging and alone, and those whose lives have been laid waste by drugs. Invariably, the song reaches beyond them as well. Listening some fifteen years on, British punk-rocker Marc Almond heard and adopted the line, "Each week we lose a hundred fine young men," as a requiem for the legions of people who were dying of AIDS.[14] Explaining in "Man in Black" why he always dresses in somber tones, Cash, in a rumbling baritone, sings, "I'd love to wear a rainbow every day / And tell the world that everything's okay / But I'll try to carry off a little darkness on my back / 'Til things are brighter, I'm the Man in Black."

Just as it was for Curtis Mayfield, Cash's was essentially a prophetic and eschatological orientation toward the world. His was a posture rooted in empathy, but ultimately one that went beyond his participation in the suffering of others to call the rest of the world into account. Cash's was a world in relation to which it was and still is impossible to remain neutral, just as the monolithic specter of his lanky frame draped head-to-toe in mourner's black cannot be ignored, even now that he is gone. Like the outsized and outwardly quixotic gestures of some of the Hebrew prophets—like, Hosea, who married a prostitute to demonstrate divine love, or like Jeremiah, who, to convey hope, bought a plot of land just as it was being seized by invaders—the force of Cash's witness to what is and what could be remains undeniable. Born of the poverty that he knew as the son of Arkansas sharecroppers—and later, of the tyranny of his addiction to drugs—his vision of dignity and justice compelled him to stand unwaveringly with oppressed, beaten down people and to bid others to join him. His sometimes dour persona and the priority that he gave to the lives of downcast people might not radiate the positivity of Mayfield's "We're a Winner" or "Move On Up," yet Cash's witness offers a powerful word of uplift just the same. Throughout his embattled life he lent a voice to those without one and, with it, a glimmer of hope, a glimpse of transcendence.

Like Mayfield, Cash was a man of faith, one with deep roots in the Baptist church who, despite periods of dissipation and doubt, remained a Christian throughout his life. His identification with people on the margins, though, tended to stem more from his hard-fought inner struggle than it did from a theologically grounded vision of transcendence like that of the beloved community or train to glory that inspired Mayfield. Cash's striving was rooted in faith, certainly, and its implications for human community are many and far-reaching. Yet more than anything, his hunger for transcendence was tied to his ongoing fight for self-integration, to his basic but far from simple urge for wholeness. Only from there did his struggle seem to open outward—and prophetically—onto the larger world.

Nowhere did Cash articulate his quest for wholeness more indelibly than in "I Walk the Line," the follow-up to "Folsom Prison Blues" that became a No. 1 country and Top 20 pop hit for him in 1956. He wrote the song as a pledge of fidelity to his first wife, Vivian Liberto, while he was stationed in Germany with the US Air Force. Over the years, however, his vow to keep the ends out for the tie that binds took on much greater existential significance. His message driven home by the obdurate beat of the Tennessee Two, Cash seemed to be confessing just how desperately he wanted to unite the disparate strands of his conflicted self.

And he certainly was conflicted, as much as any American pop icon of the past half-century. He was a doubter and a believer, and he could be hip as well as square, a rebel and a voice of reconciliation. He was an addict and an evangelist, a protestor of the war in Vietnam and a guest at the Nixon White House, a singer of unexpurgated odes to murder like "Delia's Gone" and an aficionado of clodhopper cornpone whose second wife, June Carter Cash, was one of the funniest comics in the history of country music. Even his recordings, which encompassed country, folk, blues, gospel, pop, and rock even as they influenced punk, grunge, and rap, ultimately could not be pigeonholed or pinned down. Unwilling, if not at times unable, to let any one thing define him, Cash could truly say, with Walt Whitman, "Do I contradict myself? / Very well then, I contradict myself / (I am large, I contain multitudes)."[15] In the end it was Cash's hard-won multiplicity, his struggle—not nearly as facile as the admission, "I find it very very easy to be true," in "I Walk the Line" claims—to remain true to his unruly heart that afforded him whatever measure of transcendence he knew. And again, not by disavowing or collapsing the tensions that dogged and defined him, but by embracing and lifting them up, just as he embraced and lifted up people on society's margins and urged the rest of us to open our hearts to them as well.

All of which made it vexing, during the late-career resurgence that he enjoyed while working with the rock-rap impresario Rick Rubin, to watch the media, and especially the rock press, reduce Cash to a two-dimensional avatar of darkness, equal parts punk forerunner and proto-gangsta MC. This is not to say that Cash's dark side—his addictions, his early hell-raising, his bouts of emotional turbulence and self-doubt—does not define a large part of his myth. Nor is it to deny that many people identify with the outlaw hero tradition of which that myth is an extension, particularly as it is epitomized by his persona, the Man in Black. Neither is it to ignore the extent to which this latter-day fetishization of the "badass" Cash—the man who flipped off the camera at San Quentin and who kicked out the footlights at the Grand Ole Opry—is a product of how his record label has lately marketed him to younger audiences.[16]

Yet to tout Cash's darker, stormier tendencies at the expense of the more staid domestic and devotional aspects of his character obscures the immense spiritual journey that made his pursuit of transcendence so heroic. Cash made some bracing music with Rick Rubin, and some of it, from his soul-on-ice covers of Trent Reznor's "Hurt" and Nick Lowe's "The Beast Within," to his apocalyptic original "The Man Comes Around," speaks to that struggle as well as anything in his catalog. Nevertheless, the prevailing gloom-as-fashion portrayals of Cash's persona trivialize just how hard-earned any transcendence was for him. Even worse, they mask the prophetic impetus for that guise, distorting the meaning of the blackness upon which Cash's persona hinges (an ontological claim that is in many ways analogous to that of Mayfield's claim in "We People Who are Darker Than Blue"). Focusing only on its outward trappings, such portraits utterly miss how Cash's "blackness," a condition born of his own anguish and marginalization, is predicated on his ability to envision and strive for something better, a light that might dispel the darkness.

Cash reflected on these developments, amid considerable talk of family and home, when I spoke with him at the old Carter Family fold in southwestern Virginia the year before he died. He also admitted that despite his appreciation for the outlaw-hero mystique that he embodied, he felt that he too had contributed to the latter-day narrowing of his image and legacy, be it through his scowling, sepia-toned album photos, his penchant for recording graphically violent material, or his not just black but unremittingly Gothic attire. "I pigeonholed myself a lot," he began, his feet propped up to prevent swelling due to water retention brought on by diabetes.[17] "It's true that maybe I'm defining myself more as an artist, and maybe as a person, in these later years. I don't know. But looking back at myself, and at what I project out there, there seems to be a hardness and a bitterness and a coldness . . . and I'm not sure I'm too happy with that. I'm not sure that's the image I want to project."

Indeed, far from hardening to or closing himself off from the world, Cash had spent much of his life forging connections with other people and lifting them up—reaching out, as he sings in "I Walk the Line," for the tie that binds, wherever he might find it. During their life together he and his wife June blended two unwieldy families and the two prodigious cultural and artistic legacies that went with them. They also adopted all manner of musicians, actors, preachers, and celebrity ex-sons-in-law, drawing all of them into the family fold. Few people in fact have evinced the Cashes' gift for attracting *and uniting* people of so many different, seemingly conflicting backgrounds, from Bob Dylan and Kris Kristofferson to Billy Graham and Bono of the rock band U2. This is to say nothing of Cash's omnivorous taste in musical styles and songwriters, from Bruce Springsteen and Beck to Nick Cave and the late gospel powerhouse Dorothy Love Coates.

This spiritual and artistic ecumenism was writ large in the groundbreaking TV variety show that Cash hosted on ABC from 1969 to 1971. Often cited for its singular contribution to that era's Southernization of American culture, "The Johnny Cash Show" offered dazzling evidence of Cash's commitment to reaching out for the tie that binds rather than divides people. Embracing everyone from Kristofferson, Dylan, and Roy Acuff to Louis Armstrong, Mahalia Jackson, and the Who, Cash's guest list proffered a vision of community that bridged faiths, races, and musical genres, the counterculture and the cultural mainstream. All of it converged, unlikely enough (although not, of course, to Cash), at the Ryman Auditorium, the "Mother Church of Country Music" and home of the Grand Ole Opry.

Indicative of where Cash's heart was at the time—and where it would remain for the rest of his life—was his live recording, from his 1969 concert at San Quentin, of "A Boy Named Sue." Written by *Playboy* cartoonist Shel Silverstein, the song is a wry talking-blues about the generation gap. Yet unlike Merle Haggard's "Okie from Muskogee," a similarly themed joke (turned fightin' words) from the same year, "A Boy Named Sue" was a joke that rang out like an anthem. Communication, even to the point of conflict, Cash and Silverstein were saying, is the best way to breed the tolerance and understanding needed to bridge any gap.

The record's narrative comes to a head during its final scene, in which the character played by Cash happens upon his father dealing a hand of poker in a dingy saloon. "My name is Sue / How do you do? / Now you gonna die!" the young man thunders from across the room. A brawl of Rabelaisian proportions ensues, with the two men kicking, gouging, and bloodying themselves beyond recognition as the jabbing rhythm section provides rollicking ringside commentary. It is not until the younger man pulls his gun, however, that his father finally explains why he named him Sue (although not why he abandoned him and his mother in the first place). "Son, this world is rough / And if a man's gonna make it, he's gotta be tough," his father tells him. "And it's that name that's made you strong."

The implication here is that by giving his son a name like Sue, its "sissy" connotations just the sort implied in Merle Haggard's gibes at sandal wearing hippies in "Okie from Muskogee," the father made the boy the man that he had become. The son puts away his gun after his father says his piece. The two reconcile, but it is not so much because the son believes that his father made him the person that he is. It is that after scuffling with him and hearing him out, he finally knows, right or wrong, where the man he now calls "Pa" is coming from. Speaking not only to members of the era's conservative silent majority who presumably tuned in country stations, but also to the younger generation that listened to pop radio, "A Boy Named Sue" nearly topped both the country (No. 1) and pop (No. 2) charts in 1969. By contrast, "Okie from Muskogee," which spoke only to one side of the debate, became a No. 1 country hit but stalled just outside the pop Top 40.

Cash's quest for the tie that binds was and remains prophetic—a matter of standing with people on the margins of society. This was the case whether it meant siding with those who were at odds with members of their family, like the father and the son in "A Boy Named Sue," or with those who were at odds with society, like those who were homeless or in prison, or with those who were at odds with themselves, whether due to drugs, mental illness, or crises of faith. Much as liberation theologians have observed of the Jesus of the gospels, who kept company with tax collectors, prostitutes, and other social lepers as a means of reflecting God's "preference" for the poor and disenfranchised, Cash stood steadfastly with those who were cast out, oppressed or forgotten. Through his music and persona he lifted up and gave voice to their struggles, modeling a vision of community that transcended the suffering and injustice that he witnessed in his midst.

## U2: Trying to Throw My Arms Around the World

> "I can't say where it is but I know I'm going home. That's where the hurt is."
>
> —Bono, "Walk On"

> "One love, one blood, one life. . . . Sisters, brothers . . . we get to carry each other."
>
> —Bono, "One"

Curtis Mayfield and Johnny Cash witnessed to greater possibilities for human communion and urged people to embody them to create a more just and humane world. When the Irish rock band U2 emerged in the early 1980s, they made music of such immense yearning that it sounded like they were trying to usher in those new possibilities all by themselves. Emerging from the UK's jaded post-punk scene, here was a band of earnest Christians who embraced lofty communal ideals and who were out to save the planet. They even made a reverberating din that seemed mighty enough to do it, their guitarist eschewing single-note leads for a chordal lyricism that rang out like the music of the spheres and their rhythm section churning out pummeling body-rock with a melodicism not heard since the Who. All of this with a singer whose sensual, neo-operatic delivery was so over-the-top that it seemed inevitable that he would one day record with Pavarotti.

It was all very unfashionable, and polarizing, as grand gestures often are. And the band's then-twenty-year-old singer was as pretentious as his adopted name, Bono Vox. Yet there was no denying the anthemic sweep of U2's bombast: a cavernous, seemingly sui generis supplication that, despite the mystical vagaries of the lyrics, gave voice to an urge for transcendence as epic as any in the post-punk era. "[U2] had something to share with the world and needed to get it out," Ann Powers wrote. "U2's music is and always has been about the search for God—or to give credit to its own ambiguities, about the spirit's struggle to articulate."[18]

The group's first single, "I Will Follow," bears out this observation with the ardor of acolytes. Fired by the keening, bagpipe-like ostinatos of guitarist the Edge (aka David Evans) and the chunky propulsion of bassist Adam Clayton and drummer Larry Mullen Jr., the record is a naked and nascent statement of faith. Yet, however naïve U2's post-adolescent convictions might have been, their faith in God and humanity was grounded in social and political realities as lived, foremost among them the civil war in Northern Ireland. A song like "Two Hearts Beat as One" might express a romantic ideal, but it also is hard not to hear it, if only obliquely, as a prayer for a united Ireland. And when, over the marching, charging funk of "Sunday Bloody Sunday," Bono moans, "Tonight we can be as one," he definitely is not just speaking to a lover. He is appealing to Irish Protestants and Catholics to make peace with each other in the wake of two Sundays of carnage there. Bono and the band even changed the song's opening line from, "Don't talk to me about the rights of the IRA," to "I can't believe the news today," so that it would not be misconstrued as divisive.[19]

U2's grandiose music might have been out of step with the stripped-down indie-rock and frothy new-wave aesthetics of the early 1980s, but the band certainly was attuned to what was going on in their midst. "I'm wide awake / Wide awake / I'm not sleeping," Bono cries, alluding to this social consciousness in 1984's "Bad," a glorious track punctuated by the hawklike screeches of the Edge's expressionistic guitar fills. The luminous "New Year's Day" could be about any number of things—being separated from a lover, feeling cut off from God, the rift between Catholics and Protestants in Northern Ireland or the one between Eastern and Western Europe. Or, given the apocalyptic imagery that pervades the song's verses, the end of the world. Whatever the case—and likely it is a composite of several things—"New Year's Day" is very much of its historical moment, right down to the synchronous events that attended its release. Bono was thinking about Lech Walesa, the detained leader of the Polish Solidarity movement, when he wrote the song, only to learn—and only after U2 recorded it—that martial law would be lifted in Poland on New Year's Day 1984.[20]

As a lyricist, Bono has at times grasped haphazardly at whatever inspiration lay at hand, even to the point of making up his lyrics on the spot. Yet undergirding much of what he writes, even now, is the conviction to which he gives voice toward the end of "Sunday Bloody Sunday": "The real battle has begun / To claim the victory Jesus won." This couplet's sectarian, militaristic cast notwithstanding, it is neither an inducement to convert people to Christianity nor a summons to arms for "Christian soldiers." It is an eschatological imperative in keeping with Curtis Mayfield's "We're a Winner" or Johnny Cash's "Man in Black." Bono is promoting peace through justice here, a peace that can be won only by standing in solidarity with the poor and the outcast the way that the Jesus of the gospels did. Bono's is a claim in much the same spirit as the central tenet of liberation theology: that God sides with the oppressed, and that to be aligned with God and God's purposes—to usher in God's reign, aka "the victory Jesus won"—means taking the side of disenfranchised people as well. When on the stirring "Walk On" Bono sings, "I can't say where it is but I know I'm going home / That's where the hurt is," he is talking not about being with God in some distant realm. He is talking about encountering the divine *within* the world, and specifically, among those who struggle, those who, as Curtis Mayfield put it in "People Get Ready," are "loved the most."

This impulse to lift up those on the margins is evident not just in Bono's singing and his lyrics, or in U2's restless, urgent playing, but also in the causes that they espouse. Much like Moby, the group use the liner notes of their records to appeal to their fans, urging them to join organizations like Greenpeace and Amnesty International and to support other justice-oriented causes. This commitment goes well beyond lip service and sloganeering. The group gave epochal performances of "Sunday Bloody Sunday" and "Bad" at the Live Aid concert that singer Bob Geldof organized to raise money for famine assistance in Africa in 1985. They also headlined Amnesty International's "Conspiracy of Hope" tour the following year. Royalties from the sales of their 1991 EP *One* went to AIDS research, and proceeds from Bono's collaboration with Pavarotti on 1995's "Miss Sarajevo" funded relief efforts in Bosnia. This list of activities goes on and, in

Bono's case, it goes beyond fundraising and charity work to resemble what liberation theologians call praxis, the integration of faith and action aimed at changing the structures and conditions that oppress people.

Poverty and the spread of AIDS in the third world have been Bono's main focus since the late 90s. As a member of the organization Jubilee 2000, an international nonprofit that has lobbied wealthy countries to retire third world debt in the current millennium, he has met with everyone from then-US President Bill Clinton to British Prime Minister Tony Blair to the late Pope John Paul II. As well-intentioned, however, as these initiatives are, some people, such as the music critic and activist Dave Marsh, argue that when prophetic musicians enter the political fray and in effect become politicians, they compromise their ability to speak the truth and frequently do more harm than good.

As an example, Marsh cites Bono's decision, with Bob Geldof, to work with the World Bank, the International Monetary Fund, and the Bush administration "to 'solve' the problem of Third World debt as a means of resolving the AIDS crisis in Africa."[21] The upshot of this process has not been to incite the powers involved to adopt more liberating policies toward the third world, but instead to let those powers off the hook by making them appear munificent for offering certain nations nominal debt reduction. Three years after the original negotiations took place, Bono, Geldof, and their good intentions seem to have been co-opted, while the AIDS crisis in Africa has worsened and the nations that were granted "relief" still are strapped with debts that they likely never will be able to pay. That Bono and Geldof might want to play the part of politicians is understandable, and perhaps inevitable, given their celebrity. Yet in this case, using that celebrity to address complex, global problems merely compromised their voices as prophets.

In most cases, though, the worst thing that Bono is guilty of as an activist is grandstanding and demagoguery. Sometimes he becomes so enamored of his own voice that he points more to himself and his burgeoning myth than to the greater good for which he stands. This at times messianic impulse—"Have you come here to play Jesus," he asked in a more earthbound moment during the early 90s—was already conspicuous by the time that U2 released *The Unforgettable*

*Fire* in 1984. Ironically enough—and due in large part to the Edge's imaginative guitar colors and to the ambient production of Brian Eno and Daniel Lanois—U2's music was more nuanced and intimate than ever. Tackling such outsized subjects as Martin Luther King and the civil rights movement, Bono's pronouncements were anything but. Grandiloquent meditations like "Elvis Presley and America" were indicative of Bono's tendency not just to overreach but to get lost in the sound of his voice, more often than not vitiating the force of whatever truth he might be trying to impart. To his credit, Bono eventually acknowledged his rock-god impulse to inflict himself on people, admitting, in 2004's "All Because of You," "I like to hear the sound of my own voice / I didn't give anyone else a choice."

Bono's pompous air also mars at least half of *The Joshua Tree*, the 1987 album that then made U2 the biggest band on the planet, or at least consolidated their hold on that claim. Even on the incandescent, genuinely searching "I Still Haven't Found What I'm Looking For," Bono's melodramatic depiction of his quest is enough to give all but the most indulgent of listeners pause, especially when, poetic license aside, he proclaims, "I have spoke with the tongue of angels." Like *The Unforgettable Fire*, which contains "Pride (In the Name of Love)," U2's impassioned yet oddly-timed requiem for Martin Luther King, the album has some exquisite moments, from the surging "Where the Streets Have No Name" to the haunting "Mothers of the Disappeared." And the playing and the production are, once again, sublime. Too often, though, Bono's self-important bellowing, sighing, and screeching just grate, like someone stomping through a performance of Brahms's Requiem wearing combat boots.

*Rattle & Hum*, which serves as the title both of a narcissistic 1988 documentary about U2 and of the de facto soundtrack album that accompanies it, does little to dispel this impression. The implication of having pop music royalty like B. B. King, Bob Dylan, and Johnny Cash (Bono and Cash would go on to become good friends) appear on the project is all too transparent, or in any case feels that way. Less a tribute to the band's heroes than an argument for U2's greatness by association, it is as if the group is campaigning for induction into the august ranks of their collaborators. Meanwhile, ill-fitting paeans to Billie Holiday and the blues suggest that U2 believed that they were as big as their followers and the press made them out to be—and that the band thought it was big enough to engage the entire universe.

Ironically, it took the hipster indirection of 1991's *Achtung Baby*, which saw the group pointing away from their myth and their sacrosanct if worthy ideals, for U2 to regain their focus, or at least for Bono to find his balance. More preoccupied here with putatively worldly concerns like sex, love, and desire than anything else—and with a muted, murky electronic sound to match—Bono's songs and persona come spiraling auspiciously down to earth. "I'm ready / Ready for the gridlock / I'm ready to take it to the street," he announces amid the urban clatter of "Zoo Station," the album's opening track. "Bono's new role models," wrote Ann Powers, "seem to be the angels in his buddy [filmmaker] Wim Wenders' *Wings of Desire*, who, having finally managed to transcend, wish for nothing more than the messy, painful joy of earthliness."[22]

Indeed, over the sweet undulating groove of "Trying to Throw Your Arms Around the World," Bono seems not just to be owning his penchant for overreaching. He also seems to be taking his place in the world as opposed to the stratosphere. "Nothin' much to say I guess / Just the same as all the rest / Been tryin' to throw my arms around the world," he shrugs self-deprecatingly. When, addressing a lover in "Even Better Than the Real Thing," he pleads, "Take me higher / Take me higher / Can you take me higher?" he is seeking transcendence through immanence, much as sensualists like Polly Harvey and Madonna have done. U2 made *Achtung Baby* shortly after the Berlin Wall came down, and from the new musical and emotional directions that they pursue on the record, they seem to have tapped the sense of possibility—and the sleek European sophistication—that defined the era's zeitgeist. The album conveys a sense of having the freedom to venture to places that, for whatever reason, they had not previously felt the liberty to explore.

This mood of discovery likewise pervades 1993's *Zooropa*, where, instead of singing grandiosely of quests that involve scaling mountains or fortresses (like he does in "I Still Haven't Found What I'm Looking For"), Bono confronts life with modest observations like, "Some Days Are Better than Others." "Some days you hear a voice / Taking you to another place," he muses to skittering drum-and-bass-style rhythms. Underscored by the song's title, the implication here is that some days you hear nothing at all and thus have no portal to transcendence. "Dark Day," which is dedicated to the hard-boiled poet and novelist Charles Bukowski, offers further evidence of this dampened idealism, and of Bono's heightened awareness of his participation in human brokenness. "If you need somebody to blame / Throw a rock in the air," he begins, singing above the track's gnawing undertow. "You're bound to hit someone guilty."

This phase in U2's evolution is not bereft of uplift. The inspiration might be more latent than anything else, but it is grounded in a realism that serves as a tonic for Bono's persistent triumphalism. A conspicuous though salutary exception to this development is "One," the blockbuster ballad from *Achtung Baby* that shifts, midway through, from romantic concerns to those that are at once social and spiritual. The song's more or less straight-ahead rock arrangement, as well as passages like, "One love / One blood / One life . . . with each other / Sisters / Brothers / One life . . . We get to carry each other," could almost pass for early U2 were it not for the weariness in Bono's exhortation. The message of solidarity and uplift is undeniable, but it is mitigated by a cloud of ambiguity and doubt that gives a lie to facile claims to transcendence of the sort that Bono's overbearing posture had been making from the outset of the band's career.

U2 spent the 90s making records that gainsaid any claims to greatness that they or their clack previously had made on their behalf. Most notable were the mostly self-effacing *Achtung Baby* and *Zooropa*, but also the soundtrack albums (to imaginary films) that they made under the Passengers moniker, as well as 1997's kitsch-steeped, regular-issue U2 disc *Pop*. The group also continued to use its celebrity and influence to speak and to do good things on behalf of struggling people around the globe. This mix of irony and altruism might strike some as antithetical, almost as if it comprises two halves of a presumably divided collective self. Yet ultimately these impulses are consistent. They are the outgrowth of the modesty and perspective that come with the second sight gained through immersing oneself in the messiness of the world and still finding a way to hang onto one's belief in the possibility of transcendence. Or, as Ann Powers, whose observations about the band are as mordant as anyone's, put it: "Finally giving up on innocence without surrendering its impulse to the divine, U2 is now exploring the possibility of grace within the world, the body, and the legacy of pop."[23]

This second naïveté infuses *All That You Can't Leave Behind* and *How to Dismantle an Atomic Bomb*, the two albums that U2 has released since the turn of century. The music on both evinces a stylistic reach that suggests that the band is revisiting the various phases of their career. Everything from the glorious din of their youth to the textured ambience of their middle years to the oblique electronics of their hipster turn during the 90s is here. Typical of *All That You Can't Leave Behind* are pregnant meditations like "Beautiful Day," "Elevation," and "When I Look at the World," each of which reverberates with concerns that are at once personal, political, and spiritual. Indeed, each suggests that such distinctions are irrelevant. Not only that, when to the gospel-soul of "Stuck in a Moment You Can't Get Out Of" Bono declares, "I'm just trying to find a decent melody / A song that I can sing in my own company," the modesty of his claim sounds more earned than ever. His admission is not just an expression of a musical aim. It is testimony to his hunger to live with grace both inside his own skin and in a world, as he puts it elsewhere, in which "hope and history won't rhyme."

*How to Dismantle an Atomic Bomb* probes this tension between hope and history with big, dirty guitar riffs and crashing beats. The group made the album after the death of Bono's father, and from "Sometimes You Can't Make It on Your Own" to "One Step Closer," there is considerable reflection on mortality here. The record ultimately is more concerned with the living, though, and with how to live in the face of death, than anything else. When over the ardent roar of "Miracle Drug" Bono vows, "I've had enough of romantic love / I'd give it up, yeah, I'd give it up / For a miracle drug," he is praying as much for a breakthrough in AIDS research as he is for a balm for his soul. To the stately crunch of "Crumbs from Your Table" he moans, "Where you live should not decide / Whether you live or whether you die." Here, too, Bono likely is referring to AIDS, but also, if with maddening vagueness, to hunger, war, poverty, and other forms of oppression. On "City of Blinding Lights" he cries, "Blessings are not just for the ones who kneel," jabbing both at the doubter within himself who does not get down on his knees enough and at the Christian faith with which he struggles, knowing that that faith often perpetuates the misery and divisiveness that he decries.

All of this harks back to the eschatological imperative of "Sunday Bloody Sunday": "To claim the victory Jesus won." Once again—and Bono's Christocentric language notwithstanding—this exhortation is not a charge to baptize and convert people to Christianity. It is an admonition to lift up and stand in solidarity with oppressed people the way that the gospels say Jesus did, as well as an assertion that doing so is the only way to achieve the victory or measure of transcendence he did. Dogma aside—and his use of the term "Yahweh" in the album's closing prayer suggests that he wants to dispense with Christian dogma—Bono is wrestling with how to embrace the promise of transcendence symbolized by Jesus' resurrection in a world in which there are so many crosses to bear. Much as Johnny Cash did by donning mourner's black, Bono is struggling, as a person of an Easter faith, with how to live in a Good Friday world.

# chapter 7

## FIGHT THE POWER

### Spearhead, the Mekons, and Public Enemy

> "Nothing in the world is impossible to me, you can chop
> off my legs and I'll land upon my feet."
>
> —Michael Franti, "Piece o' Peace"

The chorus of "Piece o' Peace," a reggae-inflected number by the San Francisco hip-hop group Spearhead, begins on a bromidic note, with MC Michael Franti spitting the tongue-twisting lines, "A piece o' peace for you, a piece o' peace for me, a piece o' peace for every peaceful person that you see." This salutation, which Franti delivers to a head-bobbing groove spiked with funky clavinet and wah-wah guitar, comes after two stanzas of scene-setting that takes listeners to a loft where a DJ is mixing beats on a booming sound system and where people are dancing and carrying on. The police, though, are waiting outside, "hopin'," as Franti suspects, "that shit would get outta hand so that they could test their weapons on innocent civilians." Preceding this revelation is the adamant second half of the chorus: "A piece o' peace for you and a piece o' peace for me, but I don't act peaceful if you're not that way to me."

Not exactly the feel-good anthem that it at first seems to be, "Peace o' Piece" ultimately is an expression of resistance. Not that Franti is looking for trouble here. Sizing up what he and his people are up against, and specifically, the firepower of the police, he grouses, "[That] high tech shit costin' millions and millions, money [that] should've been spent on somethin' for community." Still, when he adds, "But that's OK, because we got unity," it is clear that Franti and the revelers, including "the elders in the house," are steeling themselves for a spiritual and moral face-off. They are determined not to let the intimidating presence of the police dampen their spirits, much less bully them into shutting down their harmonious party. Instead they press on, jubilantly and defiantly, "livin' life," as Franti shouts, "at the top of [their] lungs."

As studies in resistance go, "Peace o' Piece" might seem fanciful, if not a little tame. Nevertheless, recorded right after millions across the US saw the police beating of Rodney King on the evening news—and thus at a time when most people, not just those of color, were acutely aware of racial profiling and racially-motivated police brutality—the record is hard to dismiss. Hooked by indomitable, motormouth rhymes like, "Nothing in the world is impossible to me, you can chop off my legs and I'll land upon my feet," "Piece o' Peace" exuberantly encapsulates the ethic of resistance at the heart of Spearhead's music.

Much like those who seek transcendence through solidarity and uplift, musicians who give voice to the urge for transcendence through resistance envision a more just and humane society than the one in which they live. Yet while those who promote solidarity trust that lifting up or calling attention to the predicaments of marginalized people can effect change, proponents of resistance are not so sure. Resistors have little faith in appeals to decency or reason to end suffering or bring about justice, or even in appeals made, as Bono sings, "In the name of love." More oppositional toward those in power, resistors believe that the only way to alter unjust systems and institutions is to confront and call them into account—and, if need be, to wrest justice from them. This distinction between uplift and antagonism is hardly absolute. More than anything, it is a matter of emphasis and approach, one akin to the philosophical and strategic differences between Martin Luther King and Malcolm X on the issues of equality and civil rights. Musicians in both of these camps have similar aims. They just pursue social change, on the one hand, by lifting up the plight of oppressed people, and, on the other, by resisting the structures and values that keep people down.

"Dream Team" is another of Spearhead's high-spirited assertions of resistance, inspired, in this case, by the dissonance that Franti experienced while watching the 1992 Olympics on TV. The song's title is a reference to the US men's basketball squad, a unit known as the

Dream Team because it was the first to include professionals like Michael Jordan and Magic Johnson on its roster. "Fans were wavin' the red white and blue / It seemed strange to me, was it strange to you?" Franti wonders over the track's bumping backbeat. "Brothas on the street and everyone is scared a ya, so how could ten Africans represent America?"

To balance the account, Franti, a former basketball star at the University of San Francisco, puts together a dream team of his own, an imaginary lineup comprised of celebrated African American voices of resistance. Franti's starters include everyone from Black Panther leader Huey Newton and black nationalist Marcus Garvey to slave-insurrectionist Nat Turner and radical black activist Angela Davis. Their coach is Malcolm X and their general manager is Chief Crazy Horse, and for bench strength they have Rosa Parks and Martin Luther King. Franti's unit routs the opposition, "set[ting] the record straight about America's past," before making their way to the medals stand to collect their gold. "We be headin' for the ceremony / Hand on the heart is a bunch of baloney / The spirit of the '68 Olympics / Black Power people, Can I get a witness?" Franti roars. "Fist in the air, *this* is proper manners," he goes on as other members of the group, invoking the colors of the African flag, chant the refrain, "Red-Black-Green, Red-Gold-Green," equating blackness with gold.

Like "Piece o' Peace," "Dream Team" is a whimsical gambol. Yet with its nods to the show of Black Power by the US sprinters at the Mexico City Olympics as well as to Jimi Hendrix's deconstruction of the national anthem at Woodstock, it is a trenchant one. Just articulating the scenario that the song does, and to music so danceable and hummable, constitutes an act of subversion. Powered by Franti's irrepressible logorrhea and spirit, "Dream Team" is a triumph of vision and will that affirms the possibility of transcending one's circumstances even as it serves as a word of resistance against anyone who would deny that hope.

"Dream Team" is just the sort of imaginative coup that Franti has been staging for the past fifteen or so years, ever since he was a member of the industrial noise outfit the Beatnigs in the late 1980s. The incipient hip-hop of that group, who were label mates with fellow guerilla-provocateurs the Dead Kennedys, employed a patchwork of beats and noise, outré skits and fictional news broadcasts, to rail against the likes of Apartheid, the Reagan Administration, corporate greed, and consumerism. The Beatnigs made just one eponymous album, a bracing record galvanized by a scathing jeremiad called "Television, the Drug of the Nation." "TV is the reason why less than ten percent of our nation reads books daily," Franti thunders over a maelstrom of beats and screeching electric guitar. "[It's] why most people think Central America means Kansas, socialism means un-American, and Apartheid is a new headache remedy."

After the Beatnigs disbanded, Franti and Rono Tse, the group's percussionist and DJ, formed the alternative rap duo Disposable Heroes of Hiphoprisy. Recorded in the aftermath of the 1990 war in the Persian Gulf ("Bush War I," as Franti subsequently dubbed it), their first single was a double-A-sided record that included a swarming, boom-bastic update of "Television." On the other side was a track called "The Winter of the Long Hot Summer," a clattering poly-rhythmic attack on the Gulf War, especially the hypocrisy of the blood-for-oil diplomacy of the first President Bush and his claims that the US had become a "kinder and gentler nation." The single's successor, a harrowing morality play called "Language of Violence," decries homophobia, a denunciation of the sort that still is fairly rare in rap. "Words can reduce a person to an object, something more easy to hate," Franti rhymes to a spongy bass line and thwacking drum beat. "An inanimate entity, completely disposable, no problem to obliterate."

*Hypocrisy Is the Greatest Luxury*, the Disposable Heroes' only album, is chockfull of noisy, Public Enemy-inspired expressions of resistance, whether directed at corporate welfare ("Financial Leprosy"), racial typecasting ("Socio-Genetic Experiment"), or misogyny, materialism, and anti-Semitism in rap ("Famous and Dandy [Amos and Andy]"). Franti's coruscating agit-prop is righteous and insightful throughout, owing a marked debt to proto-rappers of conscience like Gil Scott-Heron and the Last Poets, as well as to latter-day MCs like Chuck D and KRS-One. Over the course of an entire album, Franti's didacticism can grow wearing, even with Tse's ceaselessly inventive production, which makes use of everything from programmable drums to homemade instruments built from found objects like tire rims and fire extinguishers. The combination of Tse's imaginative soundscapes and Franti's forceful messages landed the Disposables opening slots on the tours of acts like Public Enemy and U2. Unjustifiably, it also earned the duo a reputation for being a politically correct rap act who catered to white audiences and did not have anything to say to urban blacks.

The Disposable Heroes split up the year after their album came out, with Franti forming Spearhead, a more elastic, Afrocentric collective that favored less strident messages and warmer funk and soul grooves than the Disposables did. Spearhead's inviting vibe aside, on "People in tha Middle," the opening track on the group's debut album *Home*, Franti both takes on his critics and reiterates his underlying ethic of resistance. "So tell me the definition of a 'sell out' / Cast your first stone then get the hell out," he begins over spongy, dancehall rhythms. "People say they own me, I can tell you that they won't / The left and the right, they all try to use me / But I'll be in they faces before they can abuse me." A few lines before this he warrants, "If I don't have enemies, I'm not doin' my job . . . I try to kick the truth, not just to make friends."

In the beat-down lament "Crime to be Broke in America," Franti confronts the criminalization of poverty and addiction in the United States, using "collective class and race agony," as the critic Milo Miles put it, "as a goad to resistance."[1] After reeling off cutting, evocative rhymes like, "They lockin' brothers in the poorhouse / Who can't afford Morehouse," Franti asks, "Can I kick a few facts?": "Six percent in college / From livin' on the block / Twenty-five percent in prison / The school of hard knocks." By the time that the track is over he has broadened the terms of the discussion enough to conclude that the existing social and economic disparities in the US in effect make it a crime not just to be poor and addicted in America, but to be black, Native American, Asian, Latino, and female as well.

"Crime to be Broke" is indicative of Franti's vision of community, which comes into clearer view than ever in his work with Spearhead. This vision is reflected in the expansive ranks of the multiethnic, sexually-integrated ensemble, as well as in the presence of other voices in the group, from a second MC, Ras I Zulu, to gospel-steeped singer Mary Harris. Franti's ecumenism also is evident in the way that he reaches out to and nurtures his fellow "people in tha middle," a designation not unlike Sly Stone's "Everyday People" that seems to refer to anyone caught in the moral-existential crossfire of the sort that

Franti depicts in "Crime to be Broke." Exhortations like "Stay strong" and "Be resistant / The negativity, we keep it at a distance" abound on Spearhead's records, the latter coming from the title track of 2001's *Stay Human*, an album built around the group's opposition to the death penalty.

Some critics have disparaged Spearhead, charging that the group represents a more palatable, more conciliatory version of Franti's previous agit-rap approach. Yet just because the "vibes was luvin'," as he and Harris sing at one point, does not lessen the force of Spearhead's resistance. When, on 2003's *Everyone Deserves Music*, Franti sings of "love invincible," he is testifying to a moral and spiritual force like that witnessed in the nonviolent confrontation of Gandhi and Martin Luther King, a love that is stronger than prejudice, injustice, and hatred. "I like to shoot hoops, not brothas," Franti exults during the outgoing vamp of "Dream Team." Spearhead's infectious, genial mix of hip-hop, reggae, soul, funk, and rock might go down easier than the abrading beats and noise of the Beatnigs or the Disposable Heroes, but that hardly makes it less tough-minded. If anything, the fact that the music induces people to get up and move, that it spurs them to the sort of resistance that it conveys, makes it more subversive.

The title track of *Everyone Deserves Music* is an exhilarating case in point. Set to a surging Philly Soul-inspired arrangement, Franti's lyrics brim with empathy and encouragement for hard-hit "people in tha middle" who could use a little music or uplift in their lives. "Everyone deserves music, sweet music," he sings over the exuberant guitar ostinatos and strings on the chorus, the word *music* doubling as a metaphor for justice here. "Even our worst enemies, Lord, *they* deserve music," Franti goes on, taking the notion of this sweet music of justice to its most radical and prophetic extreme.[2] He makes much the same assertion in "Crazy, Crazy, Crazy," the final track on the album. "No life's worth more than any other / No sister worth less than any brother," he rhymes to its rubber-band funk. Reverence for all life courses through the entire album—and, if Franti's comments about rocks being alive and trees being able to feel in "Of Course You Can" are any indication, it applies to all of nature as well.

Nowhere on the record is this impulse given stronger voice, though, than in "Bomb the World," Franti's prophetic reflection on the blind retaliation of the US in the Middle East after the attacks on the World Trade Center and the Pentagon in September of 2001. "We can chase down all our enemies, bring them to their knees / We can bomb the world to pieces, but we can't bomb it into peace," he avers, half-singing, half-speaking these lines to a hymnlike cadence, before chanting, "Power to the peaceful," to the ascending melody on the song's bridge. "So I sing out to masses, stand up if you're still sane," he urges in the second verse.

Judging by the militant arrangement of the second take, or "Armageddon Version," of "Bomb the World" on the album (co-produced by reggae luminaries Sly Dunbar and Robbie Shakespeare), it sounds like the uprising has already begun. "What I see, it's idiotic / The tears of one mother / Are the same as any other," Franti rants in the extended rap that opens the track. "Drop food on the kids / While you're murderin' their fathers / . . . You can say what you want propaganda television / But all bombing is terrorism." Far from soft, this is the "love invincible" of which Franti sings elsewhere on the album, and to which he gives voice, explicitly or implicitly, in virtually all of Spearhead's recordings. It is the sound of resistance, a prophetic refusal to choose death over life.

## ONLY DARKNESS HAS THE POWER

> "Offer resistance, actively and deliberately . . . against becoming habituated to death."
>
> —Dorothee Soelle, *The Silent Cry*[3]

> "It's hard to be human."
>
> —The Mekons, "Hard to Be Human Again"

The Mekons have spent the better part of thirty years resisting virtually everything—intolerance, imperialism, greed—that habituates people to death or crushes the human spirit. Architects of a shambolic, often glorious punk din, the group steadfastly has named and confronted whatever dehumanizes people, or, as they put it in the caterwauling centerpiece of their *Fear and Whiskey* LP, whatever makes it "hard to be human." Few bands in the annals of pop have embraced an ethic of resistance through disruption with as much relish and re-solve as these anarchic art-punks from Leeds.

In 1985, the year that the Mekons issued the epochal country-punk of *Fear and Whiskey*, the social and political breach in the United States and England was as gaping as it had been in decades. The Thatcher and Reagan regimes were waging class war with Draconian campaigns that relegated millions to the dole, to tenement housing, to prison, and to the streets. People of color, the uteruses of women, people living with mental illness and AIDS all were the targets of cen-sure and repression, as were the third world countries where US mili-tary forces and the CIA were engaged in their not-so-covert operations. "We know that for many years there's been no country here / Nothing here but the war and again and again we say / 'I'm not ready for this, I am not ready for this' / Over and over and over, 'I'm really not ready at all.'" So bellows Mekon Tom Greenhalgh, feeling like an exile in his own homeland in the hurtling, fiddle-charged "Country." "This is the start of our freedom," Mekon Jon Langford roars into the ominous silence at the close of "Trouble Down South," a surrealistic communiqué from the front targeting US treachery in Central America. A squall of harmonica and skittering rimshots fol-lows, detonating "Hard to be Human Again" as the Mekons, "clutch-ing for resistance with [their] red, red wine," make for the trenches.[4]

"When we were growing up, men went to the moon and everyone was getting vacuum cleaners and new dishwashers and fantastic new plastic utensils," Mekons co-founder Langford told writer Greg Kot in an interview that he did with the *Chicago Tribune* in 1991.[5] "But in the late 70s, some of the cracks started appearing. Men weren't going to the moon anymore and Thatcher became Prime Minister of Britain. People were turning the clock back. You had to fight for what you believed in, because all you thought and accepted was being threatened: education, health, the boring bread-and-butter values of socialist politics."

And fight the Mekons have, even to the point of sabotaging record deal after record deal, and, with each missed opportunity, any hope of commercial success or financial stability. "Destroy your safe and happy lives before it is too late," Langford decrees, wearing those misfires like a badge, to kick off *The Mekons Rock 'n' Roll*, the band's 1989 bushwhacking of capitalism and the music business. Langford's call to trash all that is near and dear echoes the search-and-destroy ethic of the Sex Pistols, but ultimately it is more humane. There is no assailing of passersby here. The Mekons' appeal is more that of snakebitten skeptics who, perennially staving off cynicism, believe that there still could be a future. Ever since the group's original core of Greenhalgh and Langford, fortified by punk's "anybody can do this" credo, started monkeying with the instruments of their fellow art students the Gang of Four, the Mekons have, despite the odds, believed that resistance could make a difference.

The group came together during the politically-charged climate that surrounded the 1977 race riots in Leeds, where, as the British writer Hew Bucknell reported, "racist violence at their early gigs crystallized an uncompromisingly radical attitude." This radicalism extended to punk itself, with early photos of the band revealing that its members eschewed the movement's de rigueur safety-pins, slashed jeans, and spiked hair in favor of more conventional dress and hair-cuts. Even the Mekons' penchant for humor ran counter to punk pro-tocol. The ideology of punk, not its fashions or conventions, is what mattered the most to them. This certainly is apparent in the group's collectivist practice of letting anyone, talent notwithstanding, get on-stage with them. Their commitment to punk ideology likewise was evident in their debut single, "Never Been in a Riot." A scuffling, spewing rush of atavistic noise, the record lampoons the disingenuous bravado of the Clash's "White Riot," in which punk's unimpeach-ables hold forth about the sort of fray that their upper-middle class ranks had never gone near, much less been in.

The bollocks that the Mekons scattered definitely were not the gar-den-variety *épater les bourgeois* of your average Sex Pistols *manqué*. Nor was their disruption just a rejoinder to the misery propagated by the long arm of Thatcherism. The Mekons' tactics were informed by a vision—part-socialist, part-dadaist, part-deconstructionist, part-kitchen sink—of social conditions that transcended the inhumanity of racism, sexism, and the nonexistent choice that many in Britain faced between drudgery and the dole. "32 Weeks," another of the group's early singles, screams that there must be a better way, its title an allu-sion to the number of weeks that someone would have to work at a menial wage to afford a car or a household appliance. Even the name Mekons, which the band took from an alien in a 1950s comic strip about a space hero named Dan Dare, suggested that they saw themselves as a breed apart.

Impossibly crude spurts of amateurist verve, the Mekons early singles testified, as Luc Sante memorably put it, to the "fact that people who couldn't have played 'Chopsticks' on a bet sometimes manage to contrive remarkable things, little epiphanies of pure will or nerve or soul or fucked-upness."[6] Nevertheless, and despite the endearingly skronky artlessness of their second LP—a study in resistance that originally listed neither the band's name nor the record's title—the Mekons' early albums hardly were as galvanizing as their singles. No less than Greil Marcus and Lester Bangs have made great claims for *The Mekons Story*, a middling collection of odds and ends from 1982, but by that point, the group seemed to have gone the way of most punks, apparently disbanding after playing a benefit for the Anti-Nazi League the previous summer. True to form, it took the prospect not of lucre or renown, but the chance to join another resistance movement, the English minors' strike of 1984, for the band to regroup, of all things as a post-apocalyptic hillbilly band.

Punk in the UK was by this time a very different species, having calcified into the ham-fisted soccer hooligan—and often skinhead—nonsense of Oi! Music. This just made the resurgent Mekons more crucial and relevant than ever. "With punk's claims as much a hyperbolic absurdity as any *Big Chill* soundtrack, the Mekons were the only 1977 leftovers with an answer to Reagan-Thatcher," wrote the critic Eric Weisbard.[7] "Their longtime commitment to small-scale realism and amateurish artistry were the perfect ingredients for re-creating community in the teeth of mass indifference. 'It's hard to be human again,' an inspirational chorus railed, and live, the band made the effort to find a common humanity an act of risky, inspirational struggle." The reconstituted Mekons feverishly nurtured this community, "rolling along," as Huw Bucknell wrote, "with an unstoppable [and long since legendary] alcoholic impetus. They gigged incessantly, spreading the word at benefits up and down the country, and lent tracks to compilations in support of the homeless, the stricken National Union of Miners, pro-choice campaigns and AIDS charities."[8]

The Mekons' rebirth as a slantwise country band made perfect sense, and not just because of the music's association, at least in the

United States, with the group's beloved miners. The band's country turn—and this is to say nothing of the tonic effect of the two-steps and fiddle breakdowns that they stomped out—also tapped the resilience that is inherent in so much honky-tonk music, which of course descends, in part, from old Anglo-Celtic ballads. Though often dismissed as fatalistic, country's plainspoken exhortations to walk the line, to keep the circle unbroken, and to keep on the sunny side are steeped in a hard-won and class-conscious realism that prides itself on not giving in to what one is up against. That is, in a sensibility that prides itself on struggle and resistance, however much those values might be veiled or conveyed between the lines.

None of which is to deny that country music frequently witnesses to people being driven to drink by their circumstances. Yet doubtless this, too, resonated with the Mekons, who called the first album that they released after regrouping *Fear and Whiskey*. Indeed, beset by "darkness and doubt" and taking refuge in knowing that "there's got to be one breath after which there doesn't come another," sometimes, as Greenhalgh coarsely croons in "Chivalry," only "fear and whiskey [*can* keep you] going." Or cat food, as Langford howls, by way of Raymond Chandler, in "Big Zombie" (aka "I'm Just Not Human Tonight") from 1986's *The Edge of the World*.

Whether fortified by Bushmill's or Purina, the Mekons always seem to press on. "Zip your suits, take your pills, secure full masks," one of their ranks barks into a walkie-talkie on "Trouble Down South" as tom-toms burst like anti-aircraft fire and shards of guitar noise go off like air-raid sirens in the background. "Pull back the branches and tear up the roots, that's the part I like the best," Langford shouts to Suzie Honeyman's hoedown fiddle and the slamming waltz-time of "Flitcraft." And Greenhalgh—even after walking through barbed wire, stepping over broken bodies, and sinking in the mud—still manages to issue the challenge, "Come on, cruel world, show me what you've got" at the close of "Hello Cruel World."

These scenes from the front are more than just vivid backdrops for fortifying music; they are reportage, however surreal, from actual wars. "Dream Dream Dream," a forcebeat rant from *The Edge of the World*, assails the American Dream, that "vile child freedom" who was weaned on social policies that fill homeless shelters and prisons and who grows up to be a global bully. On the class-conscious

"Shanty," Langford longs for a captain who will chart a course through perilous icebergs, fog, and hail. When his mates join him for a woozy round of "A yo and a ho and there's one thing I know, we're not in the same boat at all," the implication is clear. They want a leader, someone, other than a Reagan or a Thatcher, who will steer the boat that *they* are in and keep it from sailing "off the edge of the world."

In "Ugly Band," a "dance band on the edge of time" that cannily resembles the Mekons is holed up in a bunker beneath the surface of a world "distorted by greed." Bracing for Armageddon, they are "tired of their music and licking their teeth." They are not weary, though, of the song that *they* are playing. They are sick of the bitter music of the freedom that they decry in "Dream Dream Dream." They are sick of the freedom, as they sang in "32 Weeks," to work seven-and-a-half months at a drone's wage to be able to afford a refrigerator; sick of the freedom, as a nation, to invade or bomb other countries and not see it as terrorism; sick of the freedom, as the liberation theologian Dorothee Soelle put it, to become habituated to death.

No matter how beaten or broken, the ugly band, like their creators, never concedes defeat. They doggedly persist, resisting inhumanity and death, whether in the form of injustice, materialism, or aggression, while clandestinely honing their din, "in the middle of the night, with a light behind the door," waiting for the chance to rise up. Not only that, on their side is God, "tuning in His radio and listening for the sounds" that are emanating from the basement of their desert outpost, just as God, at least as theologians like Soelle would have it, is attuned to the outpourings of all who cry out from the underside of history.[9] This is not to suggest that the Mekons are theists—their affinity with Marxism suggests the opposite—just to note that their penchant for resistance shares much with Marxist-bred liberation theology. Even the group's musical arrangements during this country-inspired phase—Cajun, Zydeco, and Tex-Mex inflections abound—favor the music of marginalized people, typically that of people of color.

*Honky Tonkin'* and *So Good It Hurts*, the final two albums that the Mekons made during this "country" period, brought more fiddle and accordion, and even some dub-style reggae, to the party. And, not surprisingly, more resistance: everything from a tribute to the author

Dashiell Hammett and his refusal to succumb to pressure during the McCarthy witch hunts to a plaint in which Greenhalgh identifies with Fletcher Christian, the seditious first mate from *Mutiny on the Bounty.* "Keep on Hoppin'," a jaunty ditty about the crippled, disinherited veterans of foreign wars doubles as the group's monument to their own perseverance after repeatedly having their career cut off at the knees. "Little stunted arms and legs" indeed. The band's reward, for all their shows of resistance and solidarity, was to be consigned to the commercial margins, a sort of solidarity-as-lived, and a cruelly ironic case of it at that.

The perennially disenfranchised underdogs responded with 1989's *The Mekons Rock 'n' Roll,* an excoriating attack on capitalism and rock 'n' roll that they manage, in Mekonian fashion, to link to everything from the razing of the Berlin Wall to the CIA's dealings with Colombian drug lords. "We know the devil and we have shaken him by the hand / Embraced him and thought his foul breath was fine perfume / Just like rock 'n' roll," Greenhalgh intones beneath waves of crashing, cascading synthesizer and guitar in "Memphis, Egypt." Over the infernal fiddle runs and surging guitars of "Club Mekon," singer Sally Timms bemoans how rock 'n' roll has become a commodity, like sex, to be bought and sold, as well as how the industry that surrounds it is but "a world where the dead are worshipped."

"Amnesia" likens rock 'n' rollers to white slave traders, charging that they stole the music from the cargo holds of their ships as they made their way from the Ivory Coast to Jamaica and the US. "Truth, justice, and Led Zeppelin," Langford roars, both demanding reparations and impugning one of the music's blatant offenders. The sullied image of Elvis Presley embedded in the album's cover art points a similarly accusatory finger, while "Blow Your Tuneless Trumpet" gets in a dig at U2's at times self-aggrandizing lead singer Bono, referred to here as "the Dublin Messiah." That the Mekons drive all of this home with rousing, indomitable rock 'n' roll that lives up to the album's monolithic title, and that they never fail to implicate themselves in the process, makes the proceedings all the more enthralling.

Not that A&M Records, the company that released the album, saw it that way. After doing little to promote *Rock 'n' Roll* (perhaps due to its incriminating contents), the label urged the Mekons not to take themselves so seriously. The group seized on this advice with a vengeance, issuing *F.U.N.'90*, an EP of covers and original material wrapped in Euro-disco beats, including one track featuring vocals from the late rock critic and Mekons champion Lester Bangs. The album was nothing like its rousing, though commercially underwhelming predecessor, apart from finding the Mekons as contrarian as ever, implacably resisting the forces of commerce and having enough moxie to call themselves "cursed" on the terrific agit-prop record that they turned in (and that A&M rejected) in its wake. "Call it intuition, call it trust / But we're right in all that we distrust / Call it our battle cry," Greenhalgh asserts on the title track of that album, the cover of which is embossed with a witch's counter-spell written in Nordic script.

After that the Mekons offered their take on love and sex and the commodification of both, and embarked on a prodigious yet diffuse decade of work that encompassed art expositions, novels-in-progress, performance-art pieces, migrations to the US, and a dizzying profusion of side projects. Much of this was overshadowed by Langford's prodigious output, which includes comic strips, music criticism, painting exhibitions, anti-death penalty work, and his barnstorming alt-country detachments the Waco Brothers and Pine Valley Cosmonauts. Ultimately, though, it all was of a piece, and quintessentially Mekonian. The group's muse might have eluded them on their 1994 album, *Retreat from Memphis*, and on portions of 1998's boozy, bawdy *Me*. Yet it returned sublimely for 2000's trenchant and tender *Journey to the End of Night* and for the post-9/11 heart and soul of *OOOH!* "Every day is a battle / How we still love the war," Timms intones amid allusions to "dangerous Bibles" and the US thirst for vengeance in "Hate Is the New Love" from *OOOH!* "When we say we've had enough / We know we really want more," she sighs. Though conveyed with as much weariness as the track's dirgelike cadence, the lyrics to "Hate Is the New Love" nevertheless attest to a spirit of resistance, a refusal, despite the gathering pall and mounting body count, to become habituated to inhumanity and death.

Much the same sort of resistance is evident, among other things, in 1989's "Only Darkness Has the Power," where, to torrents of fiddle and guitar, Greenhalgh sings, "Only darkness has the power / And darkness is what surrounds me as I open my heart to the world." Greenhalgh is facing the gloom, and not without his share of doubt.

Yet just like the ugly band blaring away "in the middle of the night, with a light behind the door," he refuses to give in to the darkness or grant it the power of which he sings. Even as he opens his soul to the abyss, he seems to be saying that darkness alone has the power to defeat people, and that if we only resist it, then maybe there will be nothing left for us to overcome.

## LOUDER THAN A BOMB

> "Justice evolves only after injustice is defeated."
>
> —Public Enemy, *Apocalypse '91 . . . The Empire Strikes Black*

Public Enemy's uncompromising music and politics are all about fighting injustice, and specifically, about combating the racism inherent in America's white power structure. The group's albums are rife with Afrocentric inducements to resistance, from "Bring the Noise" and "War at 33 1/3" to "Shut 'Em Down" and "Rebel Without a Pause." Nevertheless, it was "Fight the Power," the 1989 single that they recorded for the Spike Lee movie *Do the Right Thing*, that put mainstream America on alert. "Elvis was a hero to most but he never meant shit to me / Straight up racist that sucker was / Simple and plain," thunders rapper Chuck D, taking aim at white America's reigning cultural icon. "Mother fuck him *and* John Wayne," snipes Flavor Flav, Chuck's trickster foil, to a piercing loop of a siren going off before Chuck storms back in: "'Cause I'm black and I'm proud / I'm ready and hyped, plus I'm amped / Most of my heroes don't appear on no stamps." James Brown, for instance. Not that Chuck and Public Enemy have to come out and say it, having interpolated a shuffling vamp from one of Brown's records into the track and having cribbed his line about being black and proud from another.

"Fight the Power" does more than just rage against the hegemony of the white power machine. In the stanza that precedes Chuck D's excoriation of Elvis and those who worship him, he also has an urgent word for black America. "People, people we are the same / No, we're not the same / 'Cause we don't know the game," he begins, alluding to the rules that apply to "getting over," to transcending one's circumstances. "What we need is awareness, we can't get careless / You say, 'What is this?' / My beloved, let's get down to business." Chuck's use of the term "beloved" here is an allusion to the "beloved community" of Martin Luther King and the Freedom Movement, but his message is more that of Black Power in the spirit of Malcolm X and the Black Panthers. "Now that you've realized the pride's arrived," he goes on, "We've got to pump the stuff to make us tough / From the heart / It's a start, a work of art / To revolutionize." A year earlier, summing up the group's platform in "Don't Believe the Hype," Chuck booms, "Rock the hard jams, treat it like a seminar / Teach the bourgeois and rock the boulevards."

"Fight the Power" embraces this beat-wise pedagogy with a vengeance. Grafting Chuck's imperious elocution to the dense, layered grooves of the group's production team, the Bomb Squad—all of it cauterized by the ferocious turntable scratching of DJ Terminator X—these self-appointed "Prophets of Rage" offer what Chuck at one point calls "Food for the brain and beats for the feet." As much as any group in pop music ever has, Public Enemy embodies Funkadelic's manifesto, "Free your mind (and your ass will follow)." Or as Robert Christgau put it in a 1990 column in the *Village Voice*, "Not only are [Public Enemy] the most innovative popular musicians in America, if not the world, they're the most politically ambitious. Not even in the heyday of the . . . Clash has any group come so close to the elusive and perhaps ridiculous 60s rock ideal of raising political consciousness with music."[10]

Chuck D and future Bomb Squad commander Hank Shocklee first conceived of Public Enemy as a cross between Run-D.M.C. and the Clash while the two men were attending Long Island's Adelphi University together in the early 1980s. Such a synthesis is hardly surprising coming from Chuck, aka Carlton Ridenhour, the son of leftist, middle-class parents who early on was exposed to the Black Power Movement and to visionary proto-rappers like Gil Scott-Heron and the Last Poets. Public Enemy in many ways updates the Afrocentric, agit-prop tactics deployed by these antecedents, and not just through their implacable beats and rhymes, but through their militant packaging and iconography as well. The group appears in fatigues and other army garb in album and publicity photos. They call the bodyguard-like entourage that accompanies Chuck, Terminator, and Flav onstage the S1Ws, or Security Force of the First World. And their corporate logo, which Chuck, a former art student, designed, depicts a man with his arms crossed and his head cocked staring defiantly into the crosshairs of a gun sight. Though overdone at times, all of this serves the collectivist ethic of resistance—the drive to confront and disrupt the powers that thwart racial justice and uplift—that Public Enemy conveys so indomitably through their music.

This ethic, however, was barely in evidence on the group's 1987 debut, *Yo! Bum Rush the Show*. The PE logo was already in place, and the vague indictment, "The Government's Responsible," was splayed like a frozen ticker tape across the bottom of the album's cover. Yet apart from the admonitory "Timebomb," with its asides about Apartheid and the Black Panthers, and the homiletic "Right-starter (Message to a Black Man)," its chorus hooked by the catch-phrase, "Our solution—mind revolution," there is little in the way of a prophetic voice on the record. More predictable hip-hop poses, from macho boasts like "My Uzi Weighs a Ton" to sexist put-downs like "Sophisticated Bitch," predominate instead. And while the Bomb Squad, abetted by some coruscating guitar from the great Vernon Reid, knows how to bring the noise, they certainly do not know how to make it swing yet.

Not so with the record's successor, *It Takes a Nation of Millions to Hold Us Back*, an album that swings so unrelentingly and consists of collages of beats so furious, tight, and original that it sounds like no recording in rock, pop, or rap before it—or maybe since. "Bring the Noise," the album's epochal first single, was the Bomb Squad rein-venting hip-hop with colliding polyrhythms, strafing fusillades of beats, and samples of bleating horns and screeching sirens. Owing as much to the avant-garde likes of free jazz, experimental montage, and punk/industrial noise as it does to rap—and with Chuck's "bass in your face" assailing the citadels of white America—"Bring the Noise" is a watershed in every respect.

Virtually every note on *Nation of Millions* is transcendent—"Louder Than a Bomb," as the title of another of its tracks puts it. "Too black, too strong," Chuck declares, sounding the alarm, as "Countdown to Armageddon," the album-opening air-raid alert, gives way to "Bring the Noise." From "Black Steel in the Hour of Chaos" to "Terminator X to the Edge of Panic," the apocalyptic titles of the tracks that follow alone promise more of the same. Several of them, such as "Don't Believe the Hype," rail at the racist attitudes and practices of the white-controlled media. "In the daytime the radio's scared of me / Because I'm mad, plus I'm the enemy," Chuck fumes over a pumping funk vamp, referring to how Public Enemy's confrontational fury prevents them from getting airplay. Debunking the writers who hear the group's records as incitements to separatism and violence he adds, "I'm not a hooligan / I rock the party and / Clear all the madness, I'm not a racist / Preach to teach all / 'Cause some they never had this."

The likes of "Don't Believe the Hype" and "Bring the Noise" might fixate on Public Enemy's conflicts with the media (Chuck famously called rap the "black CNN"), yet even accounting for the MC's considerable ego and arrogance, they rarely are narcissistic. Peppered with lines about Nation of Islam leader Lewis Farrakhan being a prophet and about the disproportionate number of black men on Death Row in the US, Public Enemy's complaints steadfastly open outward to illuminate how racism thwarts transcendence on a larger social and cultural scale. *Nation of Millions* invested rap, the critic Michael Eric Dyson wrote, with long-overdue "ideological vitality."[11]

"Night of the Living Baseheads" might bemoan the grip that crack cocaine has on the ghetto, but its images of zombies walking the streets speak just as prophetically to the epidemic of homelessness that was being spread by the corporate welfare system of Reaganomics. "Power, equality / And we're out to get it," Chuck broadcasts to open "Party for Your Right to Fight," the inexorable funk workout that contains the line from which the title *Nation of Millions* derives. "I know some of you ain't wit'it / This party started right in '66 / With a pro-Black radical mix," he goes on, alluding again to the Black Panthers as a wailing voice tweaked and sampled from what sounds like a James Brown record testifies right in line.

By the time that "Fight the Power" appeared the following year, Public Enemy seemed impregnable, only to see their position of resistance turn to one of defensiveness after Professor Griff, the group's so-called Minister of Information, made a flagrantly anti-Semitic remark in a story that appeared in the *Washington Times*. Chuck D handled the episode clumsily, first defending Griff, then expelling him from the group before disbanding Public Enemy altogether. Even worse than Chuck's mishandling of the flap, though, was the way that the fracas exposed the chinks in Public Enemy's ideological armor. Foremost was the way that the group painted the struggle for racial justice in terms so absolute that Chuck could dismiss Elvis Presley as a racist just because he was white.

Like all white people in the United States, Elvis participated in, perpetuated, and benefited from America's racist values and institutions and was by no means free of their taint. Yet, as Craig Werner noted in his book *A Change Is Gonna Come*, Chuck's allegation that Elvis was a racist "simple and plain"—his casting of the nation's "cultural morality play in black and white"—revealed that Public Enemy had yet to learn from the mistakes inherent in the separatist ideology of the Black Power Movement. If, as Chuck would go on to argue in "Fear of a Black Planet," the mingling of black and white blood breeds blackness, then *who* is the power that he is urging his brothers and sisters to fight? Who, for that matter, *are* those brothers and sisters?

Public Enemy regrouped not long the after the incident with Professor Griff, with Chuck D firing back with "Welcome to the Terrordome," a dense, amelodic wall of abrading noise that sifts through some of the questions that the episode raised and hints at an answer. "Every brother ain't a brother 'cause of color / Just as well could be undercover / Backstabbed," Chuck argues, articulating a much subtler take on blackness and race in one of the track's several moments of truth. "Terrordome" likely would have worked as the apology for the Griff crisis that Chuck intended it to be had he not grudgingly sniped, "Crucifixion ain't no fiction / So-called chosen frozen / Apology made to whoever pleases / Still, they got me like Jesus." However, Chuck's linking of his "persecution" to the crucifixion of Jesus, an event that anti-Semites for centuries have blamed on Jewish people, only exacerbated fears about Public Enemy's prejudices. Chuck's disparaging of the Jews as the "so-called chosen" was, if anything, worse.

"Terrordome" begins with the lines, "I got so much trouble on my mind / Refuse to lose," and from "Anti-Nigger Machine" to "War at 33 1/3," *Fear of a Black Planet*, the album on which it appears, is shot through with this mix of blues and resistance. As with *Nation of Millions*, much of the antipathy expressed on the record is attributable to or leveled against white America. "Burn Hollywood Burn" rather predictably takes on racism in the movie industry while the album's title track looks incisively at miscegenation. The incendiary "911 Is a Joke," an atypically sober vehicle for Flavor Flav, savages the racially-charged reluctance of ambulance drivers and police forces to venture into urban black neighborhoods. *Fear* also contains appeals for black unity like the exhortatory "Brothers Gonna Work It Out," with its uplifting echoes of Curtis Mayfield and Marvin Gaye. And on "Revolutionary Generation," in a middling feminist turn, Chuck rhymes, "This generation generates a new attitude / Sister to you we should not be rude," a de facto apology for his sexist slurs on "Sophisticated Bitch" and "She Watch Channel Zero?!" Unfortunately, the rapper Ice Cube's gratuitous use of the term "bitch" in his cameo on "Burn Hollywood Burn" all but gainsays Chuck's about-face here.

Sonically, *Fear* is not as startling a departure from *Nation of Millions* as that album was from its predecessor, but it is no less riveting. If anything, its beats, which at points reveal the influence of dancehall reggae, are louder and harsher, its guitars more serrated, and Terminator X's scratching more furious than ever. With Armageddon-inspired titles like "Final Count of the Collision Between Us and the Damned," the album still paints the world predominately in the less than subtle shades of black and white. The fractious events that surrounded the debacle with Professor Griff nevertheless had precipitated something of a spiritual crisis and epiphany for Chuck D. When in "Terrordome" he rhymes, "It's weak to speak and blame somebody else / When you destroy yourself," he is talking as much to himself as he is to anyone else. He seems to be acknowledging that prophets, whether of rage or otherwise, must confront and name the oppressive forces that exist both within themselves and within the larger world before they can stand on the moral high ground needed to resist those powers.

The critic Marshall Berman describes Chuck's transformation in "Welcome to the Terrordome" as a breakthrough to humanism.[12] "For the first time," Berman wrote in 1991, Chuck D "lets himself sound uncertain, vulnerable, inwardly troubled. . . . 'How to fight the power? . . . / In a game, a fool without rules . . . / What you do: Get your head ready, instead of gettin' physically sweaty.' Now, for the first time, the Bomb Squad's seismic shifts and breaks can express a clashing and broken consciousness, and rap can become a mode of

*Bildung*, part of the process of soul-making." Just as critical as the line "Every brother ain't a brother" is Chuck's revelation, "My home is *your* home / Welcome to the Terrordome," a salutation that suggests possibilities for human communion that had not been possible within Public Enemy's hitherto black-and-white world.

"Fear of a Black Planet" offers more questions, if not further evidence of a breakthrough. "What is pure? Who is pure?" Chuck asks. "Is it European state of being? I'm not sure / If the whole world was to come / Through peace and love / Then what would *we* be made of?" Chuck's use of the pronoun "we" is crucial here, referring, on the one hand, to the entire mongrelized human race, but just as crucially, to the black race in particular. The upshot of his question is that not only is white "purity" a fiction, but black purity with it, a realization that, as the writer Joe Wood observed, posed not just a problem for a self-described "blackman" like Chuck D, but an out-and-out crisis of meaning.[13] *Fear of a Black Planet* ends, as Wood pointed out, with a white interviewer asking the question, "What's the future of Public Enemy?," to which Chuck begins to tender an answer, only for the music abruptly to stop. Everyone, both the white and black voices on the track—and by implication, all people—is left in a lurch.

An answer—a bona fide day of reckoning—comes with *Apocalypse '91 . . . The Empire Strikes Black*, Public Enemy's third tour de force in a row. "I don't give a fuck about the old way / This is a new day," Chuck proclaims in "Move!," referring to one of his previous black-and-white claims about race. The record's beats certainly are deeper than those on any of the group's first three albums—seemingly fathomless at times—and the grooves are steeped more in blues, gospel, and funk; they sound "blacker," so to speak, than the noisy avant-gardisms that came before them. The record also is much tougher on black people than earlier albums were. Taking the line, "Every brother ain't a brother," from "Terrordome" to heart, Chuck and Flav direct their share of the striking alluded to in the album's title largely at black communities, both bourgeois and poor. When at the end of "Move!" Chuck admonishes, "It's a black thing, you've *got* to understand / Welcome to the Goddamn Terrordome," he is not saying, "Welcome to my world, white folk," he is urging his black brothers and sisters to get *their* shit together. Witness "Nighttrain," which goes after black drug dealers and hustlers, or "1 Million Bottle Bags," which assails alcoholism and other forms of addiction that decimate the black ghetto. Then there's the staggering "I Don't Wanna Be Called Yo Niga." Here, echoed by a choir of soul sisters shouting over a yawning blues groove, Flavor Flav screeches the epithet in the song's title at least fifty times in the process of telling his thug-posing peers that he is sick of them calling him their "niga."

Not everything on *Apocalypse '91* is aimed at black America. To the heaving gospel blues of "By the Time I Get to Arizona," Chuck rails at leaders in New Hampshire and Arizona for their refusal to participate in the national celebration of Martin Luther King's birthday. In the track's prologue, Sister Souljah, Public Enemy's Director of Attitude, issues a statement saying that the group believes that the powers that be in those states find "psychological discomfort in paying tribute to a black man who tried to teach white people the meaning of civilization." In "Shut 'Em Down" Chuck confronts multinational conglomerates that cater to black buyers, but even this is as much a call for black communities to resist the pull of materialism as it is a matter of censuring big business and marketing.

"Classify us in the have nots / Fightin' haves," Chuck declaims amid the ominous tumult of "Can't Truss It." More than anywhere else on the album, his encompassing new humanism has him taking sides and identifying "good guys" and "bad guys" based on lines other than those exclusively drawn by race. Here, in a transcendental move, "Chuck distances himself," as Berman put it, "from the Black Nationalist propaganda versions of history that he seems to have grown up on, and identifies himself with the historic multinational left."[14] "All in da same gang" is how he refers to this contingent of "have nots fightin' haves" in "Lost at Birth," his insights about miscegenation from "Fear of a Black Planet" doubtless fresh in his mind. *Apocalypse* ends with Chuck and PE teaming up with the band Anthrax for a thrash-metal update of "Bring the Noise," thus uniting the "have nots" of rap's urban black audience and those of metal's white, lower-middle-class fan base. "Justice evolves only after injustice is defeated," reads the maxim printed across the bottom of the album's cover, and for just over fifty prophetic minutes, *Apocalypse '91* is its breathtaking embodiment.

*Apocalypse* was followed by *Muse Sick-N-Hour Mess Age*, a concept album that confronted the ascendancy of gangsta rap and the racial betrayal inherent in its glamorization of sex, drugs, and violence, while not overlooking the duplicity of the white-owned media in that process. "Hopefully," Chuck wrote in the liner notes, "this album will add balance to what's out there, challenge foul-at-the-root institutions, and inspire those that have it in them to make change real, before the task to save ourselves becomes impossible." Sadly, the loyalties of the young black audiences whose struggles Public Enemy's previous records had given such clarion voice by this time belonged to blockbuster West Coast rappers like Snoop Dogg and N.W.A. (aka Niggaz with Attitude). Relatively few paid much mind to the harsh music and discomfiting messages of Chuck D and Public Enemy, not with gangsta rap's slinky G-funk making misogyny, materialism, and the crack pipe seem so seductive.

Ever militant, Chuck D went on to release a solo album in 1996 and to published a book, *Fight the Power: Rap, Race, and Reality*, the following year. He also started his own record label (Slam Jamz) and founded REACH, an organization, its acronym standing for Rappers Educating All Curriculum through Hip-Hop, committed to "changing the direction that rap is going in and changing the image that has been attached to it." Public Enemy, however, was no longer a commercial force at this point. Not even their galvanizing soundtrack to Spike Lee's *He Got Game* made much of an impression when it came out in 1998, but by then Chuck D had emerged as something of the conscience and MC emeritus of hip hop. His voice of resistance persisted; it just was heard more in the talks that he gave at race relations institutes and workshops, as well as on talk radio, than on record.

A stunning exception was "A Twisted Sense of God," a recording akin to Spearhead's "Bomb the World" that Chuck made (under the banner Fine Arts Militia) in response to the Bush Administration's retaliation after the attacks on the United States in September of 2001. "It's wack when cats throw religion into the mix," Chuck bellows to the relentless march of doomsday beats. He is alluding to the arrogant manner in which everyone from al-Qaeda to the US vindicates their aggression by identifying it with the will of God—a transgression that Chuck, in a disarming, Muslim-inspired turn, equates with hurting, even "killing," God. Explaining that his "flag is always at half-mast," a show of his refusal to become habituated to death, he booms, "The pendulum is swinging both ways as far as culprits are concerned. I have a problem with some nations and their protectors, how they refuse to acknowledge their major contribution to the cycle of terror and greed," he goes on, before adding, by way of benediction, "May God bless us *all*, beyond the flags." Here Chuck acknowledges not just the humanity that people everywhere share, but by implication, the fact that all people—white and black, Christian, Muslim, and Jew—must make peace within the Terrordome that everyone must call home.

# chapter 8

## DANCE TO THE MUSIC

### Sly & the Family Stone, Bikini Kill, Women's Liberation Rock, Sleater-Kinney, and Le Tigre

FAMILY AFFAIR

> "We got to live together!"
>
> —Sly & the Family Stone, "Everyday People"

I t might be hard to hear Sly & the Family Stone's "Everyday People" afresh after all the products that it has been trotted out to sell over the last decade or two. Back when the single topped the charts for four weeks in early 1969, though, it was as prophetic and visionary as pop music gets. Longhairs were estranged from short, blacks from whites, women from men, young from old, rich people from poor, those making love from those waging war. Preaching a broadminded gospel of "Different strokes for different folks," Sly & the Family Stone created a window for dialogue and reconciliation, a portal to transcendence.

"Sometimes I'm right and sometimes I'm wrong / My own beliefs are in my song," Sly sings self-deprecatingly to open the record's first verse. The groove is so wide and light—just piano and the rhythm section, with the horns carrying the melody on top—that it is easy to overlook just how momentous his admission is. Even when his sister Rose offers her Day-Glo assessment, "There is a blue one who can't accept the green one / For living with the fat one trying to be a skinny one," the vibe is so genial and laid-back that you hardly feel the weight of what she is saying. When, after uttering the song's won-

drous adage about different strokes, she adds, "And so on and so on
and scooby, dooby, doo-bee," it is as if to say that everything that
has come before it has just been an aside. Yet not when Sly breaks
back in and, in a ravaged howl, shouts, "We got to live together!"
Now there is no mistaking his or the Family Stone's intentions. "Everyday People" might be sweet soul music, but it is also a tough-
minded prescription for the solidarity and justice that were needed to
mend the soul of a nation torn by riots, assassinations, a war abroad
and another, against poverty, at home. Rooted in the spiritualities of
blues, jazz, and gospel music, "Everyday People" articulates a vision
of what the human family, at its best, might look like.

   "Everyday People" was not just rhetoric; if only fleetingly from
1967 to 1970, Sly & the Family Stone personified its call to unity. The
band included both men and women, and of various races and ethnicities. Everyone sang, played an instrument, and traded lead and supporting roles within the group. The Family Stone also worked in, or
rather fused, all genres of popular music, everything from rock and
pop to soul and the groove-rich funk that they invented with James
Brown. And they did all of this, and with records like "Everyday
People" and "Family Affair" that topped both the pop and R&B
charts, in an era when the boundaries between types of pop music
increasingly were being drawn along the lines of race and social class.
Even the band's vocal and instrumental arrangements, which had
members of the group weaving in and out and crisscrossing rhythms
all over the place, embodied this vision of integration and equality.
An "Everyday People" in microcosm, Sly & the Family Stone transcended every conceivable barrier that cut people off from each other,
modeling possibilities for human communion that indeed must have
seemed, as the title of their 1967 debut put it, like *A Whole New
Thing*.

   Much as prophetic artists like Curtis Mayfield and Johnny Cash
who sought transcendence through uplift, Sly & the Family Stone
were committed to solidarity. And insofar as their music promotes
tolerance and unity, it resists anything that might threaten the realization of those ideals, much like that of the Mekons and Public Enemy.
Yet Sly & the Family Stone also moved beyond incitements to lift
people up or to fight the powers that keep them down. If only for
a time, Sly and company actually embodied an alternative to those

oppressive conditions. There are senses in which, say, Curtis Mayfield, Spearhead, and the Mekons have done or are doing something
similar, but while their articulations of the urge for transcendence
point primarily to what yet could be, Sly & the Family Stone in many
ways ushered in and lived those possibilities. More than just an eschatological imperative, the group's late 60s incarnation achieved a considerable measure of transcendence. It enabled legions of others to do
so as well, permanently altering popular consciousness by introduc-
ing vernacular like "Different strokes for different folks" and by
making it safe, to paraphrase George Clinton, for rock bands to play
funk, and vice versa. Sly & the Family Stone very nearly, to borrow
again from Clinton, united one nation under a groove.

The roots of Sly's visionary ecumenism are manifold. He came of
age in multicultural Vallejo, a scrappy factory town just north of San
Francisco, and it was there, in his mother's storefront church, that he
first encountered the transforming call-and-response of gospel
music.[1] Sly also was exposed to a staggering array of rock, pop, and
soul music while working in the record business during his late teens
and early twenties. While on the staff of Autumn Records, Sly, who
was still using his given name, Sylvester Stewart, wrote and produced
singles for white rock acts like Bobby Fuller, the Mojo Men, and the
Beau Brummels. He even presided over the early version of "White
Rabbit" recorded by the Great Society, Grace Slick's first band of
note. As a DJ at the soul station KSOL he would play records by the
Beatles and Bob Dylan alongside KSOL's regular programming of
the latest Stax and Motown hits. All of this, as well as the air of experi-
mentalism that pervaded the Bay Area's psychedelic milieu, nurtured
in him an overriding dialectical impulse that persistently confronted
false "either/or" scenarios, whether musical or cultural, with a freewheeling sensibility that said, "both/and, and more besides."

The Family Stone would bear the first fruits of Sly's dialectical vision, even if that vision was not fully formed when they released their
1967 debut. The group consisted of Cynthia Robinson on trumpet
(the only holdover from Sly's previous band, the Stoners), Sly's
brother Freddie on guitar, their cousin Larry Graham on bass, as well
as Jerry Martini and his cousin Gregg Errico on sax and drums, respectively. Sly played organ, guitar, and a variety of other instruments. His sister Rose joined, on piano and vocals, just in time for the

recording of "Dance to the Music," the group's second single for
Epic. "Dance" proved a marvel of rhythmic innovation and eccen-
tricity, a barely contained synthesis of jazz, rock, and funk that really
was, as more than one writer has remarked, the whole new thing that
Sly had been hyping.

"Dance to the Music" is deceptively simple in construction. The
record consists of little more than a series of vamps, the repeated
chanting of the title, a pair of doowoping vocal breaks, and a call to
each of the musicians by turns to skin back a riff and keep blowing
until the entire band is on board. Seamlessly woven together (if at
times on the brink of anarchy), Sly's jazzy organ, Freddie's freeform
rock guitar, Larry Graham's funkadelic bass, and the group's souped-
up street-corner harmonies show off more than the Family Stone's
unbounded musical reach. They also issue a moral and spiritual man-
date. "All the squares go home!" Cynthia shrieks as the group heads
into the final break and chorus. Her message is clear: "We got to live
together, and this liberating free-for-all is what living together can
sound *and look* like. Dance or find another party."

Sly & the Family Stone's 1969 single "Stand!" stirs philosophical
waxing into this exhortatory mix. After an opening drumroll, Sly,
with his usual aphoristic concision, unpacks each of the Family
Stone's inducements to listeners to rise up. "There's a cross for you
to bear / Things to go through if you're going anywhere," Sly explains at one point, before urging, at another, "(Stand) for the things
that you know are right / It's the truth that the truth makes them so
uptight." The record's groove modulates several times on its way to
its climax, with Sly echoing the group's final "Stand" by submitting,
"Don't you know that you are free / Well, at least in your mind if
you want to be." A rallying cry of "Everybody!" follows, and then
the prodigious final vamp, hooked by a funky chorus of "nah-nah's,"
a series of clipped horn squeals, and some juking guitar and bass.

The idea, of course, was to take people higher, as the title of the
flipside of "Stand," a frenzied showstopper at Woodstock, attests. Yet
there are no cheap claims to transcendence in the Family Stone's
music. Ever dialectical, Sly always held the group's gospel-bred urge
to "get over" in tension with the realities of the blues. The "do-re-
mi" of 1969's otherwise sanguine "Sing a Simple Song," for example,
comes with the admission, "A simple song might make it better," but

just "for a little while," the implication being that transcendence is
fleeting, when it comes at all. Similarly, the putative holiday in the sun
of "Hot Fun in the Summertime" is clouded by the darker reality that
summer in the *inner* city had lately meant a series of riots, not the
love-ins or Flower Power associated with the festivals staged at Mon-
terrey and Woodstock. In "Don't Call Me Nigger, Whitey," its corollary being "Don't call me whitey, nigger," Sly and company confront
this gulf directly, even as the racial and musical syntheses that they
achieved within their own ranks bridged it. This tough-minded realism, this refusal not to lose sight of the blues, ultimately is what gives
Sly & the Family Stone's claims to transcendence such traction, even
today, despite the perennial commodification of their music.

"Thank You (Falettinme Be Mice Elf Agin)," the sardonic follow-
up to the outwardly upbeat "Hot Fun," epitomized this tension. The
60s in general, but especially the unraveling of the civil rights movement as the decade wore on, had taken their toll on Sly, who had by
this time developed a bleeding ulcer. He also was getting pressure, on
the one hand, from black nationalists who wanted him to push a more
separatist agenda and, on the other, from those who wanted him to
assume the mantle of pop music's unifying black savior, particularly
with Otis Redding and Jimi Hendrix dead. The demands of being all
things to all people only exacerbated Sly's growing addiction to cocaine and the rift that was growing between him and his audience. He
still closed the concerts that he bothered to show up for with "I Want
to Take You Higher," even as it rang increasingly hollow, if not as an
out-and-out lie. "He sat down to write a song," wrote Dave Marsh,
referring to "Thank You (Falettinme Be Mice Self Agin)," "and poison spilled out. Set it to one of the grungiest guitar-bass riffs he'd ever
devised, a slinky sinister beat, then picked up the tempo just a hair.
Got more specific as the verses progressed, drew more blood from
the shards of his own hope and career, mocked his own songs."[2]

The last of these gestures, a pastiche of the group's hit titles punctuated by a monstrous snarl of "Different strokes for different folks,"
was devastating. "Dance to the music, all night long / Everyday people, sing a simple song," Sly and a couple of other Family members
chant halfheartedly over the track's snapping bass and chank-a-lank
guitar. "Papa," they scoff, is "still singin', 'You can make it if you
try,'" and given the garbled litany of social ills that follows, from fear

and hate to people being hungry and dying young, Papa must have sounded like a fool. This, after all, was no time for uplift, not while there was a riot goin' on.

"Thank You (Falettinme Be Mice Self Agin)" reached No. 1 after just six weeks on the pop chart in early 1970, but few people seemed to notice the acrimony that seethed beneath its grooves. Sly withdrew to the studio to begin work on a new album, a record that was rumored to be called *The Incredible and Unpredictable Sly & the Family Stone*. It took the better part of two years for anything to surface, an eternity for an artist as prolific as Sly, who had overseen the release of four studio LPs in just three years, plus a hits package that included visionary new material. The album that finally was announced under the provisional title *Africa Talks to You* ultimately was called *There's a Riot Goin' On*. Sly cribbed the title from "Riot in Cell Block No. 9," a hit single that Jerry Leiber and Mike Stoller wrote for the Robins (later the Coasters) back in the 50s, but Sly's riot had nothing to do with the affable shuck-and-jive of that record. All disjunction and dissipated inertia, *Riot* was as murky and enervating as the previous records of the Family Stone were shimmering and teeming with life. In a review of the album at the time of its release, Robert Christgau heard "bracing alterations of vocal register, garish stereo separations, growls, and shrieks and murmurs . . . dragged over nerve-wracking rhythms."[3] Writer upon writer has noted that Sly sounds stoned, and with him rasping, "Feel so good, feel so good, don't wanna move" over the jittery, disfigured music that triggers the album, there is no denying it. The title track clocked in at an ominous 0:00. "Time, they say, is the answer, but I don't believe it," Sly gibes elsewhere, and time certainly seemed to have run out in what increasingly felt like a countdown to Armageddon.

Released just as Richard Nixon was gearing up his run for his ignominious second term in the White House, *Riot* was Sly's black state of the nation. "Blood's thicker than mud," he declares in "Family Affair," his gravelly voice sibilant and frayed. The meaning of his claim, and of the song itself, has been debated, occasioning speculation that it could have been written about the implosion of the Family Stone, the fragmentation of the Black Power Movement, the pervasive bad faith that was paralyzing the nation, or even about Sly's immersion in the drug culture. Doubtless it was some combination of these things.

The image of blood, though, invariably evokes the black blood shed on the incendiary streets of Detroit, Chicago, Watts, and Newark, as well as that spilled in the shooting galleries of the junkie ghettos and in the jungles of Vietnam. Declarations about not being able to cry, but crying anyway, and about feeling "all broke down," each of them set to the cauldron-like gurgle of Larry Graham's bass, served as a presentiment to further dissolution. Juxtaposed with the image of mud, with its intimation of the mud-covered hippies at Woodstock, Sly's talk of blood was chilling. "When you walk, know where you're walking / When you talk, aaaah," he warns, his voice distorting to the point of being unintelligible in the ironically titled "Brave and Strong." Whereas once, with a shout of "We got to live together," he would have taken the party anywhere, now he is watching his back and urging everyone else to follow suit.

Some family affair, *Riot* was pure blues, reimagined as beatdown funk obsessed with squandered and broken connections. Many white listeners neither "got" nor liked the record, and doubtless its entropic, Afrocentric reworking of "Thank You (Falettinme Be Mice Elf Agin)" (under the title "Thank You for Talkin' to Me Africa"), proved too much for some. The burping bass line, the clawing guitar fills and wheezing organ blips, the ghoulish voices that keep missing each other: it sounded like the Family Stone was briefing for a descent into hell. "Lookin' at the devil, grinnin' at his gun / Fingers start shakin', I begin to run," coughs Sly, who actually ends up there. He wrestles with the devil and winds up "on top," but the question lingers, "At what cost?"

*Riot* and "Family Affair" both ended up on top, too, crowning the pop album and singles charts, respectively, by the end of 1971. Both deserved their elevated status, having given voice to feelings of estrangement as harrowing and absolute as previous dispatches from the brink like Robert Johnson's "Hellhound on My Trail," Skip James's "Devil Got My Woman," and Blind Willie Johnson's "Dark Was the Night, Cold Was the Ground." Greil Marcus wrote that *Riot* "was Muzak with its finger on the trigger, and it wore a death's head mask."[4] Marcus's is as indelible an evocation of the record's stygian opacities as anyone is likely to muster.

*Fresh*, the Family Stone's 1973 follow-up to *Riot*, made outward gestures that seemed to gainsay this dissipation: the album's ebullient title, the Richard Avedon photo of Sly clicking his heels on the cover, the taut, economical arrangements of its material. Yet from its opening lines, "There's a mickie in the tastin' of disaster," to Sly's and Rose's sardonic, set-closing mugging of "Que Sera, Sera," much of *Fresh* told a different story. The riot might have been over, but Sly, who admits to "switch[ing] from coke to meth" at one point, was still fighting for his life. His addictions led to arrests, as well as to reports by mid-decade that he was in financial ruin. He and various iterations of the "Family" toured and put out records on occasion, but virtually all of what they did was as still-born as the scenes from *Riot*. The disintegration was all the more crushing given the promise of transcendence that Sly & the Family Stone had previously extended, some of it realized in the likes of "Dance to the Music" and "Everyday People," some of it glimpsed in the funk and disco revolutions that followed in *Riot*'s wake.

For years now, Sly & the Family Stone's music has languished on oldies radio and in advertising jingles, contexts in which it is utterly divorced from the social and political realities that gave it birth and that it in turn gave shape. It is too easy today, Craig Werner wrote, "to evade the questions of how and why the mellow 'sha sha's that linked 'Everyday People' with the gospel politics of the early 60s gave way to the anguished moan that fades to black at the end of 'Family Affair.' There's no question which song offers a better way to live. There's even less question which paints a more accurate picture of the quarter century that's passed since Sly effectively vanished from the world. The right blames the left and the left blames the right. No one in polite society calls anyone nigger or whitey, but race dominates American politics as surely as it did in the years leading up to the Civil War."[5]

Nevertheless, and as Werner's observations elsewhere attest, very real and enduring gains were made—as well as moments of genuine transcendence achieved—by the field of force that Sly & the Family Stone loosed upon American culture. More than just a catchphrase, "Different strokes for different folks" seeped into the nation's zeitgeist, becoming an ideal for living that changed the way that people related to each other. A decade-and-a-half later, the Reverend Jesse Jackson formed his Rainbow Coalition and ran for President by gathering "everyday people" of many stripes together in a spirit of tolerance and mutual respect. All of this is to say nothing of the liberating music that Sly & the Family Stone inspired, which—from Parliament-Funkadelic, Prince, and Public Enemy to Arrested Development, Spearhead, and the Fugees—continues to reverberate with life-affirming force today. Sly's own spirit might be dissipated and broken, but the glimmers of transcendence that he and the Family Stone reflected remain, and they cannot be wiped out or otherwise taken from us.

## There's a Riot Goin' On

> "We eat your hate like love."
>
> —Bikini Kill, "Feels Blind"

A very different sort of riot was going on in Olympia, Washington two decades after Sly & the Family Stone's epochal upheaval. It, too, was a fight for identity, self-determination, and self-expression, but in this case it was being waged by young women called "riot grrrls" who were bent on being subjects as opposed to objects of history. "Revolution girl style NOW!" is how Kathleen Hanna, the indomitable lead singer of the band Bikini Kill put it, taking on patriarchy's objectification of women in order to depose it. Elsewhere she screams, "Suck my left one!" over the exhilarating, crudely proficient clamor of her bandmates. Hanna is referring to her left breast here. Provoking both a nervous titter and a gasp, her scornful come-on gives ferocious voice to the defiance of a girl who throws her rapist father's shame and brutishness in his face, even to the point of taking control of how he abuses her as he returns to her bed at night.

It all is very jarring, not the least of which because Hanna blurs the boundary between childhood and womanhood—and with it, between victimization and complicity—as a means of amplifying the dissonance that girls who are sexually abused feel. Hanna's great gift, the critic Ann Powers wrote, is "for breaking through ugliness into bitter freedom."[6] Sometimes when she used to perform "Suck My Left One" at shows, Hanna, who is herself a survivor of abuse, would tear off her top while screeching the song's catchphrase, exposing her breasts and, with them, the word slut that she had scrawled across her bare midriff.

A similar impulse, as confounding as it is bracing, was at work in Hanna's decision to work as a stripper rather than to wait tables in a restaurant. Pouring coffee for two dollars an hour plus tips, she figured, was as exploitative as dancing naked for men; it just did not pay as much. As long as she was being oppressed, she felt that she might as well be making decent money, not to mention choosing which of the two evils she was going to endure, in that way gaining some measure of transcendence over her oppressive circumstances. "We eat your hate like love" is how Hanna puts it in "Feels Blind," and, as an overriding response to patriarchy, a posture of resistance, that declaration fairly captures what she and Bikini Kill were all about.

Hanna's tactics doubtless struck many people, notably her dogmatic forebears in feminism's second wave who fought for equality and respect, as being at cross purposes with her desire to subvert patriarchy's objectification of women. Yet Hanna flaunts received notions of femininity not so much to embrace them as to deconstruct and transcend them. At her untamed best she disarms the men in her audience while freeing herself of the values, many of them male-defined, that oppress her. As gifted at staging spectacle as Johnny Rotten—or, in the radical feminist camp, as the performance artist Karen Finley—Hanna seizes on the transgressive, cathartic energy of punk and places it in the service of her "girl style" insurrection. She understands, as Emily White wrote in the groundbreaking story that she did on the Riot Girl movement, "that contradiction might be the most powerful feminist tool yet, creating a kind of paralysis, or night blindness, in the man/boy imagination."[7]

"I don't fit your dumb words," Hanna rages in "Blood One" (from 1993's *Pussy Whipped*). Her sentiment is as concise a summation as any of the impetus for Riot Girl, the early 90s torrent of "girl punk" at which she and Bikini Kill were at the forefront. Yet Riot Girl, which was more of an artistic and ethical phenomenon than a discernible political organization, was not just about rebellion. Another sort of confrontation, an examination and raising of consciousness made possible only after taking a wrecking ball to patriarchy, was underway as well. "Hey girlfriend / I got a proposition / Goes something like this / Dare ya to do what you want / Dare ya to be who you will," Hanna challenges over the atavistic grind of "Double Dare Ya." The point, as the more concrete exhortation of the Riot

Girl Manifesto put it, was to get young women to bring about revolution in their own lives "by envisioning and creating alternatives to the bullshit, Christian capitalist way of doing things."⁸ That is, to get them to cast aside their patriarchal inheritance by fashioning safe, liberating worlds of their own making.

With its putatively quixotic inducements to "resist psychic death" and to "cry in public," the rhetoric of Riot Girl might have been idealistic and naïve, even at times over the top, as Bikini Kill's equation of racism and eating meat in "Liar" attests. (Thankfully, the group's droll interpolation of John Lennon and Yoko Ono's expression of 60s idealism, "All we are saying is give peace a chance," mitigates the shrillness of "Liar.") Many of the claims of Riot Girl nevertheless were prophetic. And Hanna and her bandmates, along with groups like Huggy Bear, Bratmobile, and others in Riot Girl hubs like Olympia, Washington and Washington, DC, did more than just talk about possibilities for transcendence. They consistently moved beyond words to embody liberating alternatives scarcely imagined by their young sisters. They thought globally, but acted locally, employing the modest means at their disposal after the do-it-yourself fashion of punk.

Everything from house meetings and "girlcore" fanzines to all-ages shows and self-run record labels and micro businesses served Riot Girl's decentralized, community-building agenda. Even something as taken for granted as the mosh pit at punk clubs became a theater for revolution. Tired of seeing their sisters being shoved, groped, or squeezed out by men near the front of the stage, groups like Bikini Kill took over the mosh pit by relegating males to the back or sides of the room in order to create space for women up front. Once they had transformed the mosh pit into a place of sanctuary, redefining how and where women danced to the music, they passed out lyric sheets and fliers urging them to explore and reclaim the hitherto, largely male-defined space within themselves as well. Riot Girl was all about making room for young women. And not just at shows, or even in bands, but about creating space for women to be free to love each other (in every respect) and to be safe from the violence of men: to discover new and unforeseen physical, emotional, and spiritual possibilities for their lives. "There are no boundaries on what I can feel," Hanna declares in "Feels Blind." This went double for what she and her sisters could do.

The event that crystallized this overwhelming sense of promise was Girl Day at the International Pop Underground convention in Olympia during the summer of 1991. As epochal in its way as the Sex Pistols' "Anarchy in the UK," Girl Day was where victimization and anger blossomed into empowerment and hope—and where scores of young women started or joined bands. "It didn't matter if what the girls said was politically correct, or if they were good at their instruments," wrote Emily White. "[T]he point was simply to make some noise."[9] Bikini Kill's "Rebel Girl" would become their anthem. "When she talks, I hear revolution / In her hips, there's revolutions," Hanna exults to the garage-metal droning of her bandmates. "When she walks, the revolution's coming / In her kiss, I taste revolution."

Dubbed the "angriest girl of all" by *Spin* magazine,[10] Hanna was the embodiment of this rebel ideal. She even had the distinction of inspiring Nirvana's "Smells Like Teen Spirit" by spray painting that galvanizing slogan on Kurt Cobain's bedroom wall. Possessed of a banshee wail that can contort and caterwaul with the most feral of cock-rockers, as well as a pop-wise knack for writing musical and lyrical hooks, Hanna was the It Girl of Riot Girl. Or maybe, given how she and her peers sought to shed the baggage of capitalist culture's fetishization of celebrity, its *anti*-It Girl. Even the name of Bikini Kill's Olympia-based record label, Kill Rock Stars, gave clarion voice to this anti-corporate, anti-hierarchical ethos. "I'm the little girl at the picnic / Who won't stop pulling up her dress," Hanna proclaims in "New Radio," another of Bikini Kill's singles. "It doesn't matter who's in control now / It doesn't matter 'cause this is the new radio," she goes on, alluding, with the word "this," to the untrammeled noise that she and her rebel sisters were making, musically and otherwise, at the time.

Some charged that Riot Girl promoted separatism through its empowerment of young women to define themselves over and against the male power structure. Separatism, however, could not have been further from the movement's liberating heart, no matter how much riot girls sought to create alternate realities for themselves and their peers. Bikini Kill made room among its ranks for a man, guitarist Billy Boredom (Karren). And males typically were welcome at Riot

Girl shows, albeit at the side of the stage or toward the back of the room, and sometimes only if they presented themselves at the door wearing dresses. Yet, despite its debt to hardcore punk's didactic "straight edge" movement as typified by Ian MacKaye's Fugazi, Riot Girl ultimately was not about ideological stridency. This is perhaps most evident when the young women are compared with their precursors in feminism's second wave, an upwelling to which Riot Girl was in some respects an answer. Bikini Kill drummer Tobi Vail even coined the alternative spelling "riot *grrrl*" as a send up of the movement's doctrinaire foremothers, the most radical of whom employed the term "womyn" to ensure that the appellation "women" did not look or sound derivative of "men."[11]

Riot Girl nevertheless had much the same difficulty transcending the ghettos of race and social class that isolated its largely privileged, white, bra-burning predecessors. Yet where 70s "women's libbers" often caviled over ideology, electing to pursue either academic or cultural expressions of feminism at the expense of the other, riot girls coined a common language of girl power that united young women— and that embraced shifting definitions of sexuality and gender. Riot girls thus tended to be less hung up on things like sexual mores ("I Like Fucking" blurts the title of one of Bikini Kill's records) and pornography (the group's songs readily draw on imagery from the sex trade), both of which were issues that gave their feminist forebears fits. Riot Girl also wanted little to do with the realities of womanhood, especially insofar as the domestication of women through marriage and motherhood frequently renders them culturally invisible. Hanna and her peers wanted the anarchic, ID-driven spirit of girlhood to persist, not to wither.

No matter how confounding it might have been to outsiders, riot girls were comfortable using sexist stereotypes as weapons in order to transcend them, even to the point of playing the part of "Madonna's boy toy gone over the edge," as Emily White wrote so indelibly of Kathleen Hanna.[12] "We're the girls with the bad reputations / We are gonna have our say," Hanna warns in "Finale," the closing track on Bikini Kill's 1996 swansong, *Reject All American*. By that time Riot Girl had all but unraveled, the casualty of media misinformation and corporate co-optation, but also of the realization on the part of its proponents that they needed to dispense with the trappings of girlhood. For a brief, prophetic season, though, these rebel girls had their say, articulating and embodying possibilities for sisterly—and human—communion previously unforeseen by many.

## Mountain Moving Day

> "Ain't gonna be easy . . . / But I'm a woman / And I'll be damned if I can't do as I please."

> —The Chicago Women's Liberation Rock Band,
> "Ain't Gonna Marry"

Riot Girl had any number of "godmothers," from original rebel girls the Shangri-Las and shamanic poet Patti Smith to child-cyclone Poly Styrene of X-Ray Spex and sexy-cool Kim Gordon of Sonic Youth. Long forgotten now, though, are the short-lived but groundbreaking rock bands that grew out of the New Haven and Chicago chapters of the Women's Liberation Union that were part of feminism's second wave. These all-female ensembles and others like Redstockings and the Furies were not "girl" rock acts that recorded for major labels like Fanny or the Runaways, groups that, as their names and packaging suggested, ultimately were the instruments of male record executives and producers. Nor did these early 70s feminist bands consist of fol-kie singer-songwriter types like Meg Christian and Holly Near, pioneers in the budding women's music movement who nevertheless could not be construed as rockers. From their unwavering do-it-your-self ethic to the pamphlets and song lyrics that they passed out from the stage to the transcendental possibilities that they envisioned, these autonomous feminist rock bands are the lost precursors to the liberationist agenda of riot girl.

Both of these self-described Women's Liberation Rock Bands were products of the 60s counterculture as well as of the exploratory, jamming ethos that defined so much of the era's music. The eight-member group from New Haven had a horn section and favored vamping arrangements that evinced strong jazz and R&B leanings. Their nine-piece counterpart in Chicago employed a more shambolic approach akin to proto-hippie Bohemians like the Fugs and the Holy Modal Rounders or, at times, to hippie-identified acts like Joy of Cooking and the Jefferson Airplane. The stylistic proclivities of the two groups aside, both viewed being in a band as a political act, one that enabled them to define their experiences and their art and communities on their own terms. That is, to be the protagonists of the songs that they wrote as opposed to being objectified as groupies, nemeses, or unattainable ideals in those written by men.

The notes to 1972's *Mountain Moving Day*, a split-sided LP issued by the Rounder Collective that was the only record that the New Haven and Chicago groups ever released, abundantly capture this revolutionary zeal. Identifying themselves as "the agit-rock arm of [their] respective women's movements,"[13] the bands wrote that they were not interested in creating the female equivalent of the testosterone-infused aggression and sexist bravado of their male rock counterparts. Instead they sought, even as they endeavored to "demystif[y] the priesthood of the instrument," to make "collective, non-assaultive, joyful music" that embodied their "radical, feminist, humanitarian vision. . . . What we all want to do is use the power of rock to transform what the world *is* like into a vision of what the world *could* look like; create an atmosphere where women are free enough to struggle to be free, and make a new kind of culture that is an affirmation of ourselves and of all people."[14]

Naomi Weisstein, a driving force behind the Chicago band, spoke of the women's desire to express an "ecstatic feminism" through their music. The genially anarchic jamming of the two groups might seem to belie that claim, particularly if the women's relatively restrained sound is judged by post-punk or rap standards. Their message, however, was unmistakably radical; given the cultural wars over gay marriage and abortion now raging in the US, in many ways it still *is* radical. Take the Chicago band's "Ain't Gonna Marry," which likens marriage to slavery. "I ain't gonna marry / I ain't gonna settle down," singer Susan Abod vows, buttressed by Weisstein's barrelhousing blues piano. "Ain't gonna be easy . . . / But I'm a woman / And I'll be damned if I can't do as I please." Testifying a year before the *Roe v. Wade* decision, Abod's sister Jennifer, of the New Haven Women's Liberation Band, sings, "We're talkin' about abortion, it's against the law / But we know that it's our right / Control of our bodies we are going to win / We've got to get together and fight." Songs like "Sister

Witch" and "So Fine," meanwhile, celebrate love among women, both sisterly and sexual.

*Mountain Moving Day* teems with idealism and a spirit of self-discovery and empowerment, the fact that the two bands shared billing on the project offering further proof of their collectivist, non-hierarchical ethos. Some of the language that they employ, such as Kathy Rowley's assertion, "We're taking back every single right we never knew," in the Chicago band's strident "Dear Government," might smack today of Women's Studies 101. Yet it is worth noting that many of the sentiments expressed on the album rarely had been articulated as vociferously before, certainly not on a rock 'n' roll record.[15] The long-haul mentality of the title track, with its images of rivers steadfastly grinding stones into sand, is prophetic, as is the album's update of "We're On Our Way," a paean to perseverance that has roots in the Underground Railroad and the civil rights movement.

Just as pointed is "TGIF," the one completely new track that appears on *Papa Don't Lay That Shit on Me*, the 2005 reissue of *Mountain Moving Day*. A 2001 recording by Le Tigre, the electro-feminist rock band that Bikini Kill's Kathleen Hanna formed after she moved to New York in the late 1990s, "TGIF" decries sexual harassment in the workplace and celebrates sisterhood. "We will survive as thieves / We will survive as freaks," the trio affirms over groovy beats programmed on a low-budget drum machine. Sequenced after "Secretary," a like-spirited track by the Chicago Women's Liberation Rock Band, "TGIF" is a reminder that women in feminism's now-fading third wave—indeed, women of all ideologies and worldviews—face some of the same barriers that women did who came of age a generation ago. And not just with respect to the sexual misconduct of men, but to the persistence of unequal pay and of the insidious double standard that dogs women who juggle family responsibilities and jobs outside the home.

Two other things about *Mountain Moving Day* suggest that there is more of a convergence between the womanly liberation of the second-wave feminists and the girl-power revivalism of Riot Girl than there otherwise might seem. The first is the photo of a gaggle of untethered girls hanging upside down (subversively?) from monkey bars that appears in the CD tray of the reissue of *Mountain Moving Day*. The second is Weisstein's corresponding vision of an "ecstatic feminism," a concept that holds celebration and resistance, the anarchy of girl-hood and the order of womanhood, in tension rather than pitting them against each other. As riot girls got older, they wrestled with these tensions as well, increasingly seeking to distance themselves from the infantilizing language of girlhood even as they continued to confront patriarchy and to embody liberating alternatives to it.

## Dig Me Out

> "Not for sale. Not your girl. Not your thing."
>
>                                —Sleater-Kinney, "Taking Me Home"

> "Worth the trouble, worth the pain. . . . I'll touch the sky and say what I want."
>
>                                —Sleater-Kinney, "Things You Say"

"I'm not waiting till I grow up to be a woman," Corin Tucker roars over the tribal beats and gnawing guitars of "I'm Not Waiting," one of several statements of purpose on Sleater-Kinney's 1996 tour de force, *Call the Doctor.* Tucker's previous band, a precocious duo called Heavens to Betsy, made its debut at Girl Day at the International Pop Underground convention in 1991. Armed with purgative, punk-derived outpourings about menstruation ("My Red Self") and sexual predators ("Stay Away"), the group was, like Bikini Kill, a quintessential riot girl band. Sleater-Kinney by contrast, and as Tuck-er's pronouncement in "I'm Not Waiting" fervidly attests, arrived as riot girls come of age.

"I wanna be your Joey Ramone," Tucker declares, and then, later in the song of that name, "I wanna be your Thurston Moore." It is telling that Tucker does not aspire to be Deborah Harry, Ramone's female counterpart from the halcyon days of New York punk and new wave. Or that she does not claim to be an inheritor of riot-girl godmother Kim Gordon, Moore's partner in noise-punk avatars Sonic Youth. Tucker is not content to remain in the girl ghetto. She is out to shatter the glass ceiling above the heads of women in rock, which is just what the imperious cacophony of Sleater-Kinney did, minus the compulsory irony of Generation X, when the group assumed the role of alternative rock visionaries abdicated by Nirvana after Kurt Cobain's death.

*Call the Doctor*, Sleater-Kinney's first full-length album, proved a watershed in every respect. Where the amateurish thrash of Bikini Kill is gloriously unhinged, Sleater-Kinney convey a fierce rage for order; they wrest control from the tumult with angular, blues-steeped guitar exchanges, no-fuss forcebeats, and Tucker's cavernous, vibrato-laden wailing. Even if *Call the Doctor* had consisted entirely of instrumentals, the catharsis that Sleater-Kinney's bass-less music affords would have been epic. The trio's ferociously channeled noise is the nonverbal correlate to their lyrics' resistance of the sexism and socialization that so often erode women's spirits, domesticating them and making them functionally invisible.

*Call the Doctor* is consumed with how patriarchy diagnoses everything from expressions of independence and restlessness in women to love between them as illnesses in need of curing, rather than embracing each as the perfectly healthy impulse that it is. "They want to socialize you / They want to purify you / They want to dignify, analyze, terrorize you," Tucker spits, shrilly enunciating each syllable over the obdurate thwack of the album's title track. Her internal rhymes nod tellingly toward "It Ain't Me Babe," Bob Dylan's similarly excoriating take on identity and self-determination. Later, amid the torrent of "Anonymous," Tucker screams, "Not enough for you to know / Not enough for you to own," affirming the inexhaustibility of her self and, by implication, that of her sisters as well. "Not for sale / Not your girl / Not your thing," she goes on to warn in "Taking Me Home," serving further notice to anyone who might presume to own or objectify her.

Valerie Saiving, in her groundbreaking 1960 essay, "The Human Situation: A Feminine View," asserted that a theologian's gender affects his or her understanding of God and the world.[16] The reason, Saiving observed, that male theologians traditionally have seen sin as excessive pride stems largely from the pressure that society places on men to be perpetually self-transcending achievers. For women, Saiving went on to argue, sin should not be viewed as hubris, but rather as undue *humility*. Socialized selflessness being the value that domesticates and keeps them from reaching their potential, women should

seek redemption not through sacrificial love, but through self-asser-
tion, through claiming and exercising the power that lies within them.

Sleater-Kinney's music might not be theological, but it certainly
evinces the urge for transcendence that Saiving found so redemptive.
This impulse is evident in everything from the trio's strafing blitzes
to Tucker's claims about not waiting to grow up to be a woman or
about wanting to be our Joey Ramone. Primarily, though, *Call the
Doctor* finds Sleater-Kinney railing against socialization and intolerance. Not so much on *Dig Me Out*, its volcanic successor, where
Tucker, singer-guitarist Carrie Brownstein, and drummer Janet Weiss
are not concerned so much with resisting or defining themselves over
and against anything as they are with reveling in their own generativity and might. "Words and guitar / I got it / Words and guitar / I like
it / Way, way too loud / I got it / Words and guitar," Tucker exults,
spurred by Brownstein's stinging guitar barbs and Weiss's hammer-
like blows. "Hit the floor / Shake it baby, a little more," Tucker bids
in "It's Enough," the drums and guitar racing to keep pace. "I make
rock 'n' roll!"

Here Tucker seeks to find herself by losing herself, by letting herself get completely out of control. "Dig me out / Dig me in / Outta
my body, baby / Outta my skin," she shrieks over squalling sheets of
guitar noise on the title track. Much as Iggy Pop embodied the idiocy
and monotony of his surroundings in order to gain a degree of mas-
tery and transcendence over them, Tucker channels hysteria, a condition that the ancient Greeks blamed on the uterus, into raw,
unmitigated power. "Worth the trouble / Worth the pain / It is brave
to feel / It is brave to be alive," Tucker shouts on "Things You Say."
When she adds, "I'll touch the sky / And say what I want," it is the
embodiment of the ecstatic feminism envisioned by Naomi Weisstein
of the Chicago Women's Liberation Rock Band, a rapturous expression of transcendence that is as visceral as it is grounded in analysis
and insight.

Tucker and Brownstein, who early on went by Carrie Kinney (the
band's name comes from that of a street intersection in Olympia), met
while both were students at Evergreen State College. Weiss, a veteran
of the post-punk scene in the Pacific Northwest and the last in a series
of drummers in Sleater-Kinney, arrived in time for *Dig Me Out*, an
album, as Neva Chovin wrote, that "redefined Sleater-Kinney as a

power trio whose chops transcended gender and genre issues."[17] Even as they took their place in the larger world of rock, though, the group remained steadfast to the values and communities that nurtured them. They also continued to model possibilities for young women, and not just ways of expressing themselves onstage, but in the bedroom as well. To the heat-seeking guitar riffs of "Turn It On," Tucker, transported by her lover, warbles, "It's too hard / It's too good / It's just that when you touched me / I could not stand up." Elsewhere she and Brownstein relish their sexual potency; "It's cherry, cherry red and it beats on time," they moan in euphoric harmony. Lovers at one point, the two women nevertheless have managed to keep Sleater-Kinney together after they no longer were a couple, something that Valerie Saiving doubtless would attribute to gender. Whereas men tend to value self-differentiation for its own sake, women who exercise that freedom are less likely to lose sight of the need to maintain and strengthen community even as they define themselves within it.

This commitment to community continued to sustain Sleater-Kinney even as they became a world-class, if still semipopular, rock band on the order of, say, Television or Hüsker Dü. Even after *Call the Doctor* and *Dig Me Out* made them critics' darlings and precipitated a flood of contract offers from major labels, the trio decided to continue to record for Kill Rock Stars, the small but influential independent in Olympia for which they made *Dig Me Out*. "A lot of Sleater-Kinney has to do with musical communities we've come from, and [with] feeling part of that," Brownstein told me, talking about the band's reluctance to forsake what they had in Olympia, in an interview in 1999. "We didn't want to feel uprooted from those communities or to be taken out of that context. . . . You can work with people you care about, and people that care about you and your music, and still put out records that a lot of people are able to buy."[18]

Indeed, even as they opted for the close-knit community that they knew over the male-dominated world of corporate rock, Sleater-Kinney was named "America's Best Rock Band" by *Time* magazine.[19] The group also consistently sold albums in the six-figure range, effectively dismantling the rock myth of excess that asserts that bigger and more is always better. "An uncut stone is flawed and beautiful / Don't try to size me down to fit your tiny hands," Brownstein warns on the title track of the group's 1999 album, *The Hot Rock*. "The End of

You," a track from the record that invokes Odysseus's close encounter with the Sirens, likewise expresses wariness of the rock-star trap while also testifying to Sleater-Kinney's indie ideals. "The first beast that will appear will entice us with money and fame," Tucker shouts above the din. "If you listen long enough, you'll forget there's anything else / Tie me to the mast of this ship and of this band / Tie me to the greater things, the people I love."

This steadfastness, this spirit of kinship and accountability, strikes at the prophetic heart not just of Sleater-Kinney and their music, but of the art and social scene in Olympia from which they emerged. Ethical ideals routinely supercede aesthetic and economic considerations there, with older people encouraging and mentoring younger ones in ways that, as Sarah Dougher, Tucker's partner in the antic, neo-girl group Cadallaca, observed, transcend the profit motive.[20] "A lot of people in Olympia have taken the time, in a sort of apprentice ideology," Brownstein added, "to pass on their skills to other people, allowing them to do things for themselves."[21]

Witness "#1 Must-Have," a paean to self-determination from Sleater-Kinney's 2000 album *All Hands on the Bad One* that doubles as an indictment of corporate culture even as it employs overt pop hooks. "I've been crawling up so long on your stairway to heaven / And now I no longer believe that I wanna get in," Tucker sings, alluding to the "cockrockracy" of corporate rock before turning to more pressing communal concerns. "And will there always be concerts where women are raped? / Watch me make up my mind instead of my face / The Number One Must Have is that we are safe . . . / Culture is what we make it / Yes it is / Now is the time to invent."

Nowhere has this penchant for invention expressed itself more dramatically than on Sleater-Kinney's 2002 album, *One Beat*. "If you're ready for more / I just might be what you're looking for," Tucker vowed on "Male Model" from the record's predecessor, *All Hands on the Bad One*. She was urging more male rock bands to share the stage with their female counterparts, but her admonition just as easily could have been a segue to *One Beat*, a record informed by the attacks of September 11, 2001, and by the Bush Administration's blindly retaliatory response to them. Packing more intensity, more empathy, more defiance, more hurt, more blare, and more technique into its twelve tracks than anything in the trio's imperious catalog, *One Beat* opens outward like no Sleater-Kinney album before it. It moves beyond politics of identity and resistance to articulate a post-9/11 grammar of faith, noise, and solidarity that connects the dots between the trio's local and global concerns.

In "Sympathy," a slide-guitar and cowbell-driven blues punctuated by "ooh, ooh-oohs" lifted from the Rolling Stones' "Sympathy for the Devil," Tucker calls on heaven to protect her newborn and, by implication, all God's children, regardless of nationality or religious faith. "I'm not the best believer / Not the most deserving / But all I have, all I am, all I can / For him I'd beg you on bended knees," Tucker sings, referring to her baby. "And I'm so sorry / For those who didn't make it / And for the mommies who are left with their heart breaking." Indeed, for all hearts, which together represent the single beat referred to in the album's title.

"These are troubled times, these times are rough / There's more to come, but you can't give up," Tucker exhorts in "Step Aside," buttressed by Weiss's spiky forcebeats and a soul-searching, neo-Stax brass choir. "Why don't you shake a tail for peace and love / Move it up one time for love? / Janet! Carrie! Can you hear it?" she asks her bandmates as the three of them lay down an irrepressible dance groove, the music and the message as timely and prophetic as that of, say, Martha & the Vandellas' "Nowhere to Run" or "Dancing in the Street." "Disassemble your discrimination / When violence rules the world outside . . . / It's not the time to just keep quiet / Speak up one time, to the beat."

## I Wanna Take You There

> "Who took the Bomp from the Bompalompalomp? Who took the Ram from the Ramalamading dong?"
>
> —Le Tigre, "Deceptacon"

Shot through with celebration and resistance, and giving voice to as fierce an expression of the urge for transcendence as any, the music of Le Tigre, the electro-pop trio that Kathleen Hanna formed with two artist friends after Bikini Kill disbanded, is all about speaking up to an irrepressible beat. "Wanna see me disco?" Hanna rants, less by way of invitation than as a dare in "Deceptacon," the bopping dance track that opens the group's self-titled debut. "Let me hear you depoliticize my rhyme," Hanna goes on reprovingly, addressing anyone who would stand in her way as her bandmates Johanna Fateman and Sadie Benning count off, "One, two, three, four!" Later, on the chorus, Hanna presses, "Who took the Bomp from the Bompalompalomp? / Who took the Ram from the Ramalamading dong?" Hanna never spells out what these ineffable, onomatopoetic forces might be. She leaves no doubt, though, that she and Le Tigre intend to reawaken them, and a few more besides.

In "Hot Topic," the marching track that follows, Fateman and Benning expound what amounts to the group's credo. "Hot topic is the way that we rhyme," they chant as Hanna calls out the names of dozens of the trio's heroes. Most of them are women, including feminist icons like activist Angela Davis and author Dorothy Allison, but some of them, true to the non-hierarchical spirit engendered by riot girl, are friends and post-punk sisters like Sleater-Kinney and "lesbionic" rockers the Butchies. All three members of Le Tigre get into the namedropping act before the song is over, their voices weaving in and out to deliver a roll call of names that includes the heady likes of Gertrude Stein, Nina Simone, Ann Peebles, Hazel Dickens, James Baldwin, and the Slits, among thirty or so others.

Ann Powers, writing about Bikini Kill in the mid-90s, called Hanna "the third term emerging from the dialectical clash between Johnny Rotten and [bisexual feminist critic] Kate Millet."[22] Le Tigre represents a further refinement of that process. With their confrontational yet brainy third-wave flair, Hanna and her arty accomplices reconcile the competing cultural and academic impulses of feminism's second wave, proving them not just to be compatible, but gloriously so. Fortified by the abstruse yet evocative likes of "extensive bibliographies," "flow disruption," "wildlife metaphors," and "post-binary gender chores," Le Tigre just might augur feminism's transcendental fourth wave. They certainly qualify, as the critic Greg Kot wrote for *Rolling Stone*, as "one of the most subversive dance bands in rock history."[23]

Witness "Sideshow at Free University," where instead of either Hanna's girlish purring or her unhinged roaring—no female voice is heard on the song—we get the oleaginous voice of a man, sampled from a scratchy LP, holding forth about the nature of artistic expression. After a funky opening vamp built upon a space-age keyboard riff, double-dutch handclaps, and a trilling toy piano, the music stops and the male voice intones, "We favor the simple expression of the complex thought. We are for the large shape because it has the impact of the unequivocal." Le Tigre ramp the groove back up for another twenty seconds or so before giving way again to the spoken word. "We are for flat forms because they destroy illusion and reveal truth," the male voice drones on, only for the music to come back and for another male voice, somewhat higher in pitch, to explain, "The artists were attempting to make art more than something to be looked at. They wanted it to be something to be involved in, something too big to ignore." The track ends with more music, this time with the addition of a distorted guitar figure and the sounds of breaking glass.

It all is very high concept, if not a little arch. Yet it also is riveting and prophetic, not to mention emblematic of Le Tigre's iconoclastic, beat-happy agenda—namely, to shatter illusion with simply yet forcefully stated truths that are too momentous to ignore. Laying claim, at least in spirit, to the celebration and riot promulgated by Sly & the Family Stone a generation or so before them, Le Tigre induces listeners to dance to the music. Not only to party, but to get in step to the tune of "Everyday People" and to embrace its inclusive yet tough-minded message of "different strokes for different folks."

"For the ladies and the fags, yeah! / We're the band with the rollerskate jams," Hanna trumpets on the refrain of "LT Tour Theme," the skittering opening track from Le Tigre's 2001 album, *Feminist Sweepstakes*. And kick out the jams they do, from the subcutaneous dub of "Dyke March 2001," with its cries of "Resist, shout it out! Resist, shout it out!," to the signifying funk of "Fake French," with its debts to radical feminist theory and to James Brown's "Hot" (by way of David Bowie's "Fame"). Still, as the trio's claim to having "multiple alliances" in "Fake French" attests, Le Tigre's music is about more than just identity politics. Their agenda is so expansive that in the hypnotic "Tres Bien" it encompasses "freedom for all," with freedom being understood, after the fashion of Sly and company, as a family affair.

This does not mean that Le Tigre does not at times call some members of the family to account, even as they seek to raise the consciousness of others and incite them to action. "Ten short years of progressive change, fifty fuckin' years of calling us names," Hanna declaims, bemoaning the thorny legacy of feminism in "F.Y.R." (aka "Fifty Years of Ridicule"). "Can we trade Title IX for an end to hate crime? / RU-486 if we suck your fuckin' dick? / One step forward, five steps back," she goes on, alluding to everything from college scholarships for female athletes to the abortion pill. "Feminists, we're calling you / Please report to the front desk / Let's name this phenomenon / It's too dumb to bring us down."

"F.Y.R." leans more toward the resistance side of Le Tigre's riotous mix of celebration and confrontation than, say, the uplift of "Hot Topic" or "Fake French." Yet ultimately—and as their avowals of "Tres Bien" make plain—Hanna and her sisters want to take everyone who is willing go there higher. Le Tigre strives to embody liberating possibilities for human communion much like those realized, for a fleeting couple of years, by Sly & the Family Stone. "I wanna be there! I wanna take you there!" Hanna shouts over the grooving vamp on the chorus of "Friendship Station"; later, to the brittle, Gang of Four-inspired funk of "Keep on Livin'," she charts a way to get there. "Just please hold onto your pride," she urges as her bandmates exhort, "Keep on, keep on livin'."

"Don't let them bring you down / And don't let them fuck you around," Hanna continues, putting the Bomp back in the Bompalompalomp. "'Cause those are your arms / That is your heart / And no, no they can't tear you apart / They can't take it away, no! / This is your time / This is your life."

# EPILOGUE

## Hungry Heart

"[I]n 'Born to Run,' there's that searchin' thing; that record to me is like religiously based. . . . Not like orthodox religion, but it's about basic things, you know? That searchin', and faith, and the idea of hope."[1]

—Bruce Springsteen

Philosophers, theologians, and poets for centuries have sought to elucidate the "searchin' thing" to which Springsteen gives such idiomatic voice above. His remarks are from an interview that he did with *Rolling Stone* in 1984 and they were made with considerable benefit of hindsight. It had been nearly a decade since he had released the epochal record in question. He no longer was the wild, wide-eyed rock 'n' roller that he had been. Neither was "Born to Run" just the paean to getting in a car, getting the girl, and getting as far away as possible that it once seemed to be. Over the years the record's headlong rhythms and Springsteen's on-the-brink vocals conveyed less a desire for escape than an urge to run *toward* something. That impulse had been there all along in lines like "We're gonna get to that place where we really want to go." It just had taken awhile for it to gain traction.

Events during the intervening decade certainly played a role. Not long after *Born to Run* simultaneously landed Springsteen on the covers of *Time* and *Newsweek*, he came face to face with greed and betrayal during a bitter dispute over his recording contract. He also had begun to immerse himself in movies, music, and books that depicted the lives of hard-hit people, a process of consciousness-raising that further dampened his youthful idealism. Most recently he had fought to keep "Born in the U.S.A.," the most far-reaching expression of his emergent populism to date, from being co-opted by conservative pundits and a Republican President. Springsteen's comments in his interview with *Rolling Stone*, in other words, were colored by the second sight that comes only through the shattering of naïveté and the ensuing struggle to come to grips with what it means to live with that brokenness. Springsteen's deepened grasp of the meaning of "Born to Run" reflected not just his need to reaffirm his faith in the possibility of glimpsing something beyond brokenness. It testified to his commitment to creating something that transcended it, even if he knew that any hope of doing so was tempered by the realization that transcendence is partial and fleeting at best.

Transparently or otherwise, Springsteen had been expressing this urge for transcendence from the beginning. Witness how, as if he were a thief, he sings of "casing" the Promised Land in "Thunder Road"— indeed, how he affirms that there is a Promised Land to begin with, especially after he had passed through the badlands and been engulfed by the darkness on the edge of town. Or consider how on *Nebraska*, despite the presence of "a meanness in the world" and the persistence of "debts that no honest man can pay," he clings to a "reason to believe." Or how, in light of all of these things, he embraces the ties that bind and insists that two hearts are better than one, intimating the vision of transcendence through community that has sustained him throughout his career.

Maybe nowhere prior to his 1984 interview with *Rolling Stone*, though, did Springsteen express this urge for transcendence more resoundingly than in his 1980 single "Hungry Heart." It might seem counterintuitive to make such a claim for a record in which the protagonist is about to walk out on his wife and children. Yet with Max Weinberg's nagging backbeat driving home its point—namely, that it's not the mere existence of a family that feeds the soul, but the inbreaking of the transcendent in the home that they have made together—the chorus takes on meaning well beyond the parameters of the song's narrative. When Springsteen sings, "Everybody needs a place to rest / Everybody wants to have a home," he is empathizing with the restlessness of the song's main character, not condoning his actions. He is speaking to the dis-ease that roils every heart. He is making an existential claim, an assertion about what it means to be human, as well as about what sort of community people hunger for. "That sense of dread—man, it's everywhere," he said in a 1988 interview. "It's outside, it's inside, it's in the bedroom, it's on the street. The main thing [is] to show people striving for that idea of home: people forced out of their homes, people looking for their homes, people trying to build their homes, people looking for shelter, for comfort, for tenderness, a little bit of kindness somewhere."[2]

The empathy that Springsteen evinces here, a spiritual generosity akin to that which he affords the troubled husband and father in "Hungry Heart," is just one of the things that make his music so prophetic. Another is the way that he steadfastly identifies with and lifts up people on the margins—everyone from misfits and murderers to illegal immigrants and Vietnam War veterans. Springsteen does more, however, than just give voice to the struggles of his beaten, broken characters. Through his music and activism he resists the powers that create the conditions that keep them down, even as he moves beyond resistance to envision life-affirming alternatives to those forces and to promote the kinds of communities that can bring those possibilities about.

Much like that of Sly & the Family Stone or the women of Riot Girl, Springsteen's music comprises all three prophetic expressions of the urge for transcendence. Prophetic articulations of the urge for transcendence would be the most expansive, and most liberating, of the various expressions of this urge to get higher, if only because they subsume all others. To be prophetic, for example, a person must be able to feel empathy; likewise, he or she must be prepared to gainsay false claims to transcendence. Prophetic outpourings, though, also open outward more persistently than those of their mystical or nay-saying counterparts. Whereas the likes of contemplation, empathy, sensuality, and negation can be conveyed in isolation or in relation to just one other person, prophetic expressions hinge on the formation and nurture of some greater community. They hold out more far-reaching prospects for transformation.

Springsteen reflected on the notion of community, as well as on the transformative promise that it holds, in an interview with author Nicholas Dawidoff that appeared in the January 26, 1997, edition of the *New York Times Magazine*. Springsteen was on the road at the time, touring as a solo act in support of *The Ghost of Tom Joad*, his austere collection of meditations on life in the global Dust Bowl. "I very consciously set out to develop an audience that was about more than buying records," he told Dawidoff.[3] "I set out to find an audience that would be a reflection of some imagined community that I had in my head, [an audience] that lived according to the values in my music and shared a similar set of ideals."

Springsteen went on to reveal that this vision had guided him since the earliest days of his career, if not before. His music, however, did not betray any overt sign of this ideal until it took a more prophetic turn with *The River*, the 1980 album that included "Hungry Heart." Though still character-driven, here Springsteen's songs hinge more and more on the convergence of the personal and the political, on using the personal as a lens to illuminate larger social realities, particularly as they impact the community from which he emerged and with which he continues to identify. The blue-collar men and women of *The River* dwell not in the land inhabited by the lucky few for whom Ronald Reagan would claim it was "morning in America." Springsteen's beloved community populates the "Other America," the one beset by a seemingly endless procession of factory and mill closings—indeed, by closed doors of all kinds, whether of mental hospitals, homeless shelters, or the offices of savings and loan associations. The disinheritance that Springsteen's characters know is not just material but spiritual (spiritual, among other things, because it robs them of hope); shot through with feelings of anger, resentment, desperation, and shame, their disenfranchisement belongs to the Great Depression of the postindustrial age.

*The River*, as Mikal Gilmore argued, finds Springsteen approaching rock 'n' roll in a fundamentally different way than he had on previous records. Here Springsteen begins to use music less as "a way of making or entering history for personal validation" than "as a means of *looking* at history, as a way of understanding how the lives of the people in his songs [have] been shaped by the conditions surrounding them, and by forces beyond their control."[4] The album's title track could be the sobering sequel to "Born to Run" or "Thunder Road." The song's nineteen-year-old narrator and his high school sweetheart make their getaway easily enough (running often *is* easy), only for him to reveal that he "got Mary pregnant" and got locked into a job that has no future. That is, only for the couple to wake up to find that "morning in America" means being tethered to a life that holds out few opportunities, and even fewer prospects for transcendence. "Now I just act like I don't remember / Mary acts like she don't care," Springsteen sings in the voice of the narrator, bemoaning their still-born dreams to funereal strains of piano and organ. "Is a dream a lie if it don't come true / Or is it something worse?" he goes on to wonder, sounding eerily like the protagonist in "Hungry Heart" might have sounded had he stayed the course, his soul withering day after agonizing day.

*Nebraska*, the stark cry from the heartland that followed *The River*, typically is lauded as Springsteen's update of John Steinbeck's *The Grapes of Wrath*, or at least of director John Ford's screen adaptation of the novel. And well it should be. Springsteen's depiction of men and women beset by an overriding sense of having no way out of the binds that they find themselves in is chilling. *The River* nevertheless remains Springsteen's first evocation of Steinbeck's populist spirit, albeit one set to expansive rock, pop, and soul arrangements, as well as one set in a "neon Dust Bowl,"[5] to invoke Paul Nelson's wonderful phrase, and thus one that is less transparently in the tradition of Steinbeck and Ford than *Nebraska*. Yet, whereas apart for the likes of "Atlantic City," "Mansion on the Hill," and "Highway Patrolman," *Nebraska* ultimately was, as Robert Christgau observed, "plunged in a social despair [that Springsteen] never quite made his own," the same cannot be said of *The River*.[6] Here the despair that Springsteen taps from within silenced row houses, deserted loading docks, and the uneasy driver's seat of a stolen car both stems from and speaks to the community from which he came, and for which he still nurtures hopes and dreams.

"Born in the U.S.A.," the title track of the 1984 album that made Springsteen a megastar on the order of Elvis Presley and Michael Jackson, confronts the ongoing betrayal of this community's dreams. "Born down in a dead man's town / First kick I took was when I hit the ground," Springsteen bellows to open the first stanza, his ravaged moan a mix of anguish, rage, and spiritual abandonment like that heard in some of the recordings of blues singers Charley Patton and Howlin' Wolf. Springsteen is portraying a Vietnam veteran here, a man who fought a war that he neither understood nor believed in, only to return home and, unable to find work, find himself with "No-

where to run . . . [and] nowhere to go." Five tracks further into the
record he shows up as the backdoor lover in "I'm on Fire," out of his
head with a desire that is at once sexual and spiritual. "Sometimes,"
he confesses, "it's like someone took a knife, baby, edgy and dull, and
cut a six-inch valley through the middle of my soul."

Nevertheless, much of *Born in the U.S.A.*, from the album's anthemic sweep to rallying cries like "No retreat, no surrender," is
about resiliency, not defeat. Even the album's cover art, which uses
the United States flag as a backdrop, testifies to this durability of
spirit, albeit not in some mindlessly patriotic way, but with the hard-
won courage of those who hope against hope. Not that everyone
heard it that way. And millions upon millions *did* hear the album,
rallying around it and the blockbuster tour that followed, a spectacle
that catapulted Springsteen into the ranks of a sort of everyman in
excelsis. In many ways this ascendancy reduced him to an abstraction,
a celebrity-as-cultural-Rorschach onto which anyone could project
their vision of America, which many of course did, even if those pro-
jections were at cross purposes with Springsteen's own.

The most fateful misappropriation of his message, and the one that
triggered the events that posed the greatest challenge to Springsteen's
notion of community, was that of syndicated columnist George Will.
After hearing "Born in the U.S.A." at a concert in 1984, Will heralded
Springsteen as a proponent of "elemental American values," by
which he presumably meant the facile optimism and self-serving moralism of the Reagan White House. Speechwriters for the President,
who was then running for a second term in office, seized on Will's
comment, which utterly mistook the defeat of "Born in the U.S.A."
for triumphalism, and worked a variation of it into a speech that the
President made while campaigning in Springsteen's home state.
"America's future rests . . . in the message of hope in the songs of a
young man so many young Americans admire: New Jersey's Bruce
Springsteen," Reagan smarmily pronounced. "And helping you make
those dreams come true is what this job of mine is all about."[7]

It was as egregious a co-optation of Springsteen's vision as imaginable, the very sort of propaganda that Cold War paranoiacs like
Reagan accused their communist counterparts of spreading all the
time. Springsteen responded several nights later, while onstage in
Pittsburgh, expressing bewilderment at Reagan's ploy and sarcasti-

cally speculating that *Nebraska*, a record that mordantly portrays the casualties of Reaganomics, must be the President's favorite album. Springsteen also commented on the matter in interviews in the days and weeks that followed, including a question-and-answer session in *Rolling Stone* in which he links Reagan's manipulation of "Born in the U.S.A." and the liberties that his administration was taking with the trust of the American people. Ultimately, though, the entire mishap exposed the Achilles heel of Springsteen's broadly stated populism—and that of any celebrity who makes such sweeping gestures from the stage: virtually anyone can usurp the grand statements of public figures for their own venal, oppressive, or otherwise dishonorable ends.

Having become such a big star, Springsteen, like Sly Stone before him, increasingly communicated with his audience at greater removes. And not just from bigger, taller stages, but from what had by this time become the vast socio-economic distance that separated Springsteen the Hollywood millionaire from his working-class fan base. It was just such a tradeoff, a sacrificing of intimacy for reach, that Springsteen's successors in Riot Girl, who embraced small decentralized communities, would not be willing to make, lest their message get lost in translation. Or perverted, as with Reagan's cooptation of "Born in the U.S.A.," or with what might have happened if Chrysler CEO Lee Iacocca had managed to convince Springsteen to let him license the record to sell cars.

People were by this point hearing Springsteen's larger-than-life music however they wanted to hear it—that is, if they were listening to what he was saying at all, or if they even could make out his message amid all the hype that attended it. "I guess I identify with his patriotic thing, but I don't think about it much," a high school student told a reporter for *Rolling Stone* prior to attending Springsteen's August 21, 1984, concert at the Meadowlands in New Jersey.[8] "Bruce Springsteen is dedicated to his country, and I like that," a young ship's mate added. "That's how I feel. He seems very excited when he sings ['Born in the U.S.A.']." Even Springsteen's nickname, the Boss, accentuated this distance or disconnect, its hierarchical connotations undercutting his populism and any intimations of community that it might convey. "This boss works for us" might have been how one slogan put it. Yet no matter how much Springsteen's fans swore that this was the case, and no matter how much he dressed like them and spoke for them, he was up on a pedestal and they were down on the ground. All of which is to say nothing of the way that the term "boss" has conjured images of African American subservience to "bosses" of various kinds.

Any whiff of the latter of course never could have been further from Springsteen's mind. Those seeking proof need only look to early incarnations of his band, which numbered two African Americans, saxophonist Clarence Clemons and pianist David Sancious, and one Latino, drummer Vini Lopez. Springsteen likewise has always colored his lyrics with black, brown, yellow, and pink faces, most of them working class, and many of them models of quiet heroism in the face of injustices that people of different races and ethnicities share in common. Issues of community, particularly as they pertained to matters of race and class, have always bubbled at or just below the surface of Springsteen's work. That is why it must have haunted him each night of his 1984 tour to be greeted by a sea of white faces, even as he envisioned a richer, more diverse community of likeminded people. "I wish I could say that the 'Born in the USA' tour was about bringing people together and leave it there," wrote Craig Werner in his book, *A Change Is Gonna Come: Music, Race and the Soul of America*.[9] "But it was really about bringing *white* people together. The standing joke was that there were more black people on stage at a Springsteen concert than there were in the audience. While it wasn't quite true, it wasn't really false either."

Nor was it for any lack of effort to transcend racial and cultural divisions on Springsteen's part. As Werner also pointed out, Springsteen would go on to sing a duet with Stevie Wonder on USA for Africa's 1985 single "We Are the World," as well as to contribute to the anti-Apartheid project *Sun City* that same year. Springsteen even enlisted hip-hop producer Arthur Baker to do dance remixes of several of the hits from *Born in the U.S.A.*, some of which spoke to the harsh social and political realities that black and white people alike faced during the Reagan years. The trouble was, apart from Baker's remixes, which failed to receive airplay on radio stations that catered to black audiences, Springsteen's foursquare rock 'n' roll was increasingly out of step with the era's black (and Latin) identified dance and turntable scenes. Like the rest of the population that did not have a

stake in his music or persona, pretty much all that casual black observers witnessed were the outsized gestures and the seemingly trium-
phal roar of the music, not Springsteen's mourning for "morning" in
Reagan's America.

The upshot of all of this disjunction was that questions of what it
means to create and sustain community, and of what it means to build
a just, tolerant society, came to dominate Springsteen's thinking as
the 1980s wore on. He also began speaking more directly to political
issues, and prophetically so, weighing in on everything from homelessness and the creation of jobs to immigration policy and US mili-
tary involvement in the third world. Though the records that
Springsteen made in the late 80s and the early 90s voiced romantic and
private concerns, two of his most recent albums, 1995's *The Ghost of
Tom Joad* and 2002's *The Rising*, were highly topical.

Inspired by Woody Guthrie and John Steinbeck, *Ghost* plumbed
poverty and race on the margins of globalization. *The Rising* sought,
nobly but with mixed results, to make sense of the lives and faith lost
in the 2001 terrorist attacks on the World Trade Center. In between
the two records came "American Skin (41 Shots)," Springsteen's out-
raged response to the repeated and senseless shooting, by members
of the New York Police Department, of West African immigrant
Amadou Diallo as he reached for his wallet to present them with
some identification. (*Devils & Dust*, a stripped-down record in the
tradition of *Nebraska* and *Tom Joad* that came out after this manuscript was completed, expresses a qualified faith rooted in Catholicism, even as it witnesses to human brokenness and the elusiveness
of transcendence.)

Much of Springsteen's heightened political awareness since the
Reagan debacle has stemmed from his increasing involvement with
local, national, and international activist groups. Much like U2 has
done, Springsteen not only began to support the likes of labor unions
and civil rights organizations financially. He also met with them in
the cities where he played, as well as challenged his audiences to do
so, urging those who attended his shows to become involved in the
causes that they espoused. Springsteen, in other words, began doing
more than just "imagining" a likeminded community, as he put it to
Nicholas Dawidoff in 1997. He started engaging and supporting com-

munities that actually were working to create the more just, tolerant society that he envisioned.

The difference here is subtle but crucial. Rather than merely trying, as a rock star, to attract a sympathetic audience, Springsteen, who hitherto had been a master at maintaining distance between himself and the rest of the world, began immersing himself in these other communities and meeting them on *their* terms. He still did not consider himself an activist—a "concerned citizen" is how he has put it in interviews. And unlike Bono, he has always known and respected the difference, rarely getting into the political fray, his recent campaign appearances with Presidential candidate John Kerry and his vociferous opposition to President George W. Bush notwithstanding.

It will be interesting to see what the urgency that Springsteen expressed during the 2004 Presidential campaign holds for his future political involvement. For now, though, his concerts remain the most explicit manifestations of the community to which he aspires. Each of these marathon events—rock 'n' roll tent meetings of almost liturgical scope—afford the throngs who gather a sense of what Craig Werner described as "participation in a living community tied together by a shared vision of what it is and what it can be."[10] Indeed, Springsteen's revivals seek to take people higher by inciting them to pursue ways in which they might create a better world together.

"I can't promise you life everlasting, but I can promise you life right now," Springsteen proclaimed at the show that he and the E Street Band played in Nashville in 2000. Springsteen had lately begun employing the trappings of Pentecostal worship in his concerts, right down to the "preaching" and the talk of "rock 'n' roll baptism," all of it in the service of rallying the faithful and renewing "The Ties That Bind." From the opening performance, at their Nashville show, of the song of that name, to their second encore's interpolation of the gospel standard "This Train," Springsteen and the E Street Band gave unwavering voice to an encompassing, if idealized, vision of community. A vision akin to that of the glory-bound train of Woody Guthrie, Curtis Mayfield, and Sister Rosetta Tharpe in which there always is room for everyone to ride.

The community that Springsteen looked out upon that night in Nashville, as well as the one that typically greets him, did not resemble the racially integrated mix of socioeconomic groups that he hopes to see at his concerts. Nor was it evocative of the train to glory he often invokes. If anything, the aging white baby-boomers that he now witnesses in his audience have little in common with the hard-pressed men and women of *The River*; they share even less with those who haunt the soup kitchens and rescue missions that he steadfastly promotes from the stage. Having long since assumed the role of elder, though, Springsteen keeps testifying to his expansive vision, urging people to embrace it by getting involved in the communities where they live and making those communities their own, much as he has sought to do.

There is something prophetic, even redemptive, about Springsteen's testimony, a sense that no matter how far he and his faithful may yet have to venture, they eventually will get to that place where they really want to go. "You gotta stay hungry" is how he puts it in "Dancing in the Dark," an ode to restlessness that gives voice to that "searchin' thing" of which he once spoke, a striving for transcendence through community that he continues to affirm, even if he cannot see it and maybe never will. "You can't start a fire without a spark," he insists. "This gun's for hire / Even if we're just dancing in the dark."

Bruce Springsteen evinces this spark, this hunger for transcendence, as transparently as any musician to come along in the last three decades. Yet whether pop singers do so explicitly or not, a great many of them, like Springsteen, make records and give performances that articulate a yearning for something deeper and more abiding than the everyday. To assert as much, as I have throughout this book, is not to deny that the vast majority of pop music also is made to entertain us and make money. Nor is it to ignore that some music lacks redeeming social value or serves oppressive ends. To make such transcendental claims for pop music, however, is to recognize the extent to which much of it can take us higher and speak to the restlessness we all feel. It is to acknowledge that these things are a big part of what draws us to pop music, and of what keeps us coming back to it for insight and inspiration.

No matter how insidious religious fundamentalism might be in our world, ours nevertheless is, at least for now, an increasingly secular and global society. Ours is a world in which great numbers of people look to pop music—and to TV, movies, and pop culture in general—for guidance that conventional religious observance does not provide. This is not to impute religious value or power to the recordings of, say, Radiohead or OutKast; it is, however, to lay claim to pop music's ability to serve a portal for the transcendence we seek. Ultimately, it is to argue, as Van Morrison does in his wondrous 1982 single "Cleaning Windows," not just for a way of hearing or responding to music, but for a way of being in the world. A way of attending to the taken-for-granted or everyday in hopes of spying openings for the inbreaking of that which transcends it, that which, however fleetingly, might satisfy the hunger in our restless hearts.

# NOTES

## PROLOGUE: I WANT TO TAKE YOU HIGHER

1. The distinction that I'm making here is between rock and rock 'n' roll. The rock era did not arrive until the mid-to-late 60s, when psychedelic, progressive, and hard rock impulses increasingly divorced rock 'n' roll from the black idioms that shaped it—that is, from rhythms that made rock *roll*. The arrival of the "concept album," along with the privileging of the recordings of artists who wrote their own songs (as opposed to those who "merely" interpreted material from a revolving canon), hastened the end of the rock 'n' roll era as well.

2. Susan Sontag, "Notes on Camp," *Against Interpretation and Other Essays* (New York: Picador, 2001), p. 276.

## INTRODUCTION: CLEANING WINDOWS: OF RESTLESSNESS, RECORDS, AND TRANSCENDENCE

1. Stephen Kinzer, "Interest Surges in Voodoo, and Its Queen," *New York Times*, November 30, 2003.

2. *Buffy the Vampire Slayer: Fear and Trembling in Sunnydale*, ed. James B. South (Peru, IL: Open Court, 2003).

3. Brian Lewis, "Scholars Plan to Espouse Merits of *Buffy the Vampire Slayer*," *Tennessean*, May 25, 2004.

4. Quoted in Lewis, "Ministers Find Rap Fits Religion," *Tennessean*, March 6, 2004.

5. Augustine, *The Confessions of Saint Augustine*, translated by John K. Ryan (Garden City, NY: Image Books, 1960), p. 43.

6. From the first stanza of the poem "The Dark Night of the Soul," *The Collected Works of John of the Cross* (Washington, DC: ICS Publications, 1989), p. 113.

7. Quoted in Pat Blashill, "Tiny Dynamite," *Tracks*, February–March 2005, p. 60.

8. Quoted in the record company bio for *You Are the Quarry* (Sanctuary Records, 2004).

CHAPTER 1

1. Quoted in *The Norton Anthology of English Literature, Vol. 2*, M. H. Abrams, General Editor (New York: W.W. Norton & Company, 1979), p. 1956.

2. Lester Bangs, "Astral Weeks," *Stranded: Rock and Roll for a Desert Island*, ed. Greil Marcus (New York: Alfred A. Knopf, 1979), p. 181.

3. For further insight into the limitations of Western understandings of God as the objective referent of this fundamental human striving, see Henry Bugbee, *The Inward Morning: A Philosophical Exploration in Journal Form* (Athens, GA: University of Georgia Press, 1999), pp. 217–220.

4. Dave Marsh, *The New Rolling Stone Record Guide*, ed. Dave Marsh and John Swenson (New York: Random House/Rolling Stone Press, 1983), p. 346.

5. Greil Marcus, *Rolling Stone*, March 1, 1969.

6. Bangs, *Stranded*, p. 180.

7. All of the *Billboard* chart positions referenced in this book are taken from Joel Whitburn, *Top Pop Singles, 1955–1996* and *Top Pop Albums, 1955–1996* (Menomonee Falls, WI: Record Research Inc., 1997).

8. Marsh, *The New Rolling Stone Record Guide*, p. 345.

9. Ralph Ellison, "Richard Wright's Blues," *Shadow and Act* (New York: Vintage, 1995), pp. 78–79. For Albert Murray's take on this reading of the blues, see *Stomping the Blues* (New York: Vintage, 1976).

10. Robert Shelton, *No Direction Home: The Life and Music of Bob Dylan* (New York: Ballantine Books, 1986), p. 463.

11. M. Mark, "It's Too Late to Stop Now," *Stranded*, p. 26.

12. Marcus, *The Rolling Stone Illustrated History of Rock & Roll*, ed. Jim Miller (New York: Random House, 1980), p. 322.

13. Mark, *Stranded*, p. 21.

14. The phrase "behind the sun" regularly appears in blues recordings, which could be where Morrison first heard it, particularly given his early exposure to the music through his father's record collection. Used by blues singers, "behind the sun" connotes things unseen, things obscured by the sun that might somehow be glimpsed. The fact that the sun rises in the east, a direction that often is associated with mysticism, likely resonated with Morrison as well.

15. Robert Christgau, *Christgau's Record Guide: The '80s* (New York: Pantheon Books, 1990), p. 281.

16. From an interview that I did with Gilmore at his home outside Austin, Texas, in 2001.

17. Terri Sutton, *Spin Alternative Record Guide*, ed. Eric Weisbard with Craig Marks (New York: Vintage, 1995), p. 149.

18. Walpola Rahula, *What the Buddha Taught* (New York: Grove Press, 1974), p. 29.

19. From a telephone interview that I did with Ely in 2001.

20. Nicholas Dawidoff, *In the Country of Country: People and Places in American Music* (New York: Pantheon Books, 1997), p. 297.

21. Ellison, *Shadow and Act*, pp. 78–79.

22. From a telephone interview that I did with Gilmore in 2001.

23. Christgau, *Christgau's Consumer Guide: Albums of the '90s* (New York: St. Martin's Griffin, 2000), p. 248.

24. Posdnuos made this assertion in "Breakadawn," a track on De La Soul's *Buhloone Mind State* (Tommy Boy, 1993).

## CHAPTER 2

1. Quoted in Michael Eric Dyson, *Mercy, Mercy Me: The Art, Loves & Demons of Marvin Gaye* (New York: Basic Civitas Books, 2004), p. 108.

2. David Ritz, "Significant Sex," in the liner notes to Marvin Gaye, *Let's Get It On* (Motown Deluxe Edition, 2001).

3. Quoted in Ann Powers, "Houses of the Holy," *Village Voice*, June 1, 1993.

4. Teresa of Avila, *Interior Castle*, trans. and ed. by E. Allison Peers (Garden City, NY: Image Books, 1961).

5. Liner notes to the soundtrack to the movie *The Harder They Come* (Mango, 1972).

6. Liner Notes to Marvin Gaye, *Anthology* (Motown, 1974).

7. Dyson, *Mercy, Mercy Me*, p. 205.

8. Ibid., p. 120.

9. Ritz, liner notes to *Let's Get It On*.

10. Mikal Gilmore, *Night Beat: A Shadow History of Rock & Roll* (New York: Anchor Books, 1998), p. 357.

11. Dyson, *Mercy, Mercy Me*, p. 167.

12. Ritz, liner notes to *Let's Get It On*.

13. Dyson, *Mercy, Mercy Me*, pp. 106–107.

14. Quoted in Alex Stimmel, "Questions for Al Green," *New York Times Magazine*, November 23, 2003.

15. Christgau, *The Rolling Stone Illustrated History of Rock & Roll*, p. 363.

16. Christgau, *Albums of the '90s*, p. 122.

17. Steve Anderson, "Forgive Me, Father," *Village Voice*, April 4, 1989.

18. Vince Aletti, "Soda Pop," *Village Voice*, April 4, 1989.

19. bell hooks, "Madonna: Plantation Mistress or Soul Sister," *Rock She Wrote*, ed. Evelyn McDonnell and Ann Powers (New York: Delta, 1995), p. 321.

20. Barbara Victor, *Goddess* (New York: Cliff Street Books, 2001).

21. Barbara O'Dair, "Voodoo Child," *Rolling Stone*, March 9, 1995. Also see Evelyn McDonnell's terrific "Stones in My Passway: PJ Harvey Gets the Blues," *Option*, March–April 1995.

22. Ibid.

23. Powers, "Houses of the Holy."

24. Ibid.

25. Marsh, *The Heart of Rock & Soul: The 1001 Greatest Singles Ever Made* (New York: Plume, 1989), p. 200. Marsh's entry on Madonna's "Papa Don't Preach" states that both the Parents Music Resource Center and *Rolling Stone* referred to Madonna as "a porn queen in heat."

26. Susan McClary, *Feminine Endings: Music, Gender, and Sexuality* (Minneapolis: University of Minnesota Press, 1991), pp. 149–150.

27. Anderson, "Forgive Me, Father."

28. McClary, p. 150.

29. Aletti, "Soda Pop."

30. Isaac Bashevis Singer, "The Séance," *The Séance* (New York: Farrar, Straus & Giroux. 1968), pp. 5–6.

CHAPTER 3

1. Emmanuel Levinas, *Otherwise Than Being or Beyond Essence* (Boston: Kluwer Academic Publishers, 1974).

2. Quoted in Gilmore, *Night Beat*, p. 330.

3. Powers, *Trouble Girls: The Rolling Stone Book of Women in Rock*, ed. Barbara O'Dair (New York: Random House, 1997), p. 379.

4. Gilmore, *Night Beat*, p. 314.

5. Ibid., p. 316.

6. Powers, *Trouble Girls*, pp. 377–378.

7. O'Connor is unabashedly syncretistic. In addition to Rastafarianism, she embraces aspects of Buddhism and nature mysticism and was recently ordained as a priest in the Latin Tridentine Church, a dissenting branch of Catholicism.

8. O'Connor's retirement from recording appears to have been short-lived. As this book was going to press, reports were circulating that she was working on a reggae album in Jamaica.

9. From an interview that I did with Miller at the couple's Nashville home in July of 2001.

10. John Mogabgab, "Editor's Introduction," *Weavings*, September–October 1998, p. 3.

11. From an interview that I did with the Millers at their home in 1999.

12. From a telephone interview that I did with Earle in July of 1999.

13. From an interview that I did with the Millers at their home in 1999.

14. Quoted in Michael Hornburg, "Moby Saves," *Spin*, June 1995.

15. Christgau, *Albums of the '90s*, p. 207.

CHAPTER 4

1. Marcus, *Lipstick Traces: A Secret History of the Twentieth Century* (Cambridge, MA: Harvard University Press, 1989), p. 16 (italics mine).

2. Paul Tillich, *The Protestant Era*, trans. by James Luther Adams (Chicago: University of Chicago Press, 1966), p. ix.

3. David Sprague, *The Trouser Press Record Guide to '90s Rock*, ed. Ira A. Robbins (New York: Fireside, 1997), p. 514.

4. Reznor's confessional songwriting is unusual for industrial music, where lyrics generally express social, political, and other commentary. They typically reveal little in the way of personal detail about the people who are singing them.

5. Quoted in Eric Weisbard, "Sympathy for the Devil," *Spin*, February 1996. Some of the biographical information included in this discussion was drawn from Weisbard's interview with Reznor as well.

6. Ibid.

7. Levine used the term "fierce wisdom" to describe punk's anti-establishment ethic in an interview that aired on Wisconsin Public Radio's "To the Best of Our Knowledge." *Dharma Punx* traces Levine's passage, as a punk, through anger, aggression, and addiction to Buddhism. It was published by Harper San Francisco in 2004.

8. Charles Aaron, review of *Pre-Millennial Tension*, *Spin*, December, 1996.

9. Quoted in Lorraine Ali, "The Tricky Question," *Option*, September–October 1996.

10. Steven Grant, *The New Trouser Press Record Guide*, ed. Ira A. Robbins. (New York: Charles Scribner's Sons, 1985), p. 213.

11. Gilmore, *Night Beat*, p. 161.

12. Ibid., pp. 158–159.

13. Ibid., p. 159.

14. McDonnell, *Spin Alternative Record Guide*, p. 203.

15. Ibid., p. 204.


## CHAPTER 5

1. Heard another way, Iggy could be talking about submitting to the tyranny of heroin, the drug to which he became addicted.

2. Lester Bangs, "Of Pop and Pies and Fun," *Creem*, November–December 1970, reprinted in *Psychotic Reactions and Carburetor Dung*, ed. Greil Marcus (New York: Alfred A. Knopf, 1987), p. 32.

3. Quoted in Gilmore, *Night Beat*, p. 190.

4. Bangs, *Psychotic Reactions and Carburetor Dung*, p. 32.

5. Mark Coleman, *Rolling Stone Album Guide*, ed. Anthony DeCurtis and James Henke with Holly George-Warren (New York: Random House, 1992), p. 676.

6. Ibid.

7. Writing in the April 21, 2005, issue of *Rolling Stone*, Thurston Moore of Sonic Youth recalled what it was like seeing Iggy at the Stooges reunion show at Coachella in 2003. "[T]he first thing Iggy did was start jumping in the air, flipping the bird to the crowd—'Fuck you, fuck you and fuck you.' Then Iggy turned to the side of the stage, where the elite were standing—Sonic Youth, Queens of the Stone Age, the Red Hot Chili Peppers and the other all-access rock stars—and he gave us the jerk-off motion. It was great. After all this time, he's still at war."

8. Langford e-mailed these comments to me. Some version of this passage will appear in a forthcoming book of his art to be published by Verse Chorus Press.

9. Foremost among the books that chronicle punk and discuss its significance are Greil Marcus's aforementioned *Lipstick Traces* and Jon Savage's *England's Dreaming: Anarchy, Sex Pistols, Punk Rock, and Beyond* (New York: St. Martin's Griffin, 2002). For a more ethnographical account, see *Please Kill Me: The Uncensored Oral History of Punk*, ed. Legs McNeil and Gillian McCain (New York: Penguin Books, 1997).

10. Marsh, *The Heart of Rock & Soul*, p. 72.

11. Christgau, *Rock Albums of the '70s: A Critical Guide* (New York: Da Capo, 1981), p. 350.

12. Coleman, *Rolling Stone Record Guide*, p. 628.

13. Marsh, *The Heart of Rock & Soul*, p. 307.

14. Quoted in Gilmore, *Night Beat*, p. 154.

15. Ibid.

16. Christgau, "Uncontainable, Uncontrollable, Incomprehensible," in *City Pages*, 2000.

17. Sasha Frere-Jones, "Fifth Grade: Eminem's Growing Pains," *The New Yorker*, December 6, 2004.

18. Christgau, "What Eminem Means—and Doesn't," *Los Angeles Times*, 2001.

19. Frere-Jones, "Fifth Grade: Eminem's Growing Pains."


## CHAPTER 6

1. David Nathan, liner notes to *People Get Ready! The Curtis Mayfield Story* (Rhino, 1996).

2. For more about the prophetic disposition, see *The Prophets* (New York: Perennial Classics, 2001), Abraham J. Heschel's indispensable study of the phenomenon.

3. This constructive vision is one that naysayers, who are similarly oppositional, typically lack, even those who betray a social or political bent.

4. This phrase appears in the version of "We're a Winner" that appears on *Curtis/Live!* (Rhino, 2000).

5. Quoted in "The 500 Greatest Songs of All Time," *Rolling Stone*, December 9, 2004.

6. Ernest Hardy, in the liner notes to Curtis Mayfield, *Gospel* (Rhino, 1999).

7. Ibid.

8. Craig Werner, *A Change Is Gonna Come: Music, Race & the Soul of America* (New York: Plume, 1999).

9. Ibid., p. 149.

10. Christgau, *Rock Albums of the '70s*, p. 247.

11. Werner, *A Change Is Gonna Come*, p. 150.

12. I first heard these stories, which had been circulating for years, at Cash's funeral at First Baptist Church in Hendersonville, Tennessee. Versions of these stories also appear in Bill Miller, *Cash: An American Man* (New York: Pocket Books, 2004), pp. 45, 89.

13. From an interview that I did with Cash at the Carter Family Fold in Maces Spring, Virginia in 2002.

14. This version of "Man in Black" appears on *'Til Things Are Brighter* (Red Rhino, 1988), a various artists compilation produced by Jon Langford and Marc Almond.

15. Walt Whitman, "Song of Myself," *Leaves of Grass*, Inclusive Edition, ed. Emory Holloway (Garden City, NY: Doubleday, 1926), p. 76.

16. It certainly was no surprise when the *Murder* volume of Cash's tripartite retrospective *Love God Murder* attracted much more attention in print— and outsold—the titles in the series that spoke to the romantic and devotional sides of his persona.

17. From the interview that I did with Cash at the Carter Fold.

18. Powers, *Spin Alternative Record Guide*, p. 423.

19. Quoted in "The 500 Greatest Songs of All Time," *Rolling Stone*, December 9, 2004.

20. Ibid.

21. Marsh, "Facing Facts," *Harp*, January-February 2005.

22. Powers, *Spin Alternative Record Guide*, p. 423.

23. Ibid., p. 424.

## Chapter 7

1. Milo Miles, *Spin Alternative Record Guide*, p. 115.

2. Franti also demonstrates Marilynne Robinson's assertion, in her novel *Gilead* (New York: Farrar, Straus and Giroux, 2004), that "Prophets love the people they chastise." This quality distinguishes those who speak in a prophetic voice from those who otherwise resist unjust or inhuman powers.

3. Dorothee Soelle, *The Silent Cry: Mysticism and Resistance* (Minneapolis: Fortress Press, 2001), p. 4.

4. The wine, in this case, would have to be red, as opposed to white, given the Mekons' staunch communitarian leanings.

5. Quoted in Greg Kot, "Curse of the Mekons," *Chicago Tribune*, November 3, 1991.

6. Luc Sante, "The Headline Below Is a Lie: Leeds Icons Sell Out Garden; Get Out of This World Alive," *Village Voice*, September 14, 1999.

7. Weisbard, *Spin Alternative Record Guide*, p. 248.

8. Huw Bucknell, *Rock: The Rough Guide*, ed. Jonathan Buckley and Mark Ellingham (London: Penguin, 1996), p. 562–563.

9. This is much the same underside of history as that inhabited by Michael Franti's "people in tha middle," Curtis Mayfield's "people who are

darker than blue," and by those for whom Johnny Cash wore mourner's black.

10. Christgau, "Jesus, Jews, and the Jackass Theory," *Village Voice*, January 16, 1990.

11. Dyson, *Spin Alternative Record Guide*, p. 314.

12. Marshall Berman, "Bass in Your Face," *Village Voice*, October 22, 1991.

13. Joe Wood, "Self Deconstruction," *Village Voice*, April 24, 1990.

14. Berman, "Bass in Your Face."


CHAPTER 8

1. Some of the biographical information related here was drawn from Dave Marsh's entry on Sly & the Family Stone in *The Rolling Stone Illustrated History of Rock & Roll*, pp. 315–319, and from Greil Marcus's chapter on the band in *Mystery Train: Images of America in Rock 'n' Roll Music* (New York: E. P. Dutton, 1982), pp. 79–82.

2. Marsh, *The Heart of Rock & Soul*, p. 137.

3. Christgau, *Rock Albums of the '70s*, p. 359.

4. Marcus, *Stranded*, p. 292.

5. Werner, *A Change Is Gonna Come*, p. 105.

6. Powers, *Spin Alternative Record Guide*, p. 42.

7. Emily White, "Revolution Girl Style Now," *L.A. Weekly*, July 10, 1992, as reprinted in *Rock She Wrote*, p. 400.

8. Ibid., p. 397.

9. Ibid.

10. Ibid., p. 399.

11. McDonnell, *Trouble Girls*, p. 458.

12. White, p. 399.

13. Liner notes to the Chicago and New Haven Women's Liberation Rock Band with Le Tigre, *Papa, Don't Lay That Shit on Me* (Rounder, 2005).

14. Ibid.

15. One exception that comes to mind is Nancy Jeffries singing, "Let me be, don't put your trip on me / Hey, I'm a woman with a heart of my own / Understand, you're just another man / Everything you touch you don't have to own," in the Insect Trust's "Trip on Me" (*Hoboken Saturday Night*, 1970).

16. Valerie Saiving, "The Human Situation: A Feminine View," *Womanspirit Rising: A Feminist Reader in Religion*, ed. Carol P. Christ and Judith Plaskow (San Francisco: Harper & Row, 1979), pp. 25–42.

17. Neva Chovin, *The New Rolling Stone Album Guide*, ed. Nathan Brackett with Christian Hoard (New York: Fireside, 2004), p. 742. Chovin's feature on Sleater-Kinney, "Where the Girls Get Off," *Option*, September–October, 1996, also explores this notion.

18. From a telephone interview that I did with Brownstein in 1999.

19. *Time*, July 9, 2001.

20. From a telephone interview that I did with Dougher in 1999.

21. From the telephone interview that I did with Brownstein in 1999.

22. Powers, *Spin Alternative Record Guide*, p. 42.

23. Kot, *The New Rolling Stone Album Guide*, p. 72.

## EPILOGUE

1. Quoted in Kurt Loder, "The *Rolling Stone* Interview: Bruce Springsteen," *Rolling Stone*, December 6, 1984.

2. Quoted in Steve Pond, "*Tunnel* Vision," *Rolling Stone*, May 5, 1988.

3. Quoted in Nicholas Dawidoff, "The Pop Populist," *New York Times Magazine*, January 26, 1997.

4. Gilmore, *Night Beat*, p. 214.

5. Paul Nelson, "Let Us Now Praise Famous Men," *Rolling Stone*, December 11, 1980.

6. Christgau, *Christgau's Record Guide: The '80s*, p. 382.

7. Gilmore, p. 211.

8. Merle Ginsberg, "Bruce Springsteen Made in the U.S.A.: The Fans," *Rolling Stone*, October 10, 1985.

9. Werner, *A Change Is Gonna Come*, pp. 298–299.

10. Ibid., p. 331.

# BIBLIOGRAPHY

Aaron, Charles. "A Riot of the Mind." *Village Voice*, February 2, 1993.
———. "Pre-Millennial Tension." *Spin*, December 1996.
Abrams, M. H., General Editor. *The Norton Anthology of English Litera-
ture, Vol. 2*. New York: W. W. Norton & Company, 1979.
Agee, James, and Walker Evans. *Let Us Now Praise Famous Men*. Boston:
Houghton Mifflin, 1969.
Aletti, Vince. "Soda Pop." *Village Voice*, April 4, 1989.
Ali, Lorraine. "The Tricky Question." *Option*, September–October 1996.
Anderson, Steve. "Forgive Me, Father." *Village Voice*, April 4, 1989.
Arnold, Gina. "Love Taps." *Village Voice*, October 6, 1998.
Augustine. *The Confessions of Saint Augustine*, trans. John K. Ryan. Garden
City, NY: Image Books, 1960.
Bangs, Lester. "Astral Weeks." *Stranded: Rock and Roll for a Desert Island*,
ed. Greil Marcus. New York: Alfred A. Knopf, 1979.
———. "Of Pop and Pies and Fun." *Psychotic Reactions and Carburetor
Dung*, ed. Greil Marcus. New York: Alfred A. Knopf, 1987.
Berman, Marshall. "Bass in Your Face." *Village Voice*, October 22, 1991.
Blashill, Pat. "Tiny Dynamite." *Tracks*, February–March 2005.
Brackett, Nathan, ed. with Christian Hoard. *The New Rolling Stone Album
Guide*. New York: Fireside, 2004.
Buckley, Jonathan, ed., and Mark Ellingham. *Rock: The Rough Guide*. Lon-
don: Penguin, 1996.
Bugbee, Henry. *The Inward Morning: A Philosophical Exploration in Journal
Form*. Athens, GA: University of Georgia Press, 1999.
Camus, Albert. *The Plague*. New York: Vintage, 1972.
Chovin, Neva. "Where the Girls Get Off." *Option*, September–October,
1996.
Christgau, Robert. "Al Green." *The Rolling Stone Illustrated History of
Rock & Roll*, ed. Jim Miller. New York: Random House, 1980.
———. *Rock Albums of the '70s: A Critical Guide*. New York: Da Capo,
1981.

————. *Christgau's Record Guide: The '80s*. New York: Pantheon Books, 1990.

————. "Jesus, Jews, and the Jackass Theory." *Village Voice*, January 16, 1990.

————. "Curse of the Mekons." *Village Voice*, May 21, 1991.

————. "Staying Alive: Tricky, Moby, and M People." *Village Voice*, June 27, 1995.

————. "Dancing with Mistah D." *Village Voice*, April 28, 1998.

————. "Thwocks and Whispers: Tricky." *Village Voice*, June 9, 1998.

————. *Christgau's Consumer Guide: Albums of the '90s*. New York: St. Martin's Griffin, 2000.

————. "Uncontainable, Uncontrollable, Incomprehensible." *City Pages*, 2000.

————. "What Eminem Means—and Doesn't." *Los Angeles Times*, 2001.

Cone, James, H. *The Spirituals and the Blues*. New York: Seabury Press, 1972.

————. *God of the Oppressed*. New York: Seabury Press, 1975.

Daly, Mary. *Beyond God the Father: Toward a Philosophy of Women's Liberation*. Boston: Beacon Press, 1973.

Dawidoff, Nicholas. "The Pop Populist." *New York Times Magazine*, January 26, 1997.

————. *In the Country of Country: People and Places in American Music*. New York: Pantheon Books, 1997.

DeCurtis, Anthony, and James Henke with Holly George-Warren. *Rolling Stone Album Guide*. New York: Random House, 1992.

Dyson, Michael Eric. *Mercy, Mercy Me: The Art, Loves & Demons of Marvin Gaye*. New York: Basic Civitas Books, 2004.

Ellison, Ralph. "Richard Wright's Blues." *Shadow and Act*. New York: Vintage, 1995.

Farley, Edward. *Good and Evil: Interpreting a Human Condition*. Minneapolis: Fortress Press, 1991.

————. *Divine Empathy: A Theology of God*. Minneapolis: Fortress Press, 1996.

Frere-Jones, Sasha. "Fifth Grade: Eminem's Growing Pains." *The New Yorker*, December 6, 2004.

Fricke, David. "U2 Drops Bomb." *Rolling Stone*, December 30, 2004.

Friere, Paulo. *Pedagogy of the Oppressed*, trans. Myra Bergman Ramos. New York: Seabury Press, 1973.

Friskics-Warren, Bill. "Raw Power: Sleater-Kinney." *Nashville Scene*, July 2, 1997.

————. "The Sound of Fury: Tricky." *Nashville Scene*, June 29, 1998.

———. "Country's Grave Condition: Jon Langford Came to Nashville to Bury Country Music, Not to Praise It," *Washington Post*, August 30, 1998.

———. "Making a Scene: Olympia Bands Balance Ideals, Music with Powerful Results." *Nashville Scene*, March 8, 1999.

———. "Hearts on Fire: Buddy and Julie Miller." *No Depression*, 1999.

———. "Defying Gravity: Jimmie Dale Gilmore Stretches His Horizons from the Flat of the Land to the Curve of the Earth." *No Depression*, March–April 2000.

———. "Hungry Heart: Bruce Springsteen's Nashville Concert a Near Religious Experience." *Nashville Scene*, April 24, 2000.

———. "Viva! La Woman." *Nashville Scene*, October 25, 2001.

———. "Spirit in the Dark: Pathos and Resistance in the Year of the Unthinkable." *Nashville Scene*, December 20, 2001.

———. "Voices of Reason: Dolly Parton and Chuck D Ask Hard Questions About God and Country." *Nashville Scene*, July 18, 2002.

———. "Living with Fear: The Mekons." *Nashville Scene*, March 28, 2002.

———. "The Man in Black and White and Every Shade in Between: Johnny Cash." *No Depression*, November–December 2002.

———. "Johnny Cash, 1932-2003: The Man in Black and Other Colors." *Nashville Scene*, September 18, 2003.

———. "God Is My Co-Pilot." *Village Voice*, December 10, 2003.

Gilmore, Mikal. *Night Beat: A Shadow History of Rock & Roll*. New York: Anchor Books, 1998.

Ginsberg, Merle. "Bruce Springsteen Made in the U.S.A.: The Fans." *Rolling Stone*, October 10, 1985.

Gutierrez, Gustavo. *A Theology of Liberation: History Politics and Salvation*, trans. and ed. Sister Caridad Inda and John Eagleson. Maryknoll, NY: Orbis Books, 1973.

Hampton, Howard. "Not of This Earth." *Village Voice*, July 12, 1988.

Hardy, Ernest. Liner notes to Curtis Mayfield, *Gospel* (Rhino, 1999).

Heschel, Abraham J. *The Prophets*. New York: Perennial Classics, 2001.

hooks, bell. "Madonna: Plantation Mistress or Soul Sister." *Rock She Wrote*, ed. Evelyn McDonnell and Ann Powers. New York: Delta, 1995.

Hornburg, Michael. "Moby Saves." *Spin*, June 1995.

John of the Cross. *The Collected Works of John of the Cross*. Washington, DC: ICS Publications, 1989.

Kot, Greg. "Curse of the Mekons." *Chicago Tribune*, November 3, 1991.

Levinas, Emmanuel. *Totality and Infinity: An Essay on Exteriority*. Pittsburgh: Duquesne University Press, 1969.

———. *Otherwise Than Being: Or Beyond Essence*. Pittsburgh: Duquesne University Press, 1998.

Levine, Noah. *Dharma Punx*. San Francisco: Harper, 2004.

Lewis, Brian. "Ministers Find Rap Fits Religion." *Tennessean*, March 6, 2004.

———. "Scholars Plan to Espouse Merits of *Buffy the Vampire Slayer*." *Tennessean*, May 25, 2004.

Kinzer, Stephen. "Interest Surges in Voodoo, and Its Queen." *New York Times*, November 30, 2003.

Loder, Kurt. "The *Rolling Stone* Interview: Bruce Springsteen." *Rolling Stone*, December 6, 1984.

Marcus, Greil, ed. *Stranded: Rock and Roll for a Desert Island*. New York: Alfred A Knopf, 1979.

———. *Mystery Train: Images of America in Rock 'n' Roll Music*. New York: E. P. Dutton, 1982.

———. *Lipstick Traces: A Secret History of the Twentieth Century*. Cambridge, MA: Harvard University Press, 1989.

———. *Ranters and Crowd Pleasers*. New York: Doubleday, 1993.

———. "Raising the Stakes in Punk Rock: Sleater-Kinney." *New York Times*, June 18, 2000.

Mark, M. "It's Too Late to Stop Now," *Stranded: Rock and Roll for a Desert Island*, ed. Greil Marcus. New York: Alfred A. Knopf, 1979.

Marsh, Dave. "Sly & the Family Stone." *The Rolling Stone Illustrated History of Rock & Roll*, ed. Jim Miller. New York: Random House, 1980.

———. *The New Rolling Stone Record Guide*, ed. Dave Marsh and John Swenson. New York: Random House/Rolling Stone Press, 1983.

———. *Glory Days: Bruce Springsteen in the 1980s*. New York: Pantheon, 1987.

———. *The Heart of Rock & Soul: The 1001 Greatest Singles Ever Made*. New York: Plume, 1989.

———. *Born to Run: The Bruce Springsteen Story, Volume 1*. New York: Thunder's Mouth, 1996.

———. "Facing Facts." *Harp*, January–February 2005.

McClary, Susan. *Feminine Endings: Music, Gender, and Sexuality*. Minneapolis: University of Minnesota Press, 1991.

McDonnell, Evelyn. "Stones in My Passway: PJ Harvey Gets the Blues." *Option*, March–April 1995.

McNeil, Legs, ed., and Gillian McCain. *Please Kill Me: The Uncensored Oral History of Punk*. New York: Penguin Books, 1997.

Miller, Bill. *Cash: An American Man*. New York: Pocket Books, 2004.

Mogabgab, John. *Weavings*, September–October 1998.

Murray, Albert. *Stomping the Blues*. New York: Vintage, 1976.

Nathan, David. Liner notes to *People Get Ready! The Curtis Mayfield Story* (Rhino, 1996).

Nelson, Paul. "Let Us Now Praise Famous Men." *Rolling Stone*, December 11, 1980.

O'Dair, Barbara. "Voodoo Child," *Rolling Stone*, March 9, 1995.

Pareles, Jon. "The Catharsis in the Cathedral." *New York Times*, November 14, 2004.

Percy, Will. "Rock and Read: Will Percy Interviews Bruce Springsteen." *DoubleTake*, Spring 1998.

Pond, Steve. "*Tunnel* Vision." *Rolling Stone*, May 5, 1988.

Powers, Ann. "Houses of the Holy." *Village Voice*, June 1, 1993.

———. "Sinéad O'Connor." *Trouble Girls: The Rolling Stone Book of Women in Rock*, ed. Barbara O'Dair. New York: Random House, 1997.

Rahula, Walpola. *What the Buddha Taught*. New York: Grove Press, 1974.

Ritz, David. "Significant Sex." Liner notes to Marvin Gaye, *Let's Get It On* (Motown Deluxe Edition, 2001).

Robbins, Ira A., ed. *The New Trouser Press Record Guide*. New York: Charles Scribner's Sons, 1985.

Robinson, Marilynne. *Gilead*. New York: Farrar, Straus & Giroux, 2004.

Rolheiser, Ronald. *The Holy Longing*. New York: Doubleday, 1999.

Ruether, Rosemary Radford. *Sexism and God-Talk: Toward a Feminist Theology*. Boston: Beacon Press, 1983.

Saiving, Valerie. "The Human Situation: A Feminine View." *Womanspirit Rising: A Feminist Reader in Religion*, ed. Carol P. Christ and Judith Plaskow. San Francisco: Harper & Row, 1979.

Sante, Luc. "The Headline Below Is a Lie: Leeds Icons Sell Out Garden; Get Out of This World Alive." *Village Voice*, September 14, 1999.

Savage, Jon. *England's Dreaming: Anarchy, Sex Pistols, Punk Rock, and Beyond*. New York: St. Martin's Griffin, 2002.

Shelton, Robert. *No Direction Home: The Life and Music of Bob Dylan*. New York: Ballantine Books, 1986.

Singer, Isaac Bashevis. "The Séance." *The Séance*. New York: Farrar, Straus & Giroux. 1968.

Smith, Huston. *The Religions of Man*. New York: Perennial Library, 1965.

Soelle, Dorothee. *The Silent Cry: Mysticism and Resistance*. Minneapolis: Fortress Press, 2001.

Sontag, Susan. "Notes on Camp." *Against Interpretation and Other Essays*. New York: Picador, 2001.

South, James B., ed. *Buffy the Vampire Slayer: Fear and Trembling in Sunnydale*. Peru, IL: Open Court, 2003.

Stimmel, Alex. "Questions for Al Green." *New York Times Magazine*, November 23, 2003.

Teresa of Avila. *Interior Castle*, trans. and ed. E. Allison Peers. Garden City, NY: Image Books, 1961.

Tillich, Paul. *The Protestant Era*, trans. James Luther Adams. Chicago: University of Chicago Press, 1966.

———. *Theology of Culture*, ed. Robert C. Kimball. Oxford: Oxford University Press, 1980.

Tribble, Phyllis. *God and the Rhetoric of Sexuality*. Philadelphia: Fortress Press, 1978.

Victor, Barbara. *Goddess*. New York: Cliff Street Books, 2001.

Weisbard, Eric, ed. with Craig Marks. *Spin Alternative Record Guide*. New York: Vintage, 1995.

———. "Sympathy for the Devil." *Spin*, February 1996.

Werner, Craig. *A Change Is Gonna Come: Music, Race & the Soul of America*. New York: Plume, 1999.

———. *Higher Ground: Stevie Wonder, Aretha, Curtis Mayfield, and the Rise and Fall of American Soul*. New York: Crown Publishers, 2004.

Whitburn, Joel. *Top Pop Singles, 1955–1996*. Menomonee Falls, WI: Record Research Inc., 1997.

———. *Top Pop Albums, 1955–1996*. Menomonee Falls, WI: Record Research Inc., 1997.

White, Emily. "Revolution Girl Style Now," *Rock She Wrote: Women Write About Rock, Pop, and Rap*, ed. McDonnell and Powers. New York: Delta, 1995.

Whitman, Walt. "Song of Myself." *Leaves of Grass*, Inclusive Edition, ed. Emory Holloway. Garden City, NY: Doubleday, 1926.

Wilmore, Gayraud S. *Black Religion and Black Radicalism: An Interpretation of the Religious History of Afro-American People*. Maryknoll, NY: Orbis Books, 1983.

Wood, Joe. "Self Deconstruction." *Village Voice*, April 24, 1990.

# SELECTED DISCOGRAPHY

The following digest is intended to serve as an evocative, epigrammatic guide to those items that form the backbone of the discussions in the book. In some cases additional titles have been listed to round out a portrait of a particular artist or to account for relevant records that they released after the manuscript was completed. Titles in this last category are noted with asterisks.

## Chapter 1

### VAN MORRISON

*The Story of Them Featuring Van Morrison* (PolyGram, 1998). The angry, early roar of Morrison's pent-up lion. As complete a document of his Belfast garage band's fusion of blues, soul, and rock 'n' roll as we are likely to get.

*Blowin' Your Mind* (Bang, 1967). Morrison's solo debut—flawed but fevered testimony to his vision and reach, from the ebullient groove of "Brown Eyed Girl" to the relentless obsessiveness of "T. B. Sheets."

*Astral Weeks* (Warner Bros., 1968). The blues in a new key, and Morrison's first masterpiece—impressionistic, introspective, singularly intense. "You breathe in, you breathe out, you breathe in, you breathe out . . . and you're high."

*Moondance* (Warner Bros., 1970). Further into the mystic, minus the weight of the world. The first outpouring of Morrison's transporting jelly-roll soul, and his second masterstroke.

*Van the Man* (Bootleg, 1971). An apocryphal wonder, the remakes of "Friday's Child" (a holdover from Them) and "Just Like a Woman" ("somebody else's tune") here are riveting. The sixteen serpentine, mostly wordless minutes of "Caledonia Soul Music," though, are transcendent.

*St. Dominic's Preview* (Warner Bros., 1972). The return of the lion, his heart on fire and aching for the motherland.

*It's Too Late to Stop Now* (Warner Bros., 1974). Morrison and his Caledonia Soul Orchestra onstage, reanimating classic blues and soul music and making a case for some of their own. Probably the best double live album of its era.

*Veedon Fleece* (Warner Bros., 1974). The lion back home in Ireland, reinventing the blues (again) by way of William Blake and "The Eternals." Twilit chamber pop as earthy and eerie as the lonesome moans of Skip James and Tommy Johnson.

*Into the Music* (Warner Bros., 1979). A glorious convergence of sexual and spiritual healing. "You know what they're talking about."

*Beautiful Vision* (Warner Bros., 1982). A mostly incandescent return to form after a period of transition. Includes "Cleaning Windows" and "Dweller on the Threshold," sublime statements of vocational and devotional intent.

*The Best of Van Morrison; The Best of Van Morrison, Vol. 2* (Polydor, 1990; 1993). Not exactly arguments for arrested artistic development (at least a handful of his later albums are terrific), but certainly the best, most expedient ways to absorb Morrison's later epiphanies.

## JIMMIE DALE GILMORE

*More a Legend Than a Band* (Rounder, 1992). Twenty years old when it finally received a proper release in the U.S., the Flatlanders' only studio album of the twentieth century is West Texas mystagogy par excellence. The Sons of the Pioneers for the Aquarian Age.

*"After Awhile"* (Elektra/Nonesuch, 1991). Gilmore's third solo album and the first on which his mix of mysticism and magical realism predominates.

*Spinning Around the Sun* (Elektra, 1993). Even better than *"After Awhile,"* this follow-up employs cavernous arrangements and a voluptuous pop romanticism to flesh out Gilmore's cosmic consciousness. Includes "Another Colorado" and the most numinous version of "Just a Wave" on record.

## P.M. DAWN

*Of the Heart, Of the Soul and Of the Cross: The Utopian Experience* (Gee Street, 1991). Far more burdened with care than its utopian subtitle lets on, this bumping, pop-wise meditation on appearance and reality never collapses the tension between the two. Exquisite.

*The Bliss Album . . . ? (Vibrations of Love and Anger and the Ponderance of Life and Existence)* (Gee Street, 1993). Far less ponderous than its subtitle lets on, this follow-up is as grounded as it is gorgeous, at once funky and transcendent.

*Jesus Wept* (Gee Street, 1995). Not as luminous as its predecessors, but not to be missed, if only for "Fantasia's Confidential Ghetto," a wildly reimagined medley of Prince's "1999," Talking Heads' "Once in a Lifetime," and Nilsson's "Coconut" that culminates in something akin to Eucharistic celebration.

## Chapter 2

## MARVIN GAYE

Compilations of Gaye's early hits for Motown abound. The best are probably the four-disc *The Master 1961–1984* (Motown, 1995), which covers his entire career and includes 1970s gems like "Trouble Man" and "You're the Man," and the two-disc *Very Best of Marvin Gaye* (Universal, 2001), a more economical set that accomplishes much the same thing. All of Gaye's early singles, from "Ain't That Peculiar" to "How Sweet It Is (To Be Loved By You)" to "I Heard It through the Grapevine," are essential, however you come by them. That goes double for his enthralling duets with Tammi Terrell, all of which can be heard on *The Complete Duets* (Universal, 2001).

*What's Going On* (Tamla, 1971). Most people cite this as Gaye's triumph in long-form—and for prophetic vision, it's plenty worthy—but I'd give the nod to *Let's Get It On* (Tamla, 1973), the presumed throwaway from which, "Keep Gettin' It On," synthesizes Gaye's sensual and social consciousness like nothing else in his catalog. Universal released deluxe editions of both albums, but apart from the essays and notes, they don't really improve on the originals.

*Live at the Palladium* (1977; Motown, 1998). A shimmering concert document, galvanized by "Got to Give It Up," twelve minutes of disco heaven.

*Here, My Dear* (Tamla, 1978). A sexy record inspired by Gaye's divorce from Anna Gordy marred only by his bizarre, petty digs at his ex.

*In Our Lifetime* (Tamla, 1981; out of print). A criminally unsung monument to Gaye's struggle to reconcile sex and salvation. Contains some of his deepest, most effortless grooves.

*Midnight Love* (Columbia, 1982). A more overt, and funk-rich adjudication of Gaye's conflicting impulses, at least until you read his liner notes.

## AL GREEN

There are any number of collections of the unassailable recordings that Green made with Willie Mitchell at Hi, with maybe the 43-track *The Hi Singles: A's and B's* (Hi UK, 2000) being the most encompassing. For sheer impact, though, start with 1975's *Greatest Hits* (1975; Motown, 1982), as beguiling and flawless an album as any ever released. The less predictable *Greatest Hits, Vol. 2*, which Motown reissued in 1983, isn't far behind.

*Call Me* (1973; Capitol 2004). Green's greatest LP with Mitchell, a fusion of gospel, soul, and country music that, from "Jesus Is Waiting" to "Funny How Time Slips Away," is as visionary and thrilling as pop music gets.

*The Belle Album* (1977; Motown 1983). Probably my favorite album of all time, a by turns burning and sublime wedding of disco, funk, gospel, and country blues produced by Green and galvanized by his stinging acoustic guitar playing. "It's you I want but Him that I need," Green explains to his lover in the title track, before proceeding to demonstrate, again and again, that the two aren't mutually exclusive. Anything but.

*Higher Plane* (Myrrh, 1981) and the slightly less miraculous *I'll Rise Again* (Myrrh, 1983) are Green's best gospel albums, some highlights of which now can be found on *One in a Million* (Word/Epic, 1991). His pop audience had forsaken him, but he continued to take those with ears to hear to the river.

*I Can't Stop* (Blue Note, 2003). Green's recent reunion with Willie Mitchell was heralded as a secular return to form, but from the title track to "My Problem Is You," there's no soul-body dualism here; just the sanctified eroticism that Green worked out a quarter-century earlier in "Belle." A second collaboration with Mitchell, *Everything's OK* (Blue Note, 2004), offers more of the same.

## PJ HARVEY

*Dry* (Indigo, 1992). This roughed-up, blues-inspired debut sounds less audacious today than it did when it first came out. Not to be missed, though, are the singles "Dress" and "Sheela-Na-Gig," one brooding, the other molten, both kicking against the pricks and laying the foundation for the wonders to come.

*Rid of Me* (Indigo, 1993). Outsized and ominous, this is Harvey reimagining the blues by way of a lacerating, rapture-inducing eroticism worthy of the shape-shifting, female mystics of the Middle Ages.

*To Bring You My Love* (Island, 1995). The majesty of the blues, replete with feral shrieks, groaning guitars, pregnant electro-pulses, and neo-Gothic saviors/seducers. Totally over the top, and enchantingly so.

*Is This Desire?* (Island, 1998) and *Stories from the City, Stories from the Sea* (Island, 2000), in which Harvey stares down the mystery that inflames her work ("Is this desire enough . . . to lift us higher, to lift above?") and then exults in it ("I can't believe life's so complex / When I just wanna sit here and watch you undress").

## MADONNA

*The Immaculate Collection* (Sire/Warner Bros., 1990). Madonna made some good-to-great albums, *True Blue* and *Like a Prayer* among them, before releasing this bravura, 17-track collection of hits. From "Like a Virgin" and "Like a Prayer" to "Into the Groove" and "Live to Tell," virtually every epiphany from the first phase of her career is here. Hearing is believing.

*Erotica* (Maverick/Sire, 1992). A gripping and largely unsung, if at times oddly glacial, reflection on the fleshly side of transcendence.

*Bedtime Stories* (Maverick/Sire, 1994). Evidence of Madonna's increasingly mystical take on sex, with deeper, warmer grooves than ever before.

*Ray of Light* (Maverick/Warner Bros., 1998). Searching and, on the surface, ethereal, this is Madonna's most sustained and transporting take on illumination and eroticism yet. The material girl as spiritual girl, as Vince Aletti once put it.

## Chapter 3

### SINÉAD O'CONNOR

*The Lion & the Cobra* (Chrysalis, 1987). O'Connor's auspicious, mostly realized debut has the astonishing method acting and vocal pyrotechnics of "Jackie" and "Troy," plus the steamy "I Want Your (Hands on Me)."

*I Do Not Want What I Haven't Got* (Chrysalis, 1990). Gauzy and subdued, yet somehow more intense than *The Lion & the Cobra*, this contains the torrents of empathy, "Three Babies" and "Black Boys on Mopeds." Also includes the ravaged Afro-Celtic soul of "I Am Stretched on Your Grave" and the epic hurt of "Nothing Compares 2 U," among other splendors.

*So Far . . . The Best of Sinéad O'Connor* (Chrysalis/EMI, 1997). A marvelously assembled retrospective, and certainly the best way to survey O'Connor's first decade of work, even if it doesn't include her majestic cover of Nirvana's "All Apologies."

*Faith and Courage* (Atlantic, 2000). An inspiring, reggae-suffused testament in which O'Connor achieves a measure of peace vis-à-vis her conflicted Irish upbringing and tumultuous years in the limelight.

*She Who Dwells . . .* (Vanguard, 2003). A sprawling double CD (one disc live, the other consisting of new studio recordings) replete with recontextualized reggae and Southern soul, plus "Brigidine Diana," a paean to the late Princess of Wales that doubles as O'Connor's most overt statement of empathetic purpose yet.

## BUDDY & JULIE MILLER

Buddy Miller, *Your Love & Other Lies* (HighTone, 1995). Miller's signal debut includes soul-deep covers of the Louvin Brothers and Tom T. Hall and soul-on-ice collaborations with Dan Penn, but nothing here can touch "My Love Will Follow You," a divine profession of faith and steadfastness.

Julie Miller, *Blue Pony* (HighTone, 1997). Roots rock for true believers, faith notwithstanding; this was the first album that Miller made outside the contemporary Christian fold. Includes a series of outpourings for wounded souls, a prodigal's plea for reconciliation (the staggering "Take Me Back," sung as a duet with her husband), and a spine-tingling version of John Sebastian and Lowell George's "Face of Appalachia."

Julie Miller, *Broken Things* (HighTone, 1999). An urgent, heartrending cycle of laments and prayers for healing, including the definitive title track.

*Buddy & Julie Miller* (HighTone, 2001). Despite collaborating extensively on their "solo" records, this is the only album that the Millers have released under both their names apart from the 2004 compilation, *Love Snuck Up*. The album is captivating throughout, but not to be missed is the closing triptych consisting of "That's Just How She Cries," "Rachel," and "Holding Up the Sky."

Buddy Miller, *Universal United House of Prayer* (New West, 2004). Non-sectarian gospel music for a world gone horribly wrong. Steeped in the outrage and wisdom of the Hebrew prophets, Miller's 9-minute update of Dylan's "With God on Our Side" should have earned a nomination for the Nobel Peace Prize.

## MOBY

*Move* (Elektra, 1993). Moby's early dance singles and remixes are collected on four overlapping/samey compilations released on the Instinct label, but as thrilling and richly textured as large portions of those sets are, this half-hour-long EP is more indicative of his vision and reach. It's also more narrative, even liturgical, in scope, ranging from diva anthems and electronic propulsion to thrashing hardcore and celestial ambience.

*Everything Is Wrong* (Elektra, 1995). Moby's first proper album witnesses gloriously to the symphonic possibilities of electronic music. The hunger for spiritual communion—with God, certainly, but also with other people and the rest of nature—in tracks like "All That I Need Is to Be Loved," "Every Time You Touch Me," and "God Moving Over the Face of the Waters" is palpable.

*Play* (V2, 1999). Employing loops of old blues and gospel performances, Moby traverses vast historical and cultural expanses to create an urgent meditation on suffering and redemption. The grooves are deep and the sweep symphonic, all of it in service of empathy and catharsis.

*18* (V2, 2002). A more conventional ambient pop record than *Play*, there's lots of heart and soul here, from the shimmering "We Are All Made of Stars" to "Sunday (The Day Before My Birthday")," an elegy for the innocence of September 10, 2001. (Moby's birthday is September 11.)

## Chapter 4

### NINE INCH NAILS

*Pretty Hate Machine* (TVT, 1989). Dance-oriented rock that scarcely hinted at the pummeling, abrading, postindustrial noise to come. Yet from "Sin" to "Terrible Lie" (the latter hooked by the admission, "I really don't know who I am . . . in this world of piss"), the antipathy was already there, and then some.

*Broken* (Halo Five, 1992). Pure torture; relentless sadomasochistic screeching.

*The Downward Spiral* (Nothing/TVT/Interscope, 1994). Seemingly anti-everything, a bracing evocation of oblivion that betrays too much humor ("Big Man with a Gun") and heart ("Hurt") to make a credible case for the self-annihilation depicted in the title track.

*The Fragile* (Nothing/Interscope, 1999). Oblivion as a way out and as a way back in—a way of dying to the world in order to survive it, and with the music that at times borders on the sublime.

**[With Teeth]* (Nothing/Interscope, 2005). More streamlined and subdued than previous NIN records, even ambient in spots, with Reznor, now 40, more pensive than angst-ridden.

### TRICKY

"Karmacoma," from Massive Attack, *Protection* (Virgin, 1994). Wickedly artful wordplay set to murky dub and Middle Eastern accents that presaged the paranoia and entropy to come.

*Maxinquaye* (Island, 1995). Dissipated and dyspeptic, but also tactile and seductive, this mesmerizing album of beatdown hip-hop blues is a testimony to dignity and resilience in a world that offers little comfort or escape.

*Pre-Millennium Tension* (Island, 1996). Tricky's first dissertation on celebrity and its discontents. Harder and colder than *Maxinquaye*, and less expansive thematically, but still gripping.

*Angels with Dirty Faces* (Island, 1998). In which Tricky propounds his philosophy of alienation and uplift for besmirched, beleaguered angels everywhere. Noisier and more industrial than its predecessors.

"Divine Comedy" (Durban Poison, 1998). Tricky's reworking of "Money Greedy," by way of Public Enemy's "You're Gonna Get Yours" after hearing an executive at his record label assert that all black people working in the music business were felons. Excoriating.

*Blowback* (Hollywood, 2001). Featuring vocals by the likes of Cyndi Lauper and Alanis Morissette, a celebrity record by the ultimate anti-celebrity. Durable, hooky funk-rock spiked with dancehall rhythms.

*Vulnerable* (Sanctuary, 2003). Tricky with a new ingénue, still hungry and wanting more.

## JOY DIVISION

*Unknown Pleasures* (1979; Qwest 1989). Charts a spiritual and emotional wilderness rendered all the more desolate by Martin Hannett's glacial production. The feelings of estrangement here border on the absolute.

*Closer* (1980; Qwest, 1989). Even more forbidding—and claustrophobic—than its predecessor. Singer Ian Curtis seems to be contemplating a life sentence in a moral and spiritual gulag.

*Heart and Soul* (Rhino, 1998). This compendium includes the band's only two studio albums, plus the transporting singles "Transmission" and "Love Will Tear Us Apart."

## NEW ORDER

*Substance* (Qwest, 1987). The faithful likely would recommend starting with the EP *1981–1982*, which includes "Temptation," and "Blue Monday," but this sprawling batch of remixes, which contains versions of both those touchstones, is electro-disco in excelsis—a nonstop, manic pop thrill. The quintessential testament to a quintessential singles band.

*Power, Corruption & Lies* (1983; Qwest, 1992). New Order's first proper album, entrancing and resplendent. (The reissue contains both sides of the original version of "Blue Monday.")

*Brotherhood* (Qwest, 1986). A rock move redolent of a post-disco Velvet Underground. With hooks galore ("Bizarre Love Triangle") and—gasp!—flashes of humor ("Every Little Counts").

## Chapter 5

## IGGY & THE STOOGES

*The Stooges* (Elektra, 1969). Sullen, bored, and staving off self-loathing, Iggy & the Stooges embody their idiot-violator ethic with an abundance of heart, smarts, and fuzz-toned insolence. They wanna be your dog.

*Fun House* (Elektra, 1970). Iggy raves about being treated like dirt (and loving it) and the Stooges, plus ringer Steve Mackay on sax, assail preconceived notions of rhythm, tone, and texture—of rock 'n' roll, for that matter—with a proto-skronk that owes as much to jazz avant-gardists as to anyone else. A watershed, in every respect.

*Raw Power* (Columbia, 1973). Iggy as "a streetwalking cheetah with a heart full of napalm" with new guitarist James Williamson carpet-bombing everything in sight.

## IGGY POP

*The Idiot* (1977; RCA/Virgin, 1990). A clean and sober Iggy crooning like a droll hedonist and survivor.

*Lust for Life* (1977; RCA/Virgin, 1990). More of the same, plus the truth-in-advertising of the title track.

*A Million in Prizes: The Iggy Pop Anthology* (Virgin/EMI, 2005). Thirty-eight tracks spread over two discs, the first of which ranges from "1969" to *Lust for Life*, the second offering much of the best of what followed.

## SEX PISTOLS

*Never Mind the Bollocks, Here's the Sex Pistols* (Warner Bros., 1977). Anarchic and apocalyptic, the end of the world as they knew it, and the welfare of their souls, if not that of modern liberal society, depended on it.

## PUBLIC IMAGE LIMITED

*Second Edition* (Island, 1980). Visceral, fathomless, and hypnotic, as thorough a negation/subversion of what came before it as *Never Mind the Bollocks*.

*Plastic Box* (Virgin, 1999). At four discs, way too much from a band that maybe made two discs worth of great music, but this has the signature theme "Public Image" from the group's first album, plus much of *Second Edition*, along with later anthems like "Rise" and "This Is Not a Love Song."

## EMINEM

*The Slim Shady LP* (Interscope, 1999). The arrival of Slim Shady—logorrheic, transgressive, comically brilliant. Dangerous, too, even if the album's only gangsta turn is Dr. Dre's bumping, hook-laden G-funk.

*The Marshall Mathers LP* (Interscope, 2000). Anger so pointed and intense it's scary, and it's meant to be. Artful, multivalent, and definitive—literally, with delineations between Slim Shady the construct, Eminem the artist, and Marshall Mathers the man.

"My Dad's Gone Crazy" from *The Eminem Show* (Interscope, 2002). More truth-telling, and from the lips of Eminem's daughter Hailie no less.

*Encore* (Interscope, 2004). A mixed bag of rock and rap with flashes of brilliance, notably "Yellow Brick Road," in which Eminem makes amends for his early racist slurs, and "Mosh," in which he takes aim at the Bush Administration's blood-for-oil diplomacy and offers an alternate take on the meaning of national security.

## Chapter 6

## CURTIS MAYFIELD

*People Get Ready: The Curtis Mayfield Story* (Rhino, 1996). A marvelous three-disc overview, this set includes a dozen of Mayfield's most crucial records with the Impressions, seventeen more from his early '70s solo peak, and the best of what came later. Great notes, too, including extensive comments from Mayfield himself. For more of the Impressions—and you need more than the twelve tracks collected here—there's *Curtis Mayfield and the Impressions: The Anthology, 1961–1977* (MCA, 1992).

*Curtis/Live!* (1971; Rhino, 2000). Three of these tracks are on *People Get Ready*, but for a snapshot of where Mayfield's head and heart were at the time, the between song "raps" are indispensable. Not to be missed as well are "We're a Winner" and "People Get Ready" recontextualized in a funk context.

*Superfly* (1972; Rhino, 1999). Mayfield's prophetic soundtrack to Gordon Parks Jr.'s blaxploitation movie serves as a vamping, sinewy "No!" to the false promise of transcendence held out by drugs, materialism, and violence. Epochal.

*Gospel* (Rhino, 1999). Thirteen spiritually transparent tracks spanning 20 years, from a handful that Mayfield made with the Impressions to 1980's lush, indispensable "Something to Believe In."

## JOHNNY CASH

*The Sun Years* (Rhino, 2002). Eighteen marvels of boom-chicka locomotion; from "Folsom Prison Blues" and "Cry, Cry, Cry" to "Big River" and "I Walk the Line," the cream of Cash's early output. *The Complete Sun Singles* (Varese Sarabande, 2002) has it all.

*The Fabulous Johnny Cash* (1959; Columbia/Legacy, 2002). Cash's debut for Columbia is as expansive musically as it is emotionally, from gospel and blues to paeans to heartbreak and home. An early snapshot of the Whitman-like multitudes he contained.

*At Folsom Prison* (1968; Columbia/Legacy, 1999). The Man in Black walking the talk in the belly of the beast. Flinty, class-conscious, and at the height of his powers, with the love of his life at his side. *At San Quentin* (1969; Columbia/Legacy, 2002), from the following year, includes the hit "A Boy Named Sue" and is nearly as great.

*At Madison Square Garden* (Columbia/Legacy 2002). A recently unearthed document from 1969 that covers more stylistic and thematic ground than either of Cash's classic prison albums, including some wry, subversive commentary about the war in Vietnam. A "dove with claws" indeed.

*The Essential Johnny Cash* (Columbia/Legacy, 2002). From Cash's sessions at Sun to his duets with June Carter and Bob Dylan to his 1994 cameo on U2's "The Wanderer," this chronologically sequenced, 36-track set is hard to beat. All of the big hits, minus Cash's subsequent "American Recordings" with producer Rick Rubin, are here. There are any number of ways to get a whole lot more Cash in a multi-disc set, none of which, despite their respective virtues, has yet to do justice to the immensity of his life and music. Maybe Columbia/Legacy's forthcoming *The Legend*, which includes DVD footage of Cash's pioneering TV show, will turn the tide.

*American Recordings; Unchained; American IV: The Man Comes Around* (American, 1994; 1996; 2002). Three of the four Rick Rubin-produced albums that Cash released during his lifetime, the first is the leanest, hardest, and had the most impact; the second, recorded with Tom Petty & the Heartbreakers, is the best; the fourth finds Cash in craggiest voice and contains the apocalyptic title track and his astounding cover of Nine Inch Nails' "Hurt" (although not the searing video).

U2

*War* (Island, 1983). The group's early attempt to throw their arms around the world, this is where U2's songwriting and bombast, as well as their faith and politics, finally converge and cohere. Includes the world-historical "Sunday Bloody Sunday," "New Year's Day," and "Two Hearts Beat as One."

*The Unforgettable Fire* (Island, 1984). Eno and Lanois lend U2's sonics greater intimacy and nuance as Bono filters Shelley by way of the civil rights movement. There is some transcendent music here, notably "Pride (In the Name of Love)," the exquisite "Bad," and the title track, but too much rock-god self-importance for comfort.

*The Best of 1980–1990* (Island, 1998). Redeems sublime tracks from albums mired in undue signifying and earnestness. The best way to hear "I Will Follow," "I Still Haven't Found What I'm Looking For," "Where the Streets Have No Name," and several others.

*Achtung Baby* (Island, 1991). Significance in retreat, or maybe just grounded. A new groove to be sure, and a sleek European sophistication to match. "Even Better Than the Real Thing" was as much a song title as a breakthrough to self-understanding for Bono.

*All That You Can't Leave Behind* (Island, 2000). Bono finding a melody that he can sing in his own company: transcendence through immanence.

*How to Dismantle an Atomic Bomb* (Island, 2004). U2 reckoning with every facet of their musical legacy while struggling with how to be post-Christians in a Good Friday world.

## Chapter 7

### MICHAEL FRANTI & SPEARHEAD

Disposable Heroes of Hiphoprisy, *Hypocrisy Is the Greatest Luxury* (4th & B'way, 1992). Noisy agit-prop anthems to resistance assailing everything from television and "Bush War I" to corporate welfare and bigotry in rap. Hard, and good.

Spearhead, *Home* (Capitol, 1994). Harder than many critics thought, this funky, humane manifesto for Franti's beloved "People in tha Middle" bears witness to how to stay human while "livin' life," as he puts it, "at the top of our lungs."

Spearhead, *Chocolate Supa Highway* (Capitol, 1997). More of the same, but where the beatdown grooves say more than the lyrics, which, while righteous, are a little pat.

Michael Franti & Spearhead, *Stay Human* (Boo Boo Wax/Six Degrees, 2001). A concept album about resisting death and the death penalty, with tunes and grooves to match.

Michael Franti & Spearhead, *Everyone Deserves Music* (Boo Boo Wax, 2003). "We can bomb the world to pieces, but we can't bomb it into peace." Franti records these lines two different ways, one subdued and funky, the other incensed and reggaefied, both of them prophetic. "Power to the peaceful."

## MEKONS

*Fear and Whiskey* (1985; Quarterstick, 2002). Apart from a handful of early singles that haven't been widely available for a good quarter-century, this is where Mekons' story really begins, or at least gains traction: post-apocalyptic country-punk that gets more relevant with each passing year. "Hard to be human" indeed.

*Edge of the World* (1986; Quarterstick, 1996). Still hard to be human, and still waltzing with abandon. Pick hits: "Ugly Band" and "Big Zombie (I'm Just Not Human Tonight)," the latter by way of Raymond Chandler.

*The Mekons' Rock 'n' Roll* (1989; Collectors Choice, 2001). The perennially marginalized underdogs burn their meal ticket, and with blazing rock 'n' roll to boot. "Only Darkness Has the Power."

*OOOH! (Out of Our Heads)* (Quarterstick, 2002). A benediction from maybe the most committed humanists on record. "Every day is a battle, how we still love the war."

## PUBLIC ENEMY

*It Takes a Nation of Millions to Hold Us Back* (Def Jam, 1988). One of the greatest albums of all time, hip-hop or otherwise. Not only is *Nation of Millions* "Louder Than a Bomb," as the title of one track puts it, it swings like mad and boasts some of the most furious beats on record. Injected rap, wrote Michael Eric Dyson, with ideological vitality.

*Fear of a Black Planet* (Def Jam, 1990). *Fear* has a broader sonic palette and is, on the whole, more subdued than *Nation of Millions*, but its peaks, from "Fight the Power" to "Welcome to the Terrordome," are as ferocious and trenchant. Another all-out wonder.

*Apocalypse '91 . . . The Enemy Strikes Black* (Def Jam, 1991). Its grooves more steeped in blues, soul, gospel, and funk than ever, PE's third straight masterstroke reflects an emerging and encompassing humanism that looks beyond black and white. "Classify us in the have nots, fightin' haves."

*Son of a Bush* (Slamjamz/Koch, 2003). This 3-track EP and bonus DVD includes "Twisted Sense of God," an excoriating jeremiad triggered by the madness that followed the attacks of September 11, 2001. Also contains the equally pointed "Son of a Bush" ("He's a baaaaad man").

## Chapter 8

## SLY & THE FAMILY STONE

*Stand!* (Epic, 1969). Much of this is also on the group's 1970 hits set, notably "Everyday People," "I Want to Take You Higher," and the title track, but this is a great album in its own right. Also contains the unassailable "Don't Call Me Nigger, Whitey."

*Greatest Hits* (Epic, 1970). A breathless romp from start to finish, this assembles all of the glories of Sly and company's "whole new thing," including the previously uncollected singles "Thank You (Falettinme Be Mice Elf Agin)" and "Hot Fun in the Summertime," the latter a lot stormier—and pointed—than it lets on.

*There's a Riot Goin' On* (Epic, 1971). An astonishing turnabout, at least for those who weren't listening between the lines of "Thank You" and "Hot Fun." Blues so dissipated and disjointed—and insanely hooky—that it sounds like yet another new thing, dispatched from hell by way of Vietnam and the ghetto. Apocalyptic.

*Fresh* (Epic, 1973). Nearly as alienated and bracing as *Riot* (cf. the woozy remake on the Doris Day hit "Que Sera, Sera" for a prophetic, if slantwise, commentary on race in America), this was a last, brilliant gasp, a staggering profusion of hooks and funk.

## BIKINI KILL

*Bikini Kill* (Kill Rock Stars, 1992). The most elemental and unabashed early blast of Riot Girl. Includes "Suck My Left One," "Double Dare Ya," and "Rebel Girl." Crucial.

*Pussy Whipped* (Kill Rock Stars, 1994). Just what the title says. Sexually pointed and gender wise: "Sugar," "Li'l Red," and "Star Bellied Boy."

*Singles* (Kill Rock Stars, 1998). Fills in the gaps the albums don't plug and contains the anthemic, Joan Jett-produced version of "Rebel Girl," cowritten by Jett.

## WOMEN"S LIBERATION ROCK

*Papa Don't Lay That Shit on Me* (Rounder, 2005). The reissue of *Mountain Moving Day*, the split-sided LP recorded by the New Haven and Chicago Women's Liberation Rock Bands, plus a new collaboration with the contemporary feminist trio Le Tigre. The music of these two all-female ensembles wasn't radical, but their message and the way they spread it was, anticipating Riot Girl, among other things, by two decades.

## SLEATER-KINNEY

*Call the Doctor* (Chainsaw, 1996). Riot girls come of age, asserting themselves with a punk-infused *Sturm und Drang* so ferocious that patriarchy doesn't stand a chance against it. Well on their way to becoming your Joey Ramone.

*Dig Out Me* (Kill Rock Stars, 1997). Ecstatic feminists reaping the whirlwind and reveling in their own generativity and might. "I'll touch the sky and say what I want."

*The Hot Rock* (Kill Rock Stars, 1999). America's soon-to-be "Best Rock Band" employs a broader, more nuanced sonic palette while resisting the siren call of celebrity and exulting in the virtues of community. "Tie me to the mast of this ship and of this band. Tie me to the greater things, the people I love."

*One Beat* (Kill Rock Stars, 2002). Where S-K moves beyond politics of identity and resistance to articulate a beat-wise, post-9/11 grammar of faith, noise, and solidarity that connects the dots between their local and global concerns. "Disassemble your discrimination. . . . It's not the time to just keep quiet. Speak up one time, to the beat."

*\*The Woods* (Sub Pop, 2005). A noisy, distorted lament for a world that ignored the salutary exhortations of *One Beat*. Words and guitar, they got it.

## LE TIGRE

*Le Tigre* (Mr. Lady Records, 1999). Third-wave feminism with "hot topics" and "extensive bibliographies," and you can dance to it. The brainiest bompalompalomp around.

*Feminist Sweepstakes* (Mr. Lady Records, 2001). More beat-happy, gender-bending celebration and resistance. "For the ladies and the fags, yeah! We're the band with the rollerskate jams."

*This Island* (Universal, 2004). Militancy infiltrates the mainstream, the message more strident, the beats more brittle.

## Epilogue

## BRUCE SPRINGSTEEN

*Born to Run* (Columbia, 1975). Springsteen's quintessential early articulation of the "searchin' thing" that underlies every note he plays and sings. "Someday, baby, we're gonna get to that place where we really want to go."

*Darkness on the Edge of Town* (Columbia, 1978). Desire in retreat, or at least obscured by the shadows. Even here, though, Springsteen affirms his belief in the existence of a promised land. Proves it all night, in fact.

*The River* (Columbia, 1980). Still centered on indelible characters, Springsteen's narratives now make the personal political, making for a sort of Jersey shore revival of the Dust Bowl populism of John Steinbeck. Prophetic.

*Nebraska* (Columbia, 1982). More explicit and more unremittingly bleak, these Steinbeckian evocations wear best when Springsteen stays closer to home, as in "Atlantic City." Nevertheless, bracing stuff.

*Born in the U.S.A.* (Columbia, 1984). A real crossroads, this is where Springsteen, now an international megastar and Hollywood millionaire, is forced to re-examine his emergent populism. A visceral, anthemic album brimming with social and existential tension.

*Tunnel of Love* (Columbia, 1987). Springsteen's "searchin' thing" in miniature, a new sort of country music.

*The Ghost of Tom Joad* (Columbia, 1995). Dust Bowl ballads for the age of globalization, with music as bereft of melody as Springsteen's protagonists are of their inheritance.

*\*Devils and Dust* (Columbia, 2005). Darkness on the edge of the world, a song cycle contemplating whether it's possible to get out alive.

# INDEX